WASHO LAND

BY

Don La Rue

For Book Reviews of WASHO LAND look to:

Los Angeles Times Book Review
Los Angeles Times calendar live.com
San Francisco Chronicle
Sacramento Bee
Seattle Times
San Diego Union
Denver Post
Dallas Morning News
New York Times Book Review
Reno Gazette-Journal
Las Vegas Sun
Portland Oregonian
Wyoming News
Idaho Statesman
Arizona Republic
Elko Daily Free Press
Oakland Tribune
Modesto Bee
Fresno Bee
Medford Mail Tribune
Eugene Register-Guard
Ontario Daily Bulletin
Prove Daily Herald
Tahoe Mountain News
North Lake Tahoe Bonanza
Tahoe World

This is a work of fiction. The characters, incidents and dialogues are products of the author's imagination and are not to be construed as real. Any resemblance to actual events or persons, living or dead, is entirely incidental.

Published by **Don La Rue STUDIO**....Since 1972
P.O. Box 1055 Tahoe City, CA 96145
e-mail ...dlarue@telis.org
(530) 583 6009

ISBN: 0- 9679614- 0- 8

Printed in the United States of America

June 2000

DEDICATION

This Book is for Sam:

.....Almost Warrior

.....Soon to be a Great Hunter

.....Destined to be a Leader of Men

AUTHOR'S INTRODUCTION

Although this is a fictional story about imaginary people, much of what you are about to read is true. The places mentioned are all real places. However, the location of the Cave of the Ancients has been altered slightly to preserve its artifacts and pictographs. The customs of the Washo Indian people are much the same today as they were at the time of our story. The monsters ONG and WATER BABY are the stuff of legends, handed down from generation to generation.

This story takes place in the year One B. C. At that time only the Wa She Shu or Washo people occupied WASHO LAND, an eight thousand square mile area along the east slope of the Sierra Nevada mountains. Lake Tahoe lies at the center. The first white man, Jedediah Smith, would not appear until 1827 A.D.

In the year One B.C. our friends the Washo were living in the stone age, as were all other native American people in this sparsely populated land. Almost all tools and weapons were made of stone. Knives, arrow heads, spear points, as well as needles, awls and scrapers, were stone. Obsidian was preferred, because of the ease with which it could be chipped into finished form. The Washos were adept at weaving and most of their utensils were basketry. Hunter-gatherers, they harvested animals such as mule tail deer, antelope and big horn sheep, as well as small game like rabbit, porcupine and sage hen. A multitude of grains, fruits, vegetables, nuts and herbs were a common part of the diet.

Other cultures, in another part of the world, were in strange contrast to the occupants of Washo Land. For example, in the year One B.C. early Britons learned it was possible to cross the River Thames at a certain spot, by wading at low tide. As it was not possible to cross elsewhere, this place became an important thoroughfare. A village that was to grow into the city of London, was born. Soon Britain was conquered by Roman Legions. They used the town Londinium as their chief port. The Roman Legions were the most advanced fighting forces in the world, using weapons made of steel and iron. Neither material would be known in the New World for almost fifteen hundred years.

At the same time the city of Rome, known as the heart of civilization, was ruled by Augustus. He built the Roman Empire to include Britain, Germany, North Africa and Persia. This realm would have become lost from sight, if dropped into the vast area of the North American continent.

Much of what you will read in this novel is fact. For example, every spot visited by our friends Ai mee, Noah and Bopo, is a real place explored by the author in years gone by. The Pine Nut Mountains, the vast Paiute Desert, Paiute Village, the stone pyramids, Honey Marsh, the great granite head wall, the Cave of the Ancients, the River of the

Feather, the tiny island in Emerald Bay where the Water Baby resides, Ribicon Peak, are all real places.

The customs and the legends you will encounter are authentic, some of them published in a wonderful little book Wa she shu, written by Joanne Nevers of the Washo Tribe. However, much of what you will read of legends and customs, comes from stories told to me and Little Joe Noah by Grandma Noah. Let me explain.

I grew up in Reno, Nevada, a quiet little desert town. Exposure to the Washo and Paiute people was an almost daily occurrence. Through out high school we developed as typical outdoor kids: hunting, fishing, swimming, hiking, ice skating, searching for arrow heads in the desert. My father endorsed summer employment for inactive youngsters during school vacations. I found a summer job during my 14th and 15th years, as a ranch hand working for August and Jennie Pedretti, a wonderful Swiss Italian couple. Their spread was some twenty miles north of Reno, in Long Valley.

What a great experience! A huge mountain meadow backed up against steeply sloped pine forests at the foot of the Sierra's. A two story frame ranch house back in the pines. A clear stream ran through the meadow. There was a huge unpainted dairy barn, corrals, immense hay stacks. A black smith shed where I turned the crank-driven grind stone and worked the bellows on the forge. A milk shed where I turned a crank on the cream separator.

August and his brother Tony milked cows, slaughtered hogs, mowed hay, made wine and sausage. Jenny canned fruit from the orchard, filled the lamps with kerosene, cooked and baked over a huge wood range. Food was stored in a cool stone cellar under the house. They milked twenty some cows daily and raised one hundred pairs of beef cattle (for the tender foot, a pair is a cow and her calf). I slept on the big screened back porch and listened to the coyotes talk all night long.

August employed a hired hand full time; his name was Joe Noah. Joe was a Washo. Short, heavy, barrel chest, booming voice, competent, an all around fine hand. He lived just over the rise in a snug house made of railroad ties, with his wife Momma, his son Little Joe Noah and Grandma Noah.

She was a wonderful little old woman with long gray-white hair, shiny black eyes, and wrinkles. Pink gums with never a tooth. She smiled a lot and smoked a short stone pipe all the time. She liked me, because I brought her pouches of Heine's Blend pipe tobacco. It was made by Sutcliff Co., located at the foot of Market Street in San Francisco. I remember the blue pouch with the white figure of a fat Dutch man in wooden shoes skating on a canal, with stocking cap, long clay pipe and hands folded behind the back. I bought the stuff for 20 cents at Southworth's Smoke Shop on Douglas Alley in Reno, on a Saturday when August took Little Joe and I to town, as a treat. I later got the devil from my mother, because she heard I'd been in Southworth's. I wasn't supposed to go there. They had magazines with pictures of ladies in tights.

Little Joe was a good guy, same age as I. He taught me a lot about ranches. He worked summers like I did. He's the model I used for the character of Bopo.

Mostly our job consisted of shoveling manure and chasing the hundred pairs out of the pasture grass. We had to keep them back up in the woods where they were supposed to be. I rode a ranch horse named Peanuts. A good cow pony, but he didn't have too much respect for a tender foot like me. He knew all about ranching and could have moved that stock around without me along. At least he always kept the rope tight when it was my turn to get the heifer out of the quick sand.

Dinner time at the ranch was just as the sun was going down. After dinner I was on my own. Every evening I'd hoof it over the hill through the tall sage brush to Little Joe's house. We'd sit on the front steps made of railroad ties. Grandma Noah relaxed on the porch in a rickety old rocking chair. She always sat on a fat pink pillow with the stuffing hanging out of it. She'd puff away on her pipe and cackle. Usually, she would kid us about what bum cowboys we were.

Pretty soon she'd start on the old time stories about how it used to be. All the stories handed down for who knows how many hundreds of years. Stories about the ceremonies and the dances and Mr. Coyote and ONG and the Water Baby. These were all very real things to her. Very serious stuff! When she said " Washo people don't go in Big Lake. Water Baby get," she meant it.

To this day, I don't think you'll find a Washo who will put a toe in that lake. It was serious stuff to Little Joe. I know, because, later I tried to get him to go swimming with me, in Lake Tahoe. He just grunted and said, " You think I'm crazy ?"

Now that I think about it, my desire to tell the world about the wonderful culture of the Washo people must have started right there on Joe Noah's front porch. It took me a while to get around to it, however. A trip through Cal Berkeley to become an engineer, followed by a career with a huge multi-national corporation where I was fortunate enough to be able to peer down at all that madness from fairly near the top of the pyramid. Retirement at age 52 included a new home overlooking Lake Tahoe with a studio where one can paint and write. Now, what more rewarding thing to do than tell the narrative of those fine people the Wa She Shu, as seen through the eyes of Ai mee, Noah and Bopo? I hope you enjoy my story!

Don La Rue

 Tahoe City, California

My sincere thanks to:

Jo Ann Nevers....for the fine little book about her people, Wa She Shu.

Dr. Warren L. d'Azevedo....leading authority on people of the Great Basin... for his friendly advice about the people, time of arrival in Washo Land, their customs, their clothing.

Lloyd Chichester...fourth generation Antelope Valley rancher, Washo basket connoisseur...for knowing all those details about the people and for sharing them with me.

Jo Ann Martinez....Respected Elder of the Washo Tribe, who graciously agreed to read a rough draft manuscript of WASHO LAND and later reported, "I found the story enjoyable." Regardless of what future acclaim may be achieved, this endorsement is more significant than all others.

Betty Long, Dick Lingle, Marge Faia, June Broili Merrilyn Bissell and Susan De Ryke, for their loyal support.

TABLE OF CONTENTS

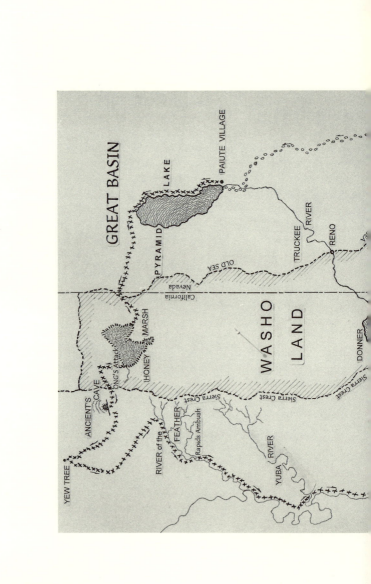

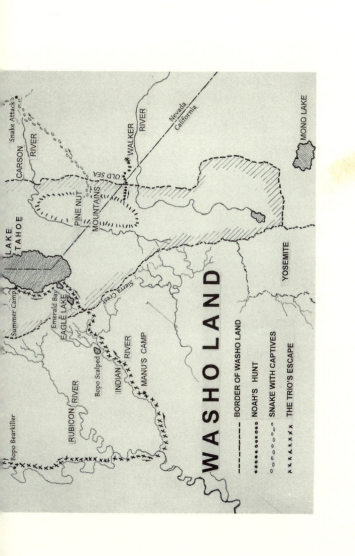

WASHO LAND

- — — — BORDER OF WASHO LAND
- •••••••• NOAH'S HUNT
- ∘∘∘∘∘∘∘∘ SNAKE WITH CAPTIVES
- xxxxxx THE TRIO'S ESCAPE

Snake Attack

CARSON RIVER

LAKE TAHOE

WALKER RIVER

OLD SEA

PINE NUT MOUNTAINS

Nevada
California

MONO LAKE

YOSEMITE

Summer Camp

Emerald Bay

EAGLE LAKE

Sierra Crest

Bopo Scalped

INDIAN RIVER

MANU'S CAMP

RUBICON RIVER

Bopo Bearkiller

CHAPTER 1   In Paiute Territory
....YEAR ONE B.C....

Deep within the slumbering brain of the Washo youth Noah, a tiny hint of faint light began to glow. Ever so slowly the ember grew. With each pulse of spreading energy the core of his brain emerged into ascending awareness. The still form slumbering on the cold, hard desert floor began to stir ever so slightly.

Noah awoke with a cold feeling of dread. Something was terribly wrong. There was complete silence. He didn't move a muscle or twitch so much as a hair. Didn't even open an eye, much as he was tempted. It was cold, the ground was hard. There wasn't a breath of air moving. In the absolute silence he knew something was very wrong. The chill along his bare spine warned he was in terrible danger. Was there someone or something lurking behind him or above him? Silence; only silence.

Ever so slowly Noah began to open his left eyelid. Carefully, very carefully, he gradually exposed the orb. No one could see the movement. He must not make a sound. Something was out there.

Peering out beyond the outline of his nose, with eye lid open only a slit, he could see nothing. There was a void of black, cold, silent night. Not a sound, not even an insect was stirring. There wasn't anything but cold silence. Still, there must be

1

something out there, poised, just waiting for him to move.

Looking down past his nose, he became aware his head was resting against the ground. Inspecting the earth just inches before his nose, he could make out a hard flat surface receding into the darkness. Pebbles, only pebbles, nothing but tiny pieces of stone, all the same size and color. There was no soil, all the residue on the desert floor had blown away. Where was he? His head was resting on the hard surface of the Paiute Desert!

At last realization struck Noah. He became fully awake. He was stretched out at full length on the cold desert floor. The dangerous Paiute Desert where he was forbidden to go. The deadly Paiute warriors were out there in the night, searching for him. Waiting for him to move, listening for him to breathe. Hoping he'd make a mistake that would reveal his hiding place.

With a feeling of stark terror, Noah slowly lifted his left eyelid a little higher. Nothing happened. No one detected the movement. His right eyelid remained closed. Slowly he moved the left eyeball, from one side to the other. His nose disappeared from view and he could see only black night. Very, very slowly, realization crept into his consciousness, the moon's down, that's why the night's so black.

The moon must have gone down somewhere behind his back. Gone down behind the crest of the mountains in Washo Land, home. It was at least a full day's walk behind him. He was deep in the heart of a vast desert that had once been Old Sea. This was the home of the deadly Paiute people. They were out there somewhere, just waiting for him to make a mistake, waiting for him to move.

Noah strained his ears, listening, listening. And then, without warning, it happened. Noah screamed,

" AHEEEEEEE !"

He screamed and screamed and screamed, a terrible sound repeated over and over again. It rattled around inside his skull. Both Noah's eyes were open now in stark terror. Open wide and yet he knew there was only silence. Silence, because the screams existed only inside his skull. Silence, because the screams had not emerged from his mouth. Silence, because his mouth was closed tight, closed by a huge hard hand. That huge hard hand suddenly covered his mouth and his nose. It twisted his head cruelly to the side.

A massive weight crushed him against the ground and he could feel the needle-like tip of a flint knife carefully searching for a joint between the vertebrae in his spine. Finding the exact spot, the sharp point penetrated slightly. Noah could feel a drop of his blood forming on the tip of the cold stone blade.

The silence was broken by a faint whisper of air. It was like a very light breeze drifting by. Unable to breath, unable to speak, unable to move, Noah became aware of the faintest of sounds borne on the breeze. Just a trace of sound, but then it came again and it was almost a whisper. The blood pounded in Noah's ears as he strained to form the whisper of breeze into a word. Then faintly, faintly the word drifted by on a puff of air.

"Quiet, quiet, don't move, don't even think of making a sound."

Relief flooded through Noah's veins like a cold, clear drink of spring water. Those words, the words that drifted past Noah's ear, softly as down, those words were spoken in the Hokan tongue!

Hokan is the ancient language of the Washo people. A language so old its origin is long forgotten. It's a language only the Washo people can speak and understand. The Paiute can neither speak nor comprehend the complex language. Communications between the two peoples are carried out only through hand sign language. Thus when Noah heard words spoken to him in the Hokan tongue he knew the speaker, his captor, must be a Washo person.

Gasping for air as the huge hand was removed from his mouth, Noah whispered over his shoulder ever so softly,

"I'm a Hokan speaker, I'm a Washo, I'm Noah, son of Much Luck the mighty hunter of the Washo people." The flint knife was removed from his back and he felt the massive weight lifted. Noah heaved a quiet sigh of relief. Silently he said thanks to his totem Mr. Coyote, for his deliverance.

Again the faintest of sounds drifted by his ear. A man's deep voice whispered. "Up this draw above you, less than a short arrow flight away, there are eight, maybe ten Paiute warriors. They're heavily armed and waiting for a herd of antelope to come over that ridge at dawn. I crossed their sign just at sunset. From the tracks, it looks to me like it may be Snake, the worst of the Paiute and his band of killers. Do you know what an evil bunch they are?" In terror-stricken silence Noah grimly nodded his head.

"If they sense you're here, you'll be dead before the sun rises. My name's Runs Swift. I'm the Washo messenger for the Pine Nut Boss. I'm out delivering news of the upcoming Pine Nut Harvest," whispered the large black shadow beside him.

Noah's only response was a sigh of relief. He didn't dare say a word. Suddenly a feeling of sickness swept over him. What a mess he was in!

"I was taking a short cut across Paiute Territory when I ran across this band of murderers," his captor hissed. "Now, if you want'a live, crawl back down this draw on your belly. Keep moving till you reach the bend. Then you can stand up and walk. If you've ever in your life been quiet, you'd better be quiet now, or you're going to be one very dead Washo. I'll be right behind you. Hurry, dawn isn't far away."

They stopped running some time around noon, as they approached the edge of Old Sea (later known as the Great Basin). This was the eastern boundary of Washo Land, home and safe haven from the Paiute.   For the first time Noah had an opportunity to steal a furtive sidelong glance at his companion. Since early dawn he'd trotted along behind the big fellow, just concentrating on keeping up with the steady ground covering pace. He'd never uttered a sound or looked back. The only time they stopped running was as they approached a crest or a ridge in the otherwise flat sweep of sage-covered desert. Then Runs Swift would kneel behind a clump of brush to avoid creating a silhouette. He'd carefully study the plain ahead, to make sure they were alone. Without a word the big messenger would then lope off into the vast desert.

Mile after mile the two tiny specs silently moved across the desert floor. It stretched from horizon to horizon. Noah was exhausted just keeping up. Never before had he run such a great distance. At last the leader drew to a halt beside a gray green clump of sage. He seated himself beside a damp spot in the sand, where a trickle of moisture dribbled noisily from the rocks to form a clear puddle of water.

This spot was typical of the ending of many a stream. Such streams were formed from snow melting in the high Sierra mountains. They flowed out into the desert to be swallowed by the thirsty sands.

With a grunt the silent leader indicated Noah was to be seated by the quiet pool. With an audible sigh of relief Noah sank to the ground. Runs Swift fumbled at the waist band of his breech clout and pulled out two long leather-like strips of jerked venison. With a scowl he regarded the jerky for a moment. He seemed to reach a decision and tossed one of the strips to Noah. Without a word the runner washed his hands in the pool, then deliberately drank water from his palm and proceeded to eat his frugal meal.

Noah studied his companion furtively. He was a large young man, taller than most Washo people. He had very long legs and broad heavily muscled shoulders. A handsome man with a strong brow, glittering black eyes, a firm chin and a hard mouth set in a fierce scowl. A full mane of jet black hair was tied behind the head with a leather thong.

Runs Swift's lithe brown body was naked except for a breech clout with leather apron, knee length leggings and moccasins. All were of snow-white ceremonial leather. At least, the color had been white when he started his journey. Now it was besmirched and soiled by some three days and one hundred miles of running. His mission, to spread the word of the upcoming Tah gum Harvest. The most important social and food gathering event of the Washo year.

In his hand the messenger carried a ceremonial lance tipped with a large black obsidian point. A leather thong, bound to the lance, had a knotted Magpie feather for each day until the Tah gum Harvest began. Ten knots indicating the harvest was scheduled to start in ten days.

Runs Swift leaned back with his elbows against the rock. He stretched out his heavily muscled legs and rubbed a hard, flat belly. The warm sun was relaxing. He heaved a gusty sigh of contentment. The run was finished. All done for this year, a good job. He'd contacted every family in the area, young people, old people, everyone. Now they all knew the Tah gum Harvest was to be on the East side of the Pine Nut Mountains, overlooking the Paiute desert country.

They all knew the tops of the trees were loaded this year. Heavy with fine ripe cones containing plenty of sweet tah gum. The Pine Nut Boss said it would be one of the best years ever!

(Tah gum is the Hokan word for Pine Nut. One of the most nutritious of all nuts, it's a staple of the Washo winter diet. The lower Eastern slope of the Sierra Nevada Mountains and the Western Great Basin is heavily forested with single needle Pinion Pine, which yields Tah gum. The Goom sa bye is the Washo autumn ritual of harvesting Tah gum. It's a ceremony directed by the Pine Nut Boss.)

The big messenger stretched out on his back in the warm sunlight. He squinted an eye at the sky, admiring the towering cumulus clouds as they slowly drifted by. The world was a good place. Everything was peace and contentment. Except! Runs Swift cocked a glittering black eye at Noah sitting there beside the pool, contentedly chewing on the last of his venison. For the first time since meeting Noah, he spoke. His voice sounded as if it were coming out of a hollow log or a cave.

" So, your name is Noah and you're the son of the mighty hunter Much Luck."

The booming voice startled Noah and he jumped.

" I know Much Luck," the booming voice continued. "He's a fine warrior, indeed, he's a great hunter, I've hunted with him many times. I have much respect for him."

Now, ever since crawling down that draw on his belly in the pitch black, Noah had been

8

experiencing an increasing feeling of guilt. As he ran along behind the big fellow all morning, a sickening sense of awareness grew within him. He'd made a serious mistake. Almost a fatal mistake! With each step throughout the long run toward home he'd became more apprehensive.

How was all of this going to turn out? Noah had a grim picture in his mind of what the big fellow might do to him, or even worse, what he might say to his father. But now, thought Noah," Here was the fellow all relaxed and easy and saying such nice things about his father. Maybe it wasn't going to turn out so bad after all. Maybe the guy was going to turn out to be a regular sort, at that. Maybe he was going to realize, a bright young man like Noah who was, after all, almost a warrior, with a lot of promise, had to get out and get some first hand experience. Had to learn how to search out a band of antelope. After all, most of the big bands of antelope were in Paiute country. It wasn't Noah's fault was it, if that was where you had to go to find antelope ?

Runs Swift fixed Noah with one cold eye and said in a loud booming voice,

"Yes, Much Luck is a fine warrior and one I really respect!   But, answer me just one little question. Where in the name of the Great Spirit, did Much Luck get such an appallingly stupid son?" Noah shriveled, disaster !

The young Washo felt terrible! He sat hunched over with knees drawn up against his chest, head hanging. For a moment there was deep silence.

Only the sound of a dragon fly buzzed across the surface of the pool.

"What were you doing out there in the desert asleep? Next to a band of Paiute cut throats?" growled the big man.

With a shake of his head, Noah reached a decision and saying a silent prayer to his totem, Mr. Coyote, he summoned all his courage. He raised his head, looking the big fellow squarely in the eye.

" I'm sorry," he said "I know I really messed up back there. I'm truly sorry for it. Did just about every thing wrong. Forgot most of the things my father taught me."

"Humphhh!" was the only reply.

"You see, I was trying to stalk a herd of antelope I'd spotted in the late afternoon, just for practice. See if I could work up on them and get close enough for a bow shot. Of course I didn't even have my new hunting bow. All I had was my sling and knife. I was really out hunting sage hen. My chore for the day was to gather enough sage hen for the whole family's evening meal. "

"Humphh! Don't imagine your family had much to eat last night," was the scowling observation.

"I know. I let 'em down. Should have been concentrating on sage hen. But, that was when I spotted the antelope. Got all excited! Worked up the draw part way. Expected the herd to come toward me. Over the crest of that draw. Only I forgot it was getting late. The antelope weren't moving that fast. They'd probably stop and graze for the night. Then they'd come over the crest at dawn. So, I lay down in the draw. Decided to wait for dawn. Guess I dropped off. Sort a went to sleep. "

The big messenger just shook his head in dismay, spread his palms skyward and rolled his eyes to the heavens in silence.

"At least you didn't snore".

"Guess I even forgot I was in Paiute country." Noah sheepishly admitted. "I didn't really mean to go so deep into forbidden territory. It was just that the farther I went the more excited I got about the antelope. You see it was all part of our plan." He continued,

" I was going to find a really good antelope hunting spot and develop a technique for stalking 'em. Then, when we got together, at the big Tah gum Harvest, we'd be all set to carry out our plan. We've been working on it ever since the summer meeting at Da ow aga," Noah explained with a note of enthusiasm creeping into his voice.

" What plan?"

"Our plan was, we'd go out to this fine hunting spot. Have a great hunt with our new bows. We'd bag two fat antelope. Then we'd casually walk back into camp with the antelope over our shoulder. Just in time for the meat to be prepared for the evening meal. The whole tribe would be there for the Harvest. They'd see we were fine hunters. They'd see we could steal sweet antelope meat right out from under the noses of the Paiutes. Then everyone'd think it was time for us to become full-fledged hunters. The tribe would declare us Warriors."

The young man held out his hands in exasperated supplication. "Don't you think we had a good plan to qualify as warriors?"

The booming voice of Runs Swift interrupted, "Who is WE? "

Scratching his head, Noah said, " I guess I forgot to tell you, 'We' is me and my cousin Bopo. You see, Bopo belongs to the Hung a lil ti clan. Lives up the mountain a ways at the place where two forks of the river come together. I first met him, of course I didn't know he was my cousin then, but I first met him at the salt licks. At the cold end of our valley."

"Is his family one of the traders who deal in salt?" the messenger asked, a note of interest creeping into his voice.

"Yeah," said Noah. "They come down to the licks to gather salt. They trade all sorts of stuff like salt. They travel around a lot doing it. Some time they even go as far as the New Sea. They put the salt in little bags made from sheep hide. They pack great loads of it in their burden baskets. Carry it all the way over the mountain. Trade it to the Tan eu for stuff like Black Oak acorns."

"Yeah, I know, I've traded some of our best flint with those fellows at times. Some of 'em are pretty sharp traders, too," said the big fellow, his demeanor warming slightly.

"Anyhow," Noah continued, "Bopo and I being cousins and all, and us being the same age, we just seem to think a lot alike. We have a very bad time being 'Almost Warriors'. Almost warriors never get to hunt the big game like deer, antelope or sheep. We always get sent out to hunt squirrels and rabbits and sage hen and blue grouse and stuff like that. What kind of a warrior hunts squirrels?"

For the first time the big fellows' eyes eased their concentration   and rolled skyward. A casual observer might suspect he was having somewhat of a problem in suppressing a smile.

"When ever it's time to hunt deer or antelope, the warriors go out and have all the fun," the lad continued seriously. "We stay home. Gather sage hen for the soup basket. So any how, at the meeting at the big lake this summer, Bopo and I worked out this plan. A plan for us to become full-fledged warriors. We'd go up over the crest of the mountain. Up where the great big old junipers grow. Up above Eagle Lake. We'd get two big slabs of old aged juniper wood. Make big, high powered hunting bows. The kind of bows that're so powerful you can drive a broad head arrow all the way through a deer."

"I can see you fellows were planning to do some serious hunting, all right," commented the older man.

"We gathered Rose wood shoots for arrow shafts and used goose feathers to make arrows with obsidian heads. Bopo became a real expert at making fine arrows. That's an art, you know! Next we planned to go out and bag two fat antelope. Show everyone we were good enough to be real warriors."

"Well, I'll agree with you,"   the big fellow nodded grudgingly "That would have been pretty impressive. IF you'd pulled it off."

"You know, " said the youth, "I made a lot of stupid mistakes out there and I don't plan to repeat any of that foolish stuff, but there's still just one thing I can't figure out. How did you know I was out there? I know you followed the tracks of that gang of Paiutes and knew exactly where they were hiding. But, how'd you know there was anyone else out there in the dark? You certainly couldn't see me !"

With a deep throaty chuckle, Runs Swift replied "At first it just didn't feel right; sixth sense, I guess. But then, when I crawled closer I could begin to smell you. Couldn't smell the others, but I could smell you. Thought maybe they'd put out a sentry."

"You could smell me," said Noah with an incredulous expression.

"You came within a breath of having your spine cut in two. Next time you decide to go antelope hunting, remember the first rule of hunting. Don't smell like a man, smell like sage or smell like the animal you're hunting. Bathe in the sacred sage smoke before you go."

In disgust Noah slapped himself on the forehead. "I knew that, why didn't I do it.?" Runs Swift stood up to full height, stretched his arms over his head and heaved a sigh.

He was rested and ready to resume his journey. He regarded Noah carefully, but with a fierce scowl. The lad really was fine looking, tall and slender, but with well-muscled long legs. He was handsome, with clean features and long shiny black hair. Best of all, he'd demonstrated he was an excellent runner. Tough as the cured tendon off the hind leg of a Big Horn Sheep. Clad in moccasins, breech clout and deer skin shirt, he made an impressive figure.

" Well, young man," said the big fellow, "our trails'll cross again. Learn to run. Maybe you'll become a messenger."

Noah raised his hand shoulder high, palm outward.   "I learned a lot from you. Thanks for what you taught me."

The big fellow smiled despite himself and said, "You better think up a good story about where you were last night, for your father." Once again he donned his fierce scowl. Then he winked at Noah and turned and walked away. Noah watched the large receding figure as it disappeared into a stand of flaming golden aspen trees.

CHAPTER 2   The Tah gum Harvest

(If you were a Bald Eagle and flew very high in the cloudless sky, you'd be able to see all of Washo Land. It's a rectangle occupying the eastern slope of a magnificent range of towering peaks, now named the Sierra Nevada Mountains. Washo Land starts at Honey Marsh in the north and extends all the way south to a pass overlooking Mono Lake. A distance so great it takes a Washo family with loaded burden baskets about fifteen days to make the trip from north to south. If the same family were to walk from east to west, it would take from three to five days. They'd go all the way from the crest of the mountains in the west, down the long slope, to the edge of the Great Basin desert in the east.

In the exact center, your sharp eagle eyes would see a large sparkling blue lake which the Washo people call Da ow aga. The first white man, who came very much later, would mistakenly call the lake Tahoe. The white man was never able to understand the complex Hokan language, which the Washo people spoke. He thought the natives were saying Tahoe when they said Da ow. A simple mistake, but then the white man was never very astute when it came to understanding the Washo people.

As you, the eagle with the sharp eyes, soared   along with great wings outstretched, you'd   notice all of Washo Land except the eastern edge was richly carpeted with towering green fir and pine, interrupted here and there with patches of quaking aspen and willow. You'd see a multitude of smaller lakes   rivers and streams all of which drain to the desert in the east. The desert along the eastern boundary of Washo Land is where the Paiute people live. The treeless belt of land along the eastern border does not receive much winter snow. It's sprinkled with a multitude of steaming hot springs. It is in this warm belt   the Washo people make their winter camps.   There, they are protected from many of the harsh storms.

While you   soared along in your fine suit of eagle feathers, you'd notice all the aspen trees had turned a rich golden color, indicating   fall time. The autumn season is the time of the Washo people's most important event, the Tah gum Harvest. Tah gum is the Hokan name for Pine Nut. It's a fine little nut in a soft shell. It is far richer in protein than most other nuts. It has a sweet taste and grows on the Pinion Pine   all along the eastern boundary of Washo Land.

The Tah gum Harvest is proceeded by a four day festival called Goom sa bye. Now, the Washo people don't have a chief; instead they appoint one of the wisest elders of the tribe to oversee each of the major tasks to be undertaken. This man is called the   Boss. This year they've appointed an elder named Stands Tall to be Pine

Nut Boss. His job is to locate the finest crop of
nuts and notify all of the Washo people when
and where to gather for the harvest.

Several days ago Stands Tall visited the
vast grove of pinion pine he's been keeping an eye
on all year long. Harvesting a few cones here and
a few cones there he's sampled the nuts and
found them to be fat and ripe and ready to pick.
This year the tops of the little pines are heavily
loaded with the small green nut bearing cones.
There are more than enough nuts to supply every
one throughout the long winter months. It's not
always so. Some years the harvest is light and the
people have a lean and hungry winter.

Stands Tall summoned six of the very best
runners in the tribe and dispatched them to every
corner of Washo Land to call each family to the
harvest. From the vantage point of the eagle, you
can see the Washo families all moving down the
mountain slope toward the pine nut forest at the
eastern edge of their home land. They've spent all
of the summer months hunting, gathering and
fishing. Now it's autumn and time to put away a
supply of food for the long cold winter ahead. If
you look closely you can just make out a
multitude of tiny little figures that look like ants.
Slowly they'd creep toward the harvest site. Men,
women and children are all converging on the
same point. Every person, even the children,
carries a loaded burden basket on his back.

The Washos have been looking forward to
the harvest all year long. What fun everyone will
have, meeting old friends and relatives whom

they haven't seen in months, sometimes years. The four days of events before the actual harvest begins will be filled with excitement. There will be games, gambling, contests, ceremonies and endless story-telling sessions that run for hours. Later there will be rituals and feasts followed by dances that keep the throbbing drums going far into the night. What an experience it will be for everyone! Afterward comes the hard work of gathering the winter's food supply. This year every one will leave with a burden basket filled to the brim with sweet Tah gum. Plenty of food for a comfortable winter.)

Bopo toiled up the last steep slope to Sun Rise pass in the Pine Nut Mountains. It was hot, the rocky trail hard on moccasin feet. He'd been walking since dawn. His burden basket, loaded with prime ripe Black Oak acorns from Tan eu land, weighed almost as much as he did. The leather straps of the basket cut into the tough muscles of his shoulders. Despite the discomfort, Bopo looked forward to reaching Sunrise Pass, the entrance to the pinion forests. At the moment, he walked through dense growths of Desert Juniper trees. These would be replaced by Pinion Pine at the pass.

The husky young Washo looked forward with anticipation to a greeting by Crow Woman, the tribal physician. She awaited at Sunrise Pass to greet everyone arriving for the harvest. It was a tradition she'd observed for years.

Bopo was a striking-looking Washo youth. Average height with shiny black hair, braided into a long pig tail that erupted from the crown of his head. It hung almost to his waist. The muscular lad was clad in breech clout, apron and moccasins of deer hide. Solid legs that resembled two tree trunks supported him. Narrow hips, a flat belly beneath a barrel chest, wide sloping shoulders and long heavily muscled arms hung low as he walked. Leaning into the heavily loaded burden basket, he was an image of great strength. Bopo's face was round, flat and expressionless, until one noticed the sparkling glint of humor in his shiny black eyes.

Sunrise Pass, a beautiful little mountain meadow surrounded by aspen, marked entry into the fertile, Pinion Pine orchard lands of the Washo. The Pinion Pine is a low bush-like tree, gray-green in color, with single needle foliage extending all the way to the ground. Its small, round cones are loaded with nuts and dripping pitch. They grow only at the top of the tree, where they take two years to mature. The trees are small, growing to a height that is two or three times as tall as a man. The surface under foot was clean sand. Deer appeared frequently and didn't seem to be alarmed at Bopo's presence.

The hillside was dotted with numerous patches of bright yellow and gold, indicating autumn aspen trees. As aspen only grow where there's moisture, the patches of bright color indicated the presence of a cold clear mountain spring. Underfoot the dried grass was a rich golden brown color. A narrow stream wound through the middle of a meadow, sparkling in bright sunlight.

The border of bright yellow aspen made a dramatic contrast with the deep green forest.

Seated in the grass at a point where a stream entered the meadow, was Crow Woman. A smile crossed her face as she waved to Bopo, slowly getting to her feet.

Crow Woman was a tall and stately person, clad in a full-length suede leather robe of dull orange-brown color. Her long, straight hair was a rich gray, drawn up and tied with a thong atop her head. Her face was long with fine high cheek bones, a thin aristocratic nose above a wide, sensitive mouth. She had smiling eyes. Eyes that were black and deep as mountain pools on a moonless night.

There was an air about Crow Woman. It suggested she was not quite real, that she's very wise and very old and of another world far, far, away. Her face was narrow at the forehead, creating an impression of aristocracy. An appearance in strange contrast to Bopo's distinctly round expressionless Washo face. Kennewick Woman? She helds out both hands and gave the young traveler a warm, back-patting hug.

Astride Crow Woman's shoulder was a huge jet black crow with glittering scarlet eyes. One is closed while the other unblinkingly followed Bopo's slightest movement. He stretched his neck and pointed his beak toward Bopo. The crow did a fancy little two step shuffle that turned into a dance. First on one foot and then on the other. He turned his back, but the eye never wavered. At last he stretched, placing his beak next to Crow Woman's ear. He muttered in a harsh, cawing voice. With a smile Crow Woman turned to Bopo and said,

"Crow says welcome! "

Crow Woman was the tribal physician, supplying herbs, potions and balms to those who were ill. Her knowledge was profound and often seemed to come from the ancient past. She also served as an instructor to the women of the tribe on all things that grew, whether they be medicinal or edible. Her wisdom was greatly respected and much sought after. Frequently tribal members asked her to serve in the roll of a judge when there's a dispute. There were many who said she was a spirit of another world and adept in matters of the occult.

Saluting the stately woman, Bopo said "Ho, Washo Mother, my father is two days behind me on the trail. He sends his greeting to you. He's given me gifts to bring to you. He wishes to thank you for the medicines you sent last winter, when the snow was deep and the wind blew cold. He's proud to have you as his friend."

"It's good to see you, Bopo, been almost a year now. Hope the medicine did the trick. You're looking fine, Bopo! You know, all of a sudden you've grown into a handsome young man. Bet the girls are beginning to make eyes at you, aren't they?" smiled the stately woman.

Blushing, Bopo lowered his heavy burden basket to the ground, saying "My father's just returned from the land of the Tan eu. He and his friends gathered many Black Oak acorns by the light

22

of the moon. The Tan eu   didn't know the Washos were collecting the acorns, so there was no battle."

(Tan eu is the Washo word for all tribes to the West)

"He's bringing   acorns here so there'll be plenty of food for all who come to   enjoy the ceremonies and the harvest."   Bopo withdrew several bundles wrapped in soft suede leather.

"Here's some of the most choice of the acorns for you and here's some beautiful blue porcupine quills. A decoration for your best robe. My mother sent those."

With a sweeping theatrical bow, like a magician performing a slight-of hand trick, Bopo extended the last of the bundles.   "And here are some delicious tarts made from fresh picked elderberries. I found 'em and my mother cooked 'em, to delight your taste."

Crow Woman expressed her pleasure with the gifts and even the Crow nodded his approval.

"Can I ask," said Bopo, "has Crow Woman seen my cousin, that skinny Washo named Noah? He's supposed to be here. He and I planned to get together for a little hunt sometime during the harvest. After we get our work done, of course."

Smiling, Crow Woman said, "Yes he's here, but he didn't say any thing about going hunting. He did say he planned to work very hard gathering tah gum. Help his father some. Enter the races, the shooting matches and the dances. Maybe chase some girls. But, no, I don't think he said any thing about going hunting." teased Crow Woman. With a smile she relented, saying,

" Noah left a message for you: he said to tell you he'd meet you at the cave tomorrow night, at sundown. I think he planned on the two of you going to the tribal dance together."

Noah sat with knees drawn up under his chin. He was on a ledge of rock jutting out from the face of the cliff. Behind him was a cave-like hollow, big enough for a person to stand upright and deep enough to shelter one in a rain storm. Far below, at the foot of the cliff, was a small grass-covered meadow surrounded by dense groves of pinion pine. It was in this meadow the tribal dance would be held just after sundown. At the moment the meadow was the scene of much activity, as people hurried back and forth.

The tribal drummers, who were brothers, carried first one and then the other big war drums into the meadow. They selected a grassy spot, carefully bedding both drums side by side. Then they were tested to be sure the booming tone was true. Others brought large pieces of fire wood and stacked it near the drums in preparation for a huge bonfire. While most Washo fires are small, this fire was going to be a large one, because this was the most important dance of the tribal year and would be attended by everyone. The whole meadow would be lighted by the fire as the people dance around it, celebrating the upcoming Tagum Harvest and thanking the gods for an abundance of fine food.

While Noah sat high on his ledge watching the busy figures far below, someone else sat above him at the very top of the cliff. That someone was watching Noah intently. He sat very still and didn't make a sound, just concentrated on watching. It was Mr. Coyote, Noah's totem.

"After all," reflected Mr. Coyote "If you're gonna be a totem, a really good totem, yuh gotta work at it. You can't just show up once in a while to check on things. You gotta be around all the while in case of an emergency or somethin' unexpected. How about the other night when that crazy Noah decided to go skylarking around a Paiute hunting party? Who do you think sent that messenger down the draw to pull that crazy young fellow out of there by the seat of his breech clout. It's a good thing ole' Mr. Coyote was on the job right then, wasn't it ?"

Seated high on the ledge with legs dandling over the edge, Noah heard a sound, then the rattling of pebbles falling. Two large brown hands appeared from below and gripped the ledge. They were followed by the top of a head, from which sprouted a long, carefully plaited pig tail of black hair. Slowly the head raised and two solemn, round black, owl eyes appeared.

" Well, what do you know?" exclaimed Noah "If it isn't the Lump! Arise great one, before you fall off that cliff."

With a grunt Bopo hauled himself over the edge of the precipice and sat down. He regarded his friend solemnly for a moment and said,

" How do, Skinny, how have you been keepin'?"

That night the two friends danced at the huge celebration, until they were so tired they were ready to drop. A tribal dance was a major event which didn't occur very often and it was important for one to participate to the fullest. The two big war drums throbbed far into the night. High above, at the edge of the cliff, Mr. Coyote raised his long pointed nose to the full moon and participated with a shrill, mournful howl.

For the next four days the fellows entered into games including foot races, hand games, ball games and archery contests. Both of them proved to be among the best archers in the tribe, helped by their powerful new hunting bows. Noah defeated all comers in the long distance foot races. It was interesting to note a large fellow standing at the finish line, proudly cheered Noah on at the top of his voice. The fellow was the tribal messenger Runs Swift! His friends called him runner.

That night the Goom say bye, which is the Hokan name given to the four day celebration, ended with a symbolic bath in the stream. Now the fun was over and many days of hard work started. The Tah gum Harvest was underway.

Tah gum is harvested by first knocking the small round cones from the tops of trees, using a long pole with a hooked antelope horn lashed to the tip. This is usually done after most of the pitch has dripped from the cone. Next the cones are collected and placed in burden baskets for transporting to a central drying area. Usually a large flat spot, which is exposed to full sunlight and a drying wind. Here, workers spread the cones out on the ground in a thin layer, so they may dry in a few days. When dry, the leaves of the cone open up, making it relatively easy to pick out the small brown pine nuts.

Picking nuts out of the cones is usually handled by the elder ladies of the tribe. They sit in a large circle and deftly tap the nuts out of the dry cones with a tool made from the tip of a deer antler. It's at this point in the operation that the ladies catch up on the news and all the latest gossip. There's much giggling and tittering as the nut pile grows!

All the while the children are busy hauling in new cones to be picked and hauling out empties. There's lots of shouting and laughter, for everyone's having fun. Through out all of this activity the Pine Nut Boss, Stands Tall, struts around issuing orders to every one. Do this, do that, go here, go there, he barks out orders in a booming voice. Of course no one really pays much attention to Stands Tall. He's really quite short with a big round belly that pops out above his apron. But, he really doesn't mind if his orders are ignored. He's having more fun than he's had all year and so are all the others. It's a happy occasion for everyone!

On the last day of the harvest the weather is cool and the first hint of a cold winter to come is in the air. The nuts are all harvested and today they will be distributed. There are immense piles of ripe nuts and the people form a long line that straggles out through the trees. Every person--man, woman and child -- has a burden basket. Every basket will be filled to the brim. As each person passes by the pile, workers load the basket. Crow Woman supervises and makes sure each basket is full. If there are any disputes or questions, Stands Tall is nearby and is the final authority.

A man's burden basket holds almost fifty pounds of nuts. He will carry it back to the family's winter camp, which may be several days' walk away. There the nuts, which are well preserved in the shell, will be stored in the ground. Later they will used as needed during the three long months of winter.

The pine nuts are very high in protein content and will supply adequate nourishment for the man over a period of three months. It works out just about right. Each man, woman or child, can carry just about enough of the rich nuts to support himself for the three months of winter.

Bopo and Noah worked very hard throughout the harvest. They pulled cones from the trees and carried baskets of cones until they never wanted to see a pine nut again. At the end of the last gathering day they went to Crow Woman and asked her to make sure their burden baskets were filled and set aside, to be claimed later. They explained their plan to go hunting and return with two antelope on the evening of the last feast. Crow Woman was understanding about 'Almost Warriors' who wanted to present the tribe with a demonstration of their hunting skills.

" However," she admonished "I won't tattle on you, but I want you to remember that you're planning to steal antelope from the Paiutes. The antelope are on Paiute land, so they belong to them. Bopo, do you understand? If someone like that horrible Snake catches you, he'll lift that fine pigtail of yours. Your scalp will go with it?"

Turning a stern eye on Noah, she said, "Noah, they'd be happy to stake you out on the ground and build a fire on your belly and let you watch it burn. You've heard about that evil fellow Snake and the ten awful warriors who follow him? They'd like nothing better than to catch two fat Washo children and fry them, slowly. I want you both to promise me, at the first sign of a Paiute, you're to turn around and run for home."

"We promise!" both fellows muttered.

The crow danced his little two step before leaning over to squawk in Crow Woman's ear. She nodded and said, " Crow says, Good Hunting !"

CHAPTER 3   The Hunt

The next morning the night sky was still pitch black, as the two youths slipped silently out of camp. Each carried his new hunting bow wrapped in a case of soft suede deer hide. Bopo's case was decorated with fine fringes, while Noah's was set off with a delicate design of blue quill work, supplied by his little sister. In addition each boy carried a quiver of broad head hunting arrows. Provisions were a pouch of jerked venison, a second pouch of pine nuts, and a flint hunting knife. They were prepared to move fast, without burden baskets and clad only in deer skin shirts, breech clouts, leggings and moccasins.

The plan was to travel light and move fast. It was anticipated they would be returning to camp with two fat antelope by sundown. No one but Crow Woman was aware they were going hunting. She had agreed not to tattle. The fellows felt very grown up and confident as they drifted off into the darkness. Neither noticed the first hint of winter slipping by on the cool predawn breeze.

The moon was well past full and sinking low in the sky, near the horizon. Long stringers of finger-like clouds drifted in. The warm fall harvest weather would change soon. The pine nuts were all harvested, assuring an adequate winter food supply. The first cold breath of winter lingered just over the horizon.

The last of the night birds chirped. Silently the boys trotted down hill toward the desert, away from the slumbering camp. They threaded their way through tightly packed clusters of pinion pine. Before them, the last of the trees bordered the edge of a meadow. Beyond, the dark ominous desert awaited.

Noah, who was leading the way, pulled up and turning to Bopo said, in a hushed voice, "I think this is as good a place as any to observe the first rule of hunting." Shrugging, Bopo commented,

"I thought the first rule of hunting was to find some animals. I don't think we're gonna jump any antelope back here in the trees."

"Of course not," whispered Noah, "the antelope are out there in the desert. But I'm surprised at you, Lump! Don't you know the first rule of hunting is to smell right? You have to be sure you don't smell like a man. You should either smell like sage brush or you oughta smell like the animal you're huntin'. I'm surprised you didn't know that!"

"I guess I knew that all the time, just sorta forgot about it for the moment. " admitted Bopo sheepishly.

" Well, if you're gonna be a big hunter Lump, you gotta remember this stuff, or you could mess up the whole hunt," counseled Noah. "Now, I think the best thing for us to do is build a fire out of sage brush. Back here in the trees where we can't be seen."

"Good idea! The tree branches'll defuse the smoke. That way no one out there in the desert, like maybe the Paiutes, can see our fire. You know, Crow Woman wasn't kidding about Snake and that mean bunch that follow him. They're just plain poison! Snake poison. We need to be real careful on this jaunt or we could lose our hair."

"Aw, that's just old lady scare talk. I don't think Snake hangs out around this country. Shucks, we'll be plenty safe."

Looking skeptical, Noah said, "I'll gather some dry wood and get a fire started. You go out and collect a big pile of nice green sage brush foliage, to make smoke with."

Noah always carried a little leather pouch at his belt. It contained a bed of dry moss, surrounding a pinch of cedar bark tinder. In the center of the tinder was a tiny coal of fire. A coal would stay alive for two and sometimes three days.

Noah constructed a substantial pile of fire wood. Behind a dense stand of pine, he kindled a small fire in the sand. Meanwhile, Bopo drifted off into the blackness, looking for a good clump of nice green sage brush foliage, to make smoke with. He wanted to collect just the fresh green top leaves of the sage. They'd cast off a dense and pungent cloud of smoke. Finding an excellent clump of rabbit brush, he began to break off the tender tips. It was a beautiful cluster of thick brush with a heavy coat of ochre blossoms. Just below the ochre blossoms was a heavy coat of bright green leaves. Just what he needed! Bopo carefully gathered an armfull of the bright gold pungent leaves. He headed back to where Noah had a small fire burning briskly.

Standing in front of the fire, Noah peeled off all his garments. Instructing Bopo to throw on some of the green leaves, he proceeded to carefully wash all of his clothes in the dense cloud of smoke. Next he stood spread-legged over the fire. Smoke billowed up around him and through his hair. The tears streamed down his cheeks. He began to cough violently. Gasping, Noah emerged from the smoke. Wiping the tears from his eyes as well as he could, in a wheezing voice he said to Bopo,

"Maybe we oughta stick to huntin' birds; they can't smell and you don't have to go through all this Sacred Smoke stuff." Bopo shook his head with a dubious frown.

Noah silently pointed at the fire. With a shrug and a reluctant grin, Bopo proceeded to immerse himself in the smoke. Noah gleefully piled handful after handful of gold rabbit brush on the flames. Next, they washed their bows and arrows in the dense cloud. Finally, they finished just as dawn was breaking. In the growing light they stood side by side at the edge of the desert. Tears streamed down their cheeks. Two Almost Warriors, ready for their first antelope hunt.

The two young men trotted briskly toward the rising sun. A light breeze began to move with them. Behind them, the dark finger-like clouds crept across the horizon, drifting out into the clear desert dawn. Throughout the morning they traveled deeper and deeper into the desert. A freshening wind was at their backs. Crossing the broad flat plain, they occasionally came to a rocky wash where there were indications of moisture, dry golden-brown patches of grass. Endless expanses of gray-green sage stretched in every direction.

There was no sign to suggest grazing antelope. Laying on their bellies at the crest of a small swell in the ground, their heads hidden behind a clump of bitter brush, they peered ahead. Carefully they scanned the vast desert floor, inch by inch. Nothing moved. No indication of game. The only movement the racing shadows of clouds, sweeping across the desert floor toward the low lying hills beyond.

" Skinny, have you noticed we're getting more and more clouds?" whispered Bopo. "When we started out this morning it looked like we were gonna have a nice clear day, but the weather seems to be gettin' worse. Did you notice? It's cooler now than when we started at dawn."

"Yeah, I noticed." said his companion. "The sky's taken on an ominous gray cast to the north. The wind's been rising and it's behind our backs. Wonder if the antelope have gotten our scent. They could just drift ahead of us, way out there so far we can't spot em."

"I don't know " mused Bopo, "If there're any antelope out ahead of us, the way we smell, with all that Sacred Smoke stuff, those animals oughta come right in here and sit in our laps!"

By noon the two Washo lads reached the low rolling hills from which the sun had emerged at dawn. Still not a sign of game, not even a bird in the gray skies. The wind freshened. It was notably colder. They crouched down behind a twisted clump of sage to eat their noon meal. Chewing on a chunk of dry jerked venison, Noah observed, "No sense in crossing this range of hills. Let's turn and head north. Maybe we'll jump some game in that direction. Can't do any worse than we've been doing."

Halfway through the afternoon the first big white flakes of snow whipped by. A gusting wind was momentarily turning stronger. Angry dark clouds were scudding across the sullen gray sky. The two lonely hunters, tiny dark dots in a vast brooding desert, hunched their shoulders against the wind. It had now turned and was coming directly into their faces, from Cold Land. Looking forward they could see a great distance across the vast sweep of the desert floor.

In the half light the colors were deep and intense. Blackish browns fading into grays, dull ocher fading into muted orange and slowly turning to a deep purple.

In the dim distance to their right, at least an hour's walk away, lay a series of dull green bluffs. The two figures, hunched against the driving wind, and turned in that direction. They hoped to find some sort of shelter at the foot of the bluffs. Suddenly the desert disappeared from view in a howling gust of wind-driven sleet. The wind had a thousand voices. It increased in velocity and emitted an audible moan. They felt the lash of wind-whipped sand. Sleet cut into face and hands.

Above the thousand voices came a   low moaning wail. Someone in intense pain! It rose to an agonizing volume. The hunters looked at each other, trying to identify the sound. With dread, they realized the sound was neither human or animal. First it seemed to come from their right. Then it faded away to a low moan. It returned from a great distance, directly behind them.

Bopo moved out at a trot, calling over his big shoulder, "Come on, Skinny. Let's get outa here. Whatever that is, it's comin' after us. I think this place's full of demons !"

Noah followed on his friend's heels, concentrating on not losing sight as Bopo disappeared into the howling black storm.

Time seemed to stand still as they ran in a windswept void of driven snow. Visibility was only a few feet. Gasping for breath, they stumbled into what must be a draw. They slid down a steep bank to the rocky bottom. Their course changed as they angled off in a slightly different direction, toward the distant bluffs. In the gloom they stumbled over rocks and brush. Following the winding path, they soon lost all sense of direction in the snow-filled void. They were only aware of the moaning wind, the driven snow and cutting sand. After what seemed an eternity, the floor of the draw widened out into a pocket. There were several huge boulders that projected up out of the sand. They'd arrived at the dull green bluffs.

Gasping for breath, Bopo said, "Far enough! Let's see if we can find a shelter where we can hunker down for a minute. I'm bushed."

"Over here" Noah groaned. "Looks like some big boulders, maybe we can get in behind 'em, out of this fierce wind."

The light was failing rapidly. Feeling their way among the boulders blindly, they discovered a sand spit where two large rocks stood back to back. A shelter, of sorts, against the violently moaning wind. With a nod of the head they silently agreed on the spot. A camp site for the night.

On hands and knees Bopo crawled into the nearby brush. He collected small twigs and blades of dry grass for a fire. Noah stripping off his leather shirt, useing it as a shield to protect a hastily dug fire pit in the sand. His companion deposited the precious fuel. Noah placed a tiny piece of glowing coal into the swirl of dry tinder. It was the very last speck of fire remaining in his pouch.

The whipping wind tore round his body and the protective shirt, scattering the few blades of grass. The youth, who was shaking with the cold, moaned in despair with his face just inches from the grass. He took a twig, coaxed the charred blades back into a tiny pile and blew on it ever so softly. Nothing happened. After a long pause he blew again very carefully, with the shirt now completely covering his head and shoulders. Hardly daring to breath, he waited for what seemed an eternity. At last there was a tiny sputter as a minute flame appeared above a single blade of grass, wavered for a moment as if about to disappear and then slowly spread to the other grass and twigs.

"Wheeeeeeooo," sighed Noah, "I didn't think we were going to make it that time. Have to thank my totem the coyote for that fire."

Suddenly the wind faded for a moment. It was deathly silent in the gloom of the sheltered camp site. From the top of an unseen bluff came an eerie, mournful, howl. Mr. Coyote was on the scene.

Out of the darkness Bopo materialized with an armful of sage brush branches. The dejected hunters hunkered down over the fire. A tiny flickering pin point of light. The only speck of warmth in a vast panorama of desert. They were desolate and alone. The howling wind made the flames dance, casting flickering shadows on the face of the boulders towering behind them. The heavy flakes of snow continued, silent and unabated. The stuff was beginning to stick now; soon it would build into a heavy blanket covering the small sea of light cast by the dancing fire. The wind moaned, rising to a soul-wrenching crescendo. Abruptly there was total, absolute silence.

Wide-eyed, Bopo turned to Noah, whose head was canted attentively to the side. He concentrated on listening, listening. There was nothing but utter silence. Then suddenly the shrieking began.

"Ow - ow - ow - owooo - oo - ooo - aghhhhhhh !!! Ow oo - oooooo ."

The two fellows sat huddled together, frozen in cold stark terror. Finally Noah hissed,

"That's the same thing we heard back down the draw. I was hopin' we'd gotten away from it or that the fire would scare it away. But now it's close, too close!"

Bopo shook his head. "No, No," he moaned "That voice isn't human and it sure isn't any animal I ever heard. That's a demon!" Again, the hideous moan rose all around them. This time echoing from the towering dark boulders. It faded off into the heavy falling snow flakes, quivering in the frozen darkness.

"Owoo - oo - oo - oo - oooo - agahhhhh!"

The night was filled with demons. Demons from another world. Out there in the black. Ready to move in and devour them.

"We're in trouble, bad trouble," hissed Bopo. "I've never been up against a demon before. Do you think we oughta run, or what?

"Maybe," gulped Noah, "maybe you could say a word to your totem. Mine doesn't seem to be listening right now."

"To tell you the truth, Skinny, I never did place much faith in that totem stuff," hissed Bopo. "When they were passing out totems, I came up sorta short. What can a fellow do at a time like this with a tree squirrel for a totem? You want I should send out an orange bellied Chickeree, to have a little chat with that demon out there?"

"Well, Lumpy ole boy, you'd better do somp'in real fast," gasped Noah. "Do you see what I see out there squatting in the snow? There. Look there!" He pointed with a shaking hand at a huge dark object emerging from the blackness. It was moving toward them.

They gasped in terror, for it was truly a demon from another world. The awful black thing rose to full height. It towered over them. With great heavy arms hanging down almost touching the snow, the monster swayed slowly from side to side. It approached and emitted a horrible spine-chilling growl. Slowly it raised one massive clawed foot. The monster shuffled a step closer, out of the howling blackness. Then another step. The thing was huge and it was almost upon them.

It moved ever closer. The trembling youths watched, speechless. The thing had a head, a gleaming white skull of a head. Empty sockets for eyes and a long white bone of a jaw with ghastly broken teeth. The jaw flapped loosely up and down with a flabby click.

Our friends retreated in horror. Hypnotized by the empty eye sockets, they began to slowly back around the fire. Noah fumbled behind his back, trying to find his bow. He never moved his gaze from those awful empty eye sockets of bare bone. The bow was gone!

Bopo moved as though in a nightmare, his mind was like jelly. His muscles wouldn't respond. They watched paralyzed with fear and fascination as the great black furry thing slouched closer and closer to the fire. From out of the darkness behind them, four large hands stealthily appeared. Abruptly, talonlike fingers closed about their unsuspecting throats. The viselike grip was chilling.

The two Washo lads found themselves on the ground, a massive weight on top of them. With his breath cut off, Bopo was sure he must be dying. He was unable to utter a sound.

Noah was powerless to move, so tightly was he pinned against the earth. Finally, in desperation he was able to drag one arm from beneath his body. Reaching back, his searching fingers gripped a leg. A leg covered with buckskin. This didn't feel like any demon. With a sudden burst of desperate energy, he was able to twist his head around. There it was, a moccasin and legging of buckskin. It had porcupine quill work running up the side.

Savagely, Noah fought to fill his bursting lungs with a deep breath. "Bopo! " he shouted. "Bopo, Fight! These aren't demons, Bopo. These are men. Fight Bopo, fight ! They're only men, Bopo. Fight them !" Noah screamed, as he was finally able to break the hold on his throat and gulp down a deep breath of air.

A grunt and a roar from Bopo's barrel chest told him his friend had made the same discovery. The two boys fought like cornered animals with hands, elbows, knees and feet. Noah was almost knocked senseless as someone smashed a hard skull into his face. With a savage growl Noah sank his teeth into some one's ear. He had the satisfaction of feeling most of the ear come away. He spit out the torn flesh and went back to the attack using the only weapon available to him, his teeth.

The fight was too one sided to last very long. Gasping and bleeding, the two Washos lay with hands bound behind their back. It was all over and they'd lost. Gathered around them were ten villainous figures, clad in buckskins. They were all somewhat the worse for their attack. Some rubbed bruises and stanched the flow of blood from a battered nose. They glared down at the two captive Washos, laying helpless on the ground. Out of the darkness stepped an eleventh figure, slightly larger than the others. He was clad in a huge cape of a black bear hide. It flapped loosely about the bare white bone mask made from the skull of a bear. Attached to the skull was a lower jaw of some large unrecognizable animal. This was the demon that had terrified the two only moments before.

Noah shook his head in disgust, as did Bopo, realizing they had been duped and even worse. They'd shown their fear before the dreaded Paiutes. Yes, their captors were the Paiutes.

The ten evil-looking warriors smirked and some laughed outright at the embarrassed fellows. However, the eleventh man did not laugh. He strode forward into the fire light with the mask still hanging from his neck and his right ear, most of which was gone, bleeding profusely. His ugly face was distorted with hate as he drew back a foot and kicked Noah in the ribs with all his strength. This was, Snake, the worst of the Paiutes.

CHAPTER 4   Captured

Snake was an ugly man with a permanent sneer. The lower part of his face was daubed with solid yellow war paint, making him look even more evil. Snake's right ear was horribly disfigured. It was apparent that Noah had marked him for life. Putting his hand to his ear and then looking at the blood on his fingers, Snake snarled at Noah. "You filthy Washo pup, I oughta kill you now. Think I'll take out my beautiful Diamond Back friend and let him fill you with venom."

Untying the small bulging bag at his waist, Snake opened the mouth of the sack. Holding the writhing rattle snake's tail through the leather, he shook it out into the open. With a leer he extended the angry snake toward Noah. The broad flat diamond shaped head twisted back and forth. The mouth was open and the gleaming fangs were bared. Its rattle tipped tail was imprisoned in the sack. The snake drew back in an attempt to coil. Then in a flash it struck at Noah's face, as he lay bound and helpless on his back. Noah gritted his teeth and braced himself. The fangs fell short of his face by the width of a finger. Noah recoiled as best he could with hands bound behind his back. Snake and his warriors howled with unholy glee at the captive's terror.

"Untie me and give me a knife," bellowed Noah. "I'll take on both you and your lousy rattler." Of course neither the evil Paiute nor the bound

Washo could understand the other. One spoke Hokan, the other the Paiute tongue.

Noah was proficient at sign language, but his hands were tied behind his back. Even so, each understood the other as they glared with hatred. It was obvious Noah's display of spirit only served to infuriate Snake. He again kicked Noah in the ribs. When the youth doubled over in gasping pain, the leering warrior launched another blow to his defenseless back. The writhing figure grunted with agony! At this, Bopo could hold his tongue no longer. He began shouting futile threats at Snake, which only earned him viscous blows from two of the Paiute warriors.

With a practiced hand Snake retrieved his writhing pet and worked it back into the sack. Holding the squirming bag in front of Noah's slightly greenish face, Snake shouted, "Snake venom's too easy a way for you to die. I'm going to take you back to our village where everyone can watch. You lousy Washo pup, I'll teach you how to die slowly. You and your noisy friend will enjoy a very, very slow death."

The Washo youths didn't understand a word of what the angry Paiute shouted. But they knew exactly what he meant to do to them. Snake signaled for his men to build up the fire, with a surly wave of his arm. The night had grown colder as the silent snow continued to fall. It collected in a thick layer on the ground. The sullen Paiute warriors drifted away and began a search for more fire wood. Soon the fire was blazing high as they gathered around, extending their hands to the flames for warmth.

One large fellow with a permanent scowl and a twisted frog like face was assigned to guard the captives. They lay bound and shivering some distance from the fire. Frog Face approached the two inert figures with pieces of braided raw hide rope. He tied hard knots around each neck. Testing the knots to be sure they were secure, he fastened the other end of the rope around his own waist. Ignoring the two lads, the ugly warrior returned to the warmth of the fire.

The Paiutes squatted on the ground around the fire and began to break out food. As soon as they felt the warmth of the fire and tasted the food, their spirits lifted. They began to talk about the events of the day. Their hunting trip had yielded unexpected but highly satisfying results. It was really a windfall to land two prized Washo captives.

"There will be great excitement at Pyramid Lake as we march into camp with our young prisoners at the end of a rope," gloated Snake, the blood still dripping from his torn face. "There will be even more excitement when I drag these two sniveling pups before the tribal elders and demanded the right to put them to death by torture."

Of course, it would probably have been more profitable if they'd made slaves of the Washo and worked them hard for the rest of what would probably be a short life. But, when the two disrespectful pups fought like cornered wild cats and the tall Washo ripped off Snake's ear, their death warrant was signed. Snake was a mean and vengeful man who would never let such an insult to his person go unpunished.

The warriors talked in low tones among themselves, occasionally laughing and muttering insults at the two youths. They lay bound and shivering in the snow, away from the fire. The worried captives remained silent as they lay in the snow, hurting all over from the beating. So cold they couldn't stop shivering, they were too depressed to make a sound.

After a while the camp became silent as the warriors one after another stretched out, pulled a robe around himself and began to snore. The youths lay there wide eyed through out the night. They uttered not a sound, trying vainly to think of some way to escape. When the first rays of dawn started to steal across the desert floor the slumbering Paiute began to stir. The two captives were still hopeless and without a plan.

Frog Face gave a cruel jerk on both the ropes around his waist, signaling the prisoners to stand. "Get up, you lazy Washo dogs."

Each managed to gulp a mouthful of snow while struggling to his feet, the first moisture either had swallowed since leaving the Pine Nut Mountains of home the morning before. Right now that seemed a long time ago and very far away.

A small snow bird busily flitted from bush to bush, looking for food. The morning sun was warm and it looked as though the early storm had come and gone. Patches of desert sand began to appear here and there through the cover of snow. For the first time in hours the captives' thoughts drifted away from freezing and turned to empty stomachs.

"That sun feels good, first time I've been able to stop shivering all night," grunted Noah, attempting to stretch his cramped shoulder muscles.

"Wonder what these delightful people are planning to serve for breakfast," said a sardonic Bopo, licking his lips.

While the Paiute warriors sleepily arose from the ground and started packing their robes in preparation to leave, Noah and Bopo stood with hanging heads and watched in silence. One by one their captors produced food and munched away at breakfast. No one paid the least heed to the two forlorn Washo youths. It was plain they didn't get anything to eat.

Snake appeared and strode toward the two captives. Instinctively they   ducked behind the protective figure of Frog Face. They retreated as far as the ropes around their throats would allow. Ignoring them, Snake strode off at a fast walk toward the bluffs with the morning sun at his face. One by one the evil ten fell in behind Snake, with Frog Face bringing up the rear. At the end of their tethers the two Washos plodded along in the dust behind Frog Face, hands still bound behind their backs.

Snake followed a faint game trail that led to the top of a bluff. Looking back across the vast desert, Noah could see a low rise of the Pine Nut Mountains in the hazy distance. Behind them the towering mountain range of Washo Land. Noah got a lump in his throat. He wished fervently he were sitting before the fire at the family camp.

Shaking his head, Bopo muttered, "I just wish I could figure out where we went wrong. Those Paiute devils couldn't have seen us in that snow storm. We couldn't see more than an arm's length ahead and they sure couldn't see any better. For some reason they just seemed to know right where we were."

"Almost as though someone had told them about us," agreed Noah.

"One thing's sure, we really messed up and now we're in deep trouble. Should have paid more attention to Crow Woman, I guess!"

"I can't understand how they found us," groaned Noah as his thoughts were interrupted by a viscous jerk on the rope around his neck. Frog Face was making it clear they weren't to fall behind.

"Yes sir," muttered Noah, "I'm coming." As an afterthought he added, "But I don't like it and one of these days I'll get a chance to show you just how much I don't like it, Mr. Frog Face."

Laying on his belly in a shadowed patch of cool snow, under a clump of sage brush, a scruffy old coyote silently watched the procession of eleven surly looking Paiutes marching along in single file. They were followed by two disreputable-looking Washos, hands bound, stumbling as they walked. The silent coyote slowly shook his head in disbelief.

"Just think, instead of this I could be back in that nice warm meadow high up in Washo Land catching plump, juicy field mice." Again he shook his grizzled head, "This totem business, bah!"

During the balance of the morning Snake kept up his fast pace, bending gradually to his left til, at last, the party was moving due north. As the silent file crested a rise they could look out for a great distance across the vast sage covered desert to a horizon of low-lying mountains vanishing into a purple haze. Straight as an arrow, Snake struck out through the center of the great plain, his destination clear to see. They were headed for a low chain of mountains in the far distance. At the foot of those mountains lay Pyramid Lake and home, Paiute Village.

The sun was high overhead as the procession came upon a small trickle of water. It originated in a tiny spring high up in an outcropping of bare lava rock. The leader approached a quiet pool of clear water and kneeling beside it, tested it for freshness. Then he proceeded to drink from a cupped hand. The other warriors followed suit. Soon they started to talk quietly among themselves and taking out food, began a spare noon meal. The two dejected captives watched every bite with hungry eyes. Bopo actually drooled, but to no avail. No one took notice or offered them so much as a crumb of food.

Bopo put on his most engaging smile, flashing a fine mouth full of strong white teeth. His attentions were directed at the guard Frog Face, who stared back with a slack-jawed   look of total disinterest.

"I say Mr. Frog Face...that is your name, isn't it? I was wondering to myself, do you happen to speak any Hokan? I'm sure a brilliant fellow like you must understand at least a few words." Cocking his head to one side and still smiling engagingly, Bopo went on talking softly to the ugly fellow.

"Oh, you say you really don't know what I'm talking about, do you? Well now, that makes you one big stupid slob of a Paiute, doesn't it ?"

Smiling all the while, Bopo nodded his head up and down at Frog Face. The big ugly Paiute, whose mouth hung slack, nodded his head up and down in response.

Never changing his smiling expression, Bopo went on in the most friendly of voices. "Well   then, Big Stupid, why don't you untie our hands and give us something to eat?" Again the big fellow nodded his head up and down, but gave no sign he understood a word.

Noah was hard pressed to keep a straight face. He turned his head away so no one could see he was losing the battle against laughter.

At last without any warning the big warrior stood up and walked over to where Bopo was squatting on his heels. Grasping the rope around Bopo's neck, he dragged him to an upright position, strangling the fellow as he did so. Next he pointed to the stream, indicating Bopo should drink. Gasping and choking, Bopo did so, gulping eagerly.

While he was drinking, Bopo's captor carefully inspected the knots in the neck rope and then proceeded to untie the leather thongs about his wrists. Bopo arose, rubbing his aching wrists to restore circulation.

"Oh Boy! Does that ever feel better!"

Next the warrior released Noah's hands, allowing him to drink as well.

" Well," muttered Bopo under his breath. "At least our hands are free and we got some water. I wonder if that fellow does understand a few words of the Hokan language after all? Hope not, or my name is Turtle. Come to think of it, my name is Turtle Without a Shell!"

Throughout the balance of the day the warriors and their captives continued to head north toward Pyramid Lake and the Paiute Village. The youths were allowed to drink whenever they passed water and their hands remained free. At dusk they reached a stream in a clump of cottonwood trees. Snake indicated with a surly grunt, this was to be the campsite for the night.

Noah, reverting to sign language, made an attempt to catch Frog Face's eye and engage him in hand talk. Their captor chose to ignore him.

"That ugly Paiute just won't talk to you, will he?" grunted Bopo as their captor dragged the two off by the neck. They were to gather wood for the evening camp fire. The two assembled a large pile of wood, sufficient for the whole night. Again Noah attempted to get the ugly Paiute to converse with him in sign language. The fellow responded grudgingly for a while, but then led them back to the camp area in silence.

"Well, you finally got the guy to talk what did he say? I couldn't see his hands from where I was?" inquired Bopo eagerly.

"Sushhhhh, I'll tell you later, I think they are listening now. That frog Face may understand more Hokan than we think."

To the captives' dismay, the Paiute again lashed hands behind their backs. He motioned them to lie down on the ground a good distance away from the fire. The neck ropes remained in place. It was another long cold night without food. Throughout the night a nearby coyote sang his mournful song to a sliver thin new moon high in the sky.

The sun rose on a second day of captivity, much as the morning before. The boys were increasingly aware of the gnawing hunger in their bellies and it was obvious the Paiutes had no intention of providing them with any food. Indeed, the surly Paiutes seemed to ignore the fact they existed, except for Frog Face whose job it was to guard them.

"Bopo," whispered Noah, "we've got to get something to eat. Start watching along the trail. Stuff we can dig and eat raw. If we don't find grub today this is gonna get serious. I'm starving! How about you?"

"Well, " said Bopo, making a gloomy face, "I watched all day long yesterday and didn't see one darned thing that was edible. Nothing growing out here in this dry desert. If we were back in Washo Land there'd be a lot more water and stuff you could eat growing all along the trail. Just have to keep watchn,' I guess. Just make sure you don't fall behind or ole Frog Face will jerk your head clean off with that darn neck rope!"

Noah nodded his head and hissed out of the corner of his mouth, "You mark my words, Lump, the time's coming when I'm gonna have a chance to even things up with that guy. I'm really gonna nail him! He's almost as mean as that fellow Snake! That's saying quite a bit. You know, when I finally got him to talk a little in sign language, he told me how they found us in that storm. You'll never believe this, Bopo! They smelled us. Can you believe that? They smelled us."

"Aw, come on Noah. I don't believe that; besides, we were all smoked up, they couldn't have smelled us in all that wind and snow. No way!"

"You know, when I asked you to collect sage brush leaves, so we could make smoke. Observe the first rule of hunting. Smell like Sage Brush, not like man. Well, you messed up, Bopo. Messed up sumpthin' awful. You got Rabbit Brush, remember? Rabbit Brush! Well the problem was, Rabbit Brush grows mostly around Washo Land where there's plenty of water, but not much of it ever grows in Paiute desert country. So to a Paiute, Rabbit Brush smells like Washo Land."

"Oh no. I can't believe this!" groaned Bopo, his massive shoulders sagging.

With a grim look Noah proceeded.   "That night in the storm Snakes gang was comin' up the wash behind us. They could smell our smoke made from Rabbit Brush. It was so strong they thought a great big hunting party of Washos must be up ahead of them, in the dark. Imagine how surprised they were when they found out it was only two stupid Washo kids. Children, who didn't know the difference between Sage Brush and Rabbit Brush. Bopo, you really messed up good when you went out picking leaves for the smoke ceremony."

For a long period there was silence. At last Bopo said in his most disgusted voice,

"Noah, don't you ever, ever, tell me again, never, about your darned First Rule of Hunting! Smelling like sage brush smoke. UGH!"

Through the long morning trek the two Washo lads concentrated on keeping up with the fast-moving group of silent warriors. At the same time they watched carefully for any sign of vegetation that appeared to be edible. Bopo picked some gray leaves from a low scrub bush. He chewed on them tentatively before spitting them out and making a wry face at his friend.

"No luck, it's just too darned dry for anything fit to eat to grow out here."

Toward noon the single file of warriors approached a small hollow at the foot of a sage-covered hill. Two dry-looking cottonwood trees, with the last remnants of yellow leaves clinging to their twisted branches, marked a likely looking spot to pause. Out in that vast desert, the presence of a cottonwood tree indicated the existence of at least a trace of moisture somewhere below the surface of the parched ground. The two youths exchanged knowing looks and smiled grimly.

Without a word the Paiutes squatted down on their haunches under the bare trees and prepared to eat a meager noon meal. In the center of the hollow were the traces of a pond, long since dried up. The bottom of the pond, at one time smooth mud, was now dried and cracked into a multitude of tiles. Around the border of the pond were the remains of a growth of cat tails intermixed with wild turnips. The foliage was a sere brown, the heads of the cat tails burst and spreading a stream of fluffy white seed on the breeze. The wind rattled the dry leaves and a small brown bird busily flitted from stalk to bare stalk.

"Come on," hissed Bopo. "I feel the urge to eat and eat and eat."

The hungry Washos armed themselves with dry sticks and, going to the end of their neck tethers, knelt down and began to dig. The roots of the tails were just below the surface, where there was still a trace of moisture. They were pale green in color, moist and succulent, the boys hastily wiped the stalks free of sandy loam and began to make a meal. After gorging themselves on roots, they moved to another spot and dug turnips which were crisp, white tapers with a delicate flavor. After a while they paused, unable to hold more, with appetites satisfied for the time being.

It soon occurred to the captive to lay away a supply of the succulent tubers as the next food might be a long way down the trail. They fell to digging again. All the while the Paiutes sat stoically under the trees, munching away at their noon meal and totally ignoring the frantic activities of the hungry Washo captives.

For the next two and a half days the party pressed on through long desert valleys. While they uncovered no more food, the weather was clear and warm with the last vestiges of snow gradually disappearing. As evening fell, they topped the crest of a sage-covered hill and looked down into a large meadow of incredible beauty. The meadow of golden brown autumn grass was long and curving, following the course of a broad sparkling river of deep clear water. Its banks were marked by huge old cottonwoods, now turned to a flaming gold color by the change of seasons.

"There it is!" said Noah in a quiet voice filled with admiration. "The Truckee River !."

The leader, Snake, designated a grassy spot on the river bank under immense spreading cottonwoods and camp was set up by the tired travelers. The river gurgled close by. The Paiutes, who were accomplished fishermen, made forked spears and soon produced large fat Cutthroat Trout from the cold waters of the river. The warriors enjoyed a rich feast far into the night. Their spirits were high. There was much laughing and talking in loud voices. Return to the home village on the following evening was a reality.

Meanwhile, the captives grabbed a hasty mouthful of wilted turnips, before their hands were bound behind their backs for the night. Laying in the darkness while listening to the music of gurgling water, Noah said to his cousin, "You know, Lump, it's hard to realize that not too many hours ago, the very water that's flowing past us now was flowing before the lodges of our northern relatives. The clan of the Wel mel ti in Washo Land. If we could just find some way to escape, we could make it back there with not much more than one day's run."

The next morning the first rays of sun to break across the eastern mountains found the party already underway. It would be a long day's walk to the Paiute Village at Pyramid Lake. The day was consumed in following the course of the winding Truckee River on its journey to the great desert lake called Pyramid. The trail, which was a well-worn route of Paiute travel, lay along the crest of a steep hill paralleling the west bank of the sparkling river.

Looking down into the deep valley between the two sage-covered hills, one could follow the winding river's course around big rocks, over sand bars and through clumps of bright green willows or flaming golden cottonwoods. It moved lazily northward out of sight into the distance. As they traveled, Mallards, Pin Tail ducks and Speckled geese would occasionally erupt from a hiding place along the waters edge. The startled birds would sound a loud cry of alarm, skimming low along the river to disappeared from sight. In the stillness of the early morning it was sometimes possible to hear the gurgling of the water in the distance, as it broke over rocky spots in the river bed. Several times, bands of gray brown sage hen appeared in the trail ahead of the party. They scrambling along for some distance before flying away in a frenzied beating of clumsy wings. The desert sky was a brilliant, cloudless blue. Gradually the morning sun warmed the air.

All day long the party forged northward. The pace gradually quickened as the sun moved across the sky. At noon there was no pause for the usual meal. The warriors kept moving. Each was eager to catch the first glimpse of the main village at Pyramid Lake. With each step northward the two tired and hungry Washo captives became more apprehensive.

Just as the sun was beginning to dim behind the western horizon the party broke over a crest to behold a panorama. It was so spectacular it was shocking. Before them stretched a huge lake. A body of water almost as large as Da ow oga. The surface a vivid opaque blue stretching off into the distance, to low purple hills at the horizon. The vast basin surrounding the lake was barren of vegetation. The shore line was void of trees. A lake of brackish water, without an outlet. To the right the abundant Truckee River flowed into the lake. Its entrance formed a large fan shaped delta of shallow green water at the mouth. On the far river bank a grassy meadow with clusters of giant cottonwood trees. Spectacular in autumn gold foliage. This was Paiute Village.

A cluster of thatched lodges scattered at random along the river bank. Noisy, excited men, women and children issued from the reed huts, anxious to catch a first glimpse of the new arrivals.

Slowly the tired party waded across the shallow river mouth. Each traveler climbed the far bank amid the howls and screams of a welcoming crowd. Everyone was there. Young people, elders, children, all screaming and shouting. They created an unbelievable din. A multitude of stamping moccasin feet created a dense cloud of yellow dust. Arm waving figures were clad in buckskin clothing. There were feathered ornaments of bright colors. Underfoot were small children, mostly naked, every one with long black hair flying. The tumult was deafening !

The two forlorn Washo captives were dragged across the shallow river ford, stumbling at the end of neck ropes. Immediately they were attacked by women and children. All were equipped with switches or hands filled with stones and dirt. Screamed insults rained down upon them. In the midst of this assault the captives were dragged to a solitary reed hut, isolated from the others by some distance. Shouting threats with a sneer on his ugly face, Snake roughly shoved the two bound captives into the dark interior. With a leer he tied the leather door flap closed.

CHAPTER 5 The Paiute Village

"It's black in here, I can't see. The floor's hard. I'm cold. Ugh!"

Noah and Bopo lay on the hard packed clay floor for a long time. Neither moved. They were stunned. The last six days had been a shattering series of events. The humiliation, beating and starvation, were new and bitter experiences.

During the long march, hope had begun to grow within both of them. Hope that the cruel treatment would be discontinued once they reached Paiute village. There, they'd be under the authority of tribal elders. However, the welcome just received dispelled any hopes they may have had.

"Ugh, these people really dislike us," groaned Noah,

"I never realized just how intense the hatred was. This is much more than just being upset about a couple of poached antelope."

"Yeah," said Bopo. "This goes all the way back to when Snake first arrived. He's the one who fanned the flames. Got an active war started between the Washos and the Paiutes."

Laying on his back and staring out of the smoke hole in the top of the reed hut, Noah could see the first star of evening appear in a darkening sky outside. The hut was well constructed of a sturdy woven willow frame work, lashed together with thin strips of green willow bark. Clumps of reed and marsh grass were lashed to the frame work in a shingled fashion, providing a covering that was both waterproof and windproof. Two antelope hides laced together formed the cover for an eastward facing doorway. At the top, the smoke hole was open to the sky. It was a secure and snug shelter, thought Noah. Built by an expert.

"You know," whispered Bopo, "I'm lying here, flat on my back with my hands and arms tied under me. I'm hurting like crazy. I'm all beaten up. I've never been so tired or hungry in my life. There are a whole bunch of crazy people outside who wanta kill me. I feel absolutely awful! But, in spite of all that my mind keeps going back to only one thing. This whole event is just exactly as if I'd been here before."

"Didn't know you'd been in Paiute Village before!"

"This whole thing, the great huge lake in this barren waste with no vegetation. The Truckee River emptying into the lake. The meadow with the big old cottonwood trees. The thatched huts with smoke coming out at dusk. This whole thing is just like it should be. Except, of course, the people should be friendly. Not a bunch of crazies getting ready to kill me."

"So, you been here before, have you?" asked a gloomy voice out of the darkness.

Bopo didn't say anything for a moment, just twisted his head around and looked questioningly at his friend. Wondering if he might have gone out of his head from all the rough treatment.

"Even this hut is exactly the way I remember it," he said. "The only trouble is, I've never been here in my life. Never before. In fact, this is the first time I've ever been in Paiute territory."

"Well," said Noah, trying to sound very calm for his friend's benefit. "Maybe you should tell me all about it. But let's sit up first, my back's killing me. Be careful not to disturb your neck rope. I have a hunch one of those nice fellows outside will jerk your head clean off if you move too quickly."

Quietly Noah got to his feet and stretched stiff muscles. Carefully he went over to the doorway and nudged the flap aside. Just enough so he could peer out of the slit.

"Shhhhhhhhhh...shhhhhhhhh," he whispered "Weasel is sitting just outside the door with his back to us. I think he's asleep. But I can't tell for sure. Anyway, he's got the two neck ropes tied around his wrist. So be careful!"

Weasel was one of the evil ten who accompanied Snake. He was a small, mean looking rat-like, little man. He'd apparently taken over Frog Face's job of guarding. Silently the two youths moved to the rear of the hut and sat with their backs to the willow frame work. They stretched as far as the buckskin neck ropes would permit. Seated close together, they whispered to each other throughout most of the night. Neither captive felt much like sleeping.

"This story goes back a long ways to when I was a pretty small kid. I can remember it as clear as if it was yesterday," whispered Bopo. "It all happened while we were sitting around the campfire.

In fact, there were lots of camp fires. My father was quite a story teller. Probably the finest of story tellers. I've heard a lot of them by now."

"Yeah, I remember hearing him tell one of his tales once. He has quite a reputation as a teller of tales."

Leaning back and squirming into a more comfortable position against the wall of the hut, Bopo prepared to tell his story. "You see, my dad is a trader. He's always been a trader because he's Hung a lil ti clan. They live by going to one place and finding something precious. They store it in their burden basket. Then they go far away to where there's someone who doesn't have any of the precious stuff. He trades some of his precious stuff for something that's needed elsewhere. They travel most of the time. Always going to far away places. Sometimes, when I was a little older, I got to go with them. I've even been all the way to New Sea. Heard the ocean roar. Listened to the waves crash. Smelled salt in the air. Not many Washo kids can say that. Anyhow, one of the places my dad used to go was the lake of the pyramids, to trade with the Paiute people."

"You mean right here,   this very village where the people are so hostile?"

"Yup! " said Bopo. "Things were peaceful way back then. He and his friends--there were other Washos--they all traveled together. So they wouldn't get ambushed. You see, their burden baskets always held lots of valuable stuff. They'd be loaded with things like Black Oak acorns and lots of abalone shell. Pieces of abalone shell were one of the best trade goods. All the people liked them. Used shell for decorations and jewelry. You could carry lots of pieces of shell without having too much weight. Even so, it was a lot of work to carry a full basket of shells. All the way from New Sea to Pyramid Lake. That's many moons of walking. But anyway, when they finally got here, all the Paiute people were glad to see 'em. There was a big feast of cutthroat trout. Everyone had a good time celebrating the arrival."

"Boy, what a change from the reception we got today. I thought they were going to kill us on the spot. What caused 'em to change?"

"In a word, Snake: he was the cause of the change, but that came later," whispered Bopo. "First let me tell you about the old time traders. The day after they arrived at Paiute Village, they'd get down to trading. The Washos would sit around on the ground with their trade goods spread out before 'em on a deer hide or a woven mat. The Paiute people would move around looking everything over, until they saw somethin' that took their eye. They'd sit down and put what they had to trade on the ground. Then the haggling began in earnest. Everybody talked in sign language. Sometimes the bargaining would go on for a long time. Finally a deal was struck."

"What kind of stuff did the Paiutes have? Doesn't look like there's much out here in the desert to trade."

"The best trading was usually abalone shells for powdered colors. The Paiutes had all sorts of wonderful colors: white and black and a variety of

red and ochre, sulphur yellow, blue and green. All
of the great desert colors. The Paiute ladies
gathered stones of all the bright colors. They have a
whole bunch of sites, each one with different color
rock. They carry the rock back to camp where they
grind it to fine powder. Use pounding stones or a
metate. Nobody had as good colors as the Paiutes!
The colors were used for dyeing and paint.
Decoration of all sorts!"

"Yeah! Our women folk use those bright
colors a lot."

"Of course, there were all sorts of things to
be found at one of those trades. Good things! Like
feathers of all colors and sizes. Chipping flint of all
kinds. Porcupine quills in every color. All kinds of
fine suede leather, salt and food. It was really a big
event."

"So what happened to change it all?" asked a
suspicious Noah.

"This was the way it used to be a long time
ago. When there was still peace between the two
tribes," whispered Bopo. He sat, arms bound behind
his back in the gloom, a captive in an enemy lodge.

"When my father returned from one of his
trips, we'd all gather around the campfire at night.
He'd tell us stories about his trading. All about the
people. What they wore. What they ate. Who'd
gotten married. Who was sick. What kind of shelters
they built. All the latest gossip! My dad's a great
story teller! He always made it sound just like you'd
been there yourself. Knew all of the people. That
way, we always felt we knew all about the places he
visited."

"All right," exclaimed an irate Noah. "So what changed all this great relationship with our neighbors the Paiutes?"

Undaunted, Bopo plunged ahead with his story. "He told us of the Paiutes when he traveled to the eastward. The Shoshone when he went to the south. Tan eu when he went west. Yanas and Yahi, our Hokan-speaking brothers, when he traveled northward. That's why I felt like I had been here before. I had a really funny feeling when we walked down the hill to this place. Seeing everything right where it should be. Looking just as he'd described it."

Bopo heaved a big sigh. "But, that was a long time ago while there was still peace between the two tribes. One day without any warning at all, Snake and the Evil Ten appeared from out of the deep desert to the east. It was rumored they came from a place very far away under the Old Sea, where Old Sea still lives; on the shores of a great lake whose waters were heavy with salt. So much salt the land there glistens white."

"I've heard rumors about that place. Never thought it really existed," agreed Noah.

"It was whispered Snake was driven out into the desert to the west. By the tribal elders. Because he was a very evil man. He was said to be a murderer who was at war with everyone. Even his own people! He and his followers would steal from anyone. Friend or enemy. Then they'd kill whom-ever complained. When he first arrived at Pyramid Village, these things were not known. The tribal elders could see he was very strong. His men were heavily armed.

"The elders thought he could help defend the village. Make the Paiute tribe much safer. So, they accepted him as a member. To show their good faith the elders offered him the fairest of their daughters, Night Bird, in marriage. And so Snake took Night Bird as his bride. Became a much respected warrior of the village."

"All sounds like sweetness and light. What happened?"

"But then," whispered Bopo "Everything began to change rapidly. People became aware the rattle snake was his totem. He kept many rattlers in his lodge. Always carried one with him in a small bag at his waist. He'd take out the vicious snake and threaten any one who disagreed with him. Several of those who chose not to agree became mysteriously ill. As though they were poisoned by their food. Eventually they wasted away and died in great pain. It was very bad medicine."

"I can begin to see this fellow was a real bad one."

"Snake beat his wife and abused the poor woman before others so often she tried to run away. But, the Evil Ten were ordered to return her to the lodge. Only to be beaten again! Snake always wore war paint. Night and day! He was never   seen without the lower half of his face daubed with glaring yellow paint. A frightening sight!"

"Yeah, you're right, he looks awful in that war paint. Didn't get any prettier when I chewed his ear off either!" chortled Noah.

"Each morning his wife's first chore, after she arose, was to replenish his facial paint. People soon became aware he was at war with everyone outside the village. Whenever Snake and his band of cutthroats returned to camp from a hunting trip, he was more apt than not to have a fresh scalp at his waist. Soon it became apparent to the elders they were at war with all their neighbors, because of indiscriminate raids carried out by the yellow faced villain."

"Man, he was a real bad warrior, wasn't he?"

"Yeah! He kept gettin' worse, too! Soon he began to return to camp with women and children captives. People taken from neighboring tribes. These captives he sold as slaves. The only exception was a beautiful young Washo girl child. He kept her as a slave in his own lodge. It was announced she was to be his number two wife, when she became of age. The girl was very unhappy! Tried to run away. She was brought back! Beaten and humiliated before the whole tribe! Everyone secretly felt sorry for the little girl, because she was so alone."

"The elders should have thrown him out right then."

"Yeah! But, they didn't. Now, even the Paiute people are ashamed of Snake and the Evil Ten. Secretly, they wish there was some way to drive him away from the village. But they're all afraid of him"

"Bopo, I wish you would stop talking. I'm sorry I asked about that devil," hissed Noah in the darkness. "The more you tell me about Snake and that gang of cutthroats, the worse I feel. In fact I feel sick. It was real bad medicine when I decided to chew on that fellow's ear. Couldn't possibly find a worse person to offend. Don't know what happened to my totem! He sure isn't bringing me much good luck right now."

After that the young Washos were silent for a long period. Each tried to think of some way to get out of their awful predicament. The longer they thought about it, the more they realized just how hopeless the situation had become.

"If only we could get these thongs off our wrists. Find some way lay hands on our knives," hissed Bopo. "At least we could go out there like men. Take on Snake and the whole bunch of em! There isn't much question how it'd turn out! At least we wouldn't be sittin' here like a piece of cold meat. Waitin' for Snake to drag us out by the neck and start torturing us. I'm not sure I'm going to turn out to be the strong silent Washo warrior type, when Snake starts to do some of the things Crow Woman told us about. I sure wish we could talk to Crow Woman right about now. She'd know just what to do. She always knows!"

"Bopo, be quiet," hissed Noah in alarm "Something's happening. Something's moving behind us. Have you gotten your hands loose?"

"Nope, tied tight as ever," whispered a frightened Bopo. "My thongs are just as tight as when they were first tied. Doesn't matter what I try. They won't loosen up a bit!"

Turning his head in a vain effort to see the thatched wall behind him, Noah hissed in desperation,

"Something's moving right behind us! Maybe they're comin' to start torturing us. Maybe it's Snake!"

Making a wry face, Bopo said plaintively "Well, Skinny, if it is Snake I can't think of anything very constructive we can do about it. Except maybe you could bite his other ear off." he said with sudden inspiration.

The rustling behind them continued as the first light of dawn began to creep through the smoke hole above their heads, diluting the gloom within the hut. In desperation both boys silently struggled to their feet, each mentally making one last plea to his totem for help, lots of help, lots of help right nowwww!

In agony the two captives stood facing the reed-thatched wall. It was deathly silent as they watched. At last there was a slight quiver of the longer reeds in the wall. The movement stopped and they strained to hear even the slightest sound. But there was nothing, the silence was ominous. Then, there it was again, the tiny movement. This time it continued, slowly, slowly. At last a thin slit of dawn light filtered through the reed covered wall. The slit was carefully enlarged with agonizing care. Now, a small brown fingertip could be seen gently working the reeds from side to side, enlarging the slit ever so slightly. The fingertip was withdrawn and silence continued, not a sound. Noah cautiously bent forward, placing his eye before the slit, in an attempt to see out. There was nothing, just the paling night sky.

For what seemed an eternity they stood frozen, transfixed, staring at the blank wall. Outside were the first faint sounds of the Paiute camp stirring to life. Suddenly, their eyes were drawn back to the wall. There it was again, the faint rustling of the reeds as the slit slowly widened.

The sharp tip of an obsidian knife blade began to gradually emerge from the reeds. At last the entire blade of a flint hunting knife appeared, followed by a small brown hand gripping the bone handle. The hand opened palm upward and the knife slipped out, falling to the floor with a soft thud.

"Noah, that's my hunting knife," gasped Bopo. He scrambled to sit in a position where his bound hands could retrieve the blade. Noah stared at the small brown hand as it slowly turned over, so the palm was downward. The fingers spread wide and the little brown thumb extended. The hand moved from side to side as if to draw attention.

"Bopo," hissed Noah, "look at this!" He pointed with his head. The extended hand displayed a web stretched between thumb and index finger. Bopo scrambled closer, placing his face close to the small hand.

"Wow! " he gasped in surprise. "What do you know! A Washo tattoo! The kind of blue tattooed mark the Washos put on their kids' hand or ankle, so they can be identified, if they're stolen."

Quickly the hand was withdrawn through the slit in the thatching. Noah placed his mouth to the slit and whispered.

" Who are you? Are you a Hokan speaker?"

Placing an ear to the slit he listened intently, but there was no sound. For a long time Noah listened in vain. He felt an agony of anxiety. What if the person had gone away? Glancing out of the corner of his eye at Bopo, he whispered urgently.

"Quick, cut your hands loose. Go over and see if Weasel's still there. See if he's awake."

Continuing to listen, ear to the slit wall, at first he heard nothing. Then at last there was a faint sound. Softly whispered words coming from far away.

"I can only stay here a minute or I'll be discovered. The camp is beginning to awaken. I'm a Hokan speaker. My name is Ai mee. I'm a captive! A slave in the lodge of Snake. He'll kill me if I am caught here. You must escape quickly, now! There isn't a minute to waste. Snake will awaken at any time now. First he'll eat. Then he'll have his face painted. Next, he'll come for you. Then the torture will begin! You must hurry! Do exactly as I tell you. There's no time to talk. Last night I made a false trail, by planting some of your things along the main path. The one that leads back up the river toward Washo Land. When he comes to this hut and finds you're gone, he'll search and find the false trail. They'll pursue you in that direction for a few moments, before they realize they've been tricked." whispered the soft voice.

"Cut yourselves loose. Keep the thongs. You'll need them. Tie your neck ropes to the frame of the lodge. One of you watch Weasel. The other cut a small passage hole, through the rear thatched wall. Watch the hut to your left. It's the one farthest from the river, closest to the lake. I'll hide there. When it's safe for you to slip out of this hut, I'll hang a red skin over the door. The door of the hut where I'm hiding. Stay low and run for the red skin hut. When you get there you'll see a group of five large rocks a ways farther on. Go to the largest of the rocks. Behind it you'll find a pit where the women dig clay. I've hidden a bundle there; the few supplies I could steal. Your bows are there too. You won't have more than a few minutes' head start over Snake and the others. So, don't stop for anything. Your life depends on it! Go along the lake shore to the north. At the end of the lake where you see the pyramids, turn to the west. Go for many days until you come to Honey Marsh. Don't enter the marsh or you're dead! Quick sand!" whispered the urgent voice of the unseen speaker.

"It's best I don't go with you," the small voice began to fade away. "So, Good Luck! I pray you make it." Then there was silence and Noah could sense she was gone.

Bopo's eye was glued to the opening at the doorway. He watched intently for the red skin to appear on the hut to their left. Nothing happened for what seemed like an eternity. It was as if Snake would loom before them in his evil yellow war paint at any instant. Then all would be lost. Time edged by slowly as the village continued to awaken. Then at last Bopo hissed,

"There it is, the red skin. Run for it! I'm right behind you!"

Silently, two figures streaked from the back of the thatched hut, as the first ray of sunlight broke over the mountain top. Gasping for breath, the two Washo youths slid to a stop behind the lone hut with the red skin over its doorway.

A small forlorn buckskin clad figure sat hunched against the rear wall of the hut, head down and arms clasped around the knees. As the runners arrived in a cloud of dust, the tiny figure raised her head and they could see it was a beautiful young girl. An expression of sadness crept across her small brown face. Without uttering a sound she raised her arm and pointed toward a large rock in the distance.

"Come on Bopo. Here we go!" shouted Noah triumphantly. "Hit the trail!"

The two struck out at full speed with Bopo in the lead. Halfway to the big rock and running hard, Noah sensed there was no one behind him. Looking back over his shoulder he saw the small brown figure, head down, still seated against the wall.

"Go ahead Bopo! " he shouted. "Wait for me behind the big rock. I'll be right there."

Turning, Noah trotted back to the hut. "Come on!" he hissed in exasperation. "We haven't got that much time."

Raising her head, Ai mee said sadly, "I'm not going. You don't have a chance with me along. Your only chance to get away from Snake is for me to stay here. Even then your chances are pretty slim. Don't you see? If you take me with you, Snake will

74

hound you to the end of the earth. You'll never get away! He thinks I'm to be his number two wife some day. He'll never let me get away! Run! Now! While you have a chance. Hurry!"

"Look" said Noah puffing, out of breath. "If it weren't for you we'd still be back there in that hut, tied up and waiting to be tortured. At least now we've got a chance. If you don't go, we don't go!" he rasped. "I mean it. Our chances are as good with you as without you. Better, in fact, because you know the country around here and we don't."

"No, you just don't understand." she sobbed.

"I understand that I'm not going without you!" Noah gritted. "You aren't very big. Even so, I may have a pretty hard time, if I've gotta pack you over my shoulder and stay ahead of Snake for very long. But, if that's the way it's gonna be, so be it."

This time there was the hard edge of two pieces of flint grating together in Noah's voice. He reached for Ai mee's huddled figure.

"You really mean that, don't you?" Ai mee said, a smile of hope beginning to spread across the beautiful little face.

" Try me," Noah said grimly.

The two ran a foot race to the big Rock where Bopo waited. Ai mee won by a hair, much to Noah's surprise.

CHAPTER 6   Escape

Snake awakened to the whining sound of Weasel's voice outside the doorway. He slowly arose and stretched his arms wide, becoming aware Weasel was babbling something about the prisoner's escape. Snarling, Snake snapped wide awake. He rushed out of the hut to confront Weasel with questions, only to find the worthless warrior had allowed the two Washo youths to escape. Through the rear of their hut. They'd cut a hole in the wall and left the neck ropes tied to the willow frame.

With an angry roar Snake swung his club-like arm, striking Weasel alongside the face, sending him flying into the dust head over heels. Quickly Snake slipped a flint knife and fighting axe into his belt. He shouldered a quiver of arrows, picked up his bow and dashed off, shouting over his shoulder,

"Quick, the river trail! Call the men. Follow me! Spread out on each side of the trail. Search for any sign of them. Hurry !"

Snake loped up the river trail at top speed. His eyes searched back and forth across the ground, looking for tell tale tracks. After a short while he spotted a quiver laying crossways on the trail. Arrows were spilled out across the ground, as though someone in a great hurry had dropped them. Didn't have time to stop to retrieve them. He recognized the fancy turquoise quill work on the quiver as belonging to the dog who'd bitten his ear off. With a loud whoop, he summoned the warriors. They spread out on either side of the trail and dashed off at top speed.

It was some time later when they discovered a single arrow laying beside the trail. Its black and white magpie feathers identified it as Bopo's. Later another arrow turned up. Then, farther along the trail a third arrow. Finally, shortly before noon they found the discarded quiver. It was at this point Snake gave a snort of disgust, saying,

"This trail's false. We've been betrayed by someone. Back to the village."

They returned to the village at top speed. There, amid much confusion and shouting, Frog Face discovered   tracks leading away in the opposite direction, along the lake shore. They were heading northward. He pointed to the clear indentations in the soft dust. Three separate set of prints were evident, all leading north. Two sets of large prints and one familiar set of small moccasin tracks. That sign could only belong to the slave Ai mee.

Slowly, the truth of the matter began to dawn upon Snake. Not only had those treacherous Washo pups escaped, but they'd   stolen his prized slave Ai mee ! In a cold rage, Snake turned to the Evil Ten and with his ugly yellowed face distorted by hate, shouted,

"Go, pack much food for the trail. Bring all of your weapons. They have many hours head start. It will be a long trail. We'll never return until all three of them are in my hands. Then they'll feel Snake's wrath!"

Meanwhile, behind the large rock where the women dig clay, three young escapees held a hurried council of war. Ai mee retrieved two small hidden bundles of supplies wrapped in soft antelope hide. They were hidden beside the boys two powerful hunting bows and Noah's flint knife.

"Here's your knife, Noah," said Ai mee shyly. "I'm sorry I couldn't pack more food. Night Bird watches me closely all of the time."

"We're lucky to have some food. You should see what we got along the trail."

Shaking her head, Ai mee said, "If we skimp there should be enough food for three, maybe four days. What worries me most is water. There're two water skins in the packs. They don't hold much. We'll be heading north into country that's very dry. We need to watch for any sign of fresh water. Replenish our precious little supply."

"Did you see any signs of our quivers and arrows?" asked Noah, an expectant look on his face. "These bows aren't much use without our arrows."

"I'm really sorry" said Ai mee, abashed. "I used them to create a false trail. Going up the river. Help to buy time. To make it believable, I needed something valuable. Something easily recognizable as belonging to you two. So Snake would be deceived and follow the trail. I'm awfully sorry, really I am! I know all those things were very important to you. I didn't know what else to do. You had to have some way to get a head start on Snake."

"Don't worry about it," said Noah. "Of course you did the right thing, I just didn't understand. Besides, Bopo here is one of the last of the great arrow makers. I'm sure he'll whip out some new ones for us before very long."

"Sure." said Bopo with great bravado. "Won't take any time at all to turn out a bunch of my finest precision arrows. All we need to do is pause long enough along the trail. Pick up some good straight rose wood shoots. Some quality obsidian, too. A few goose feathers. Then we'll be all set! However, we'd better forget about all this friendly chatter. Get down to business!"

"You're right, Bopo. I have an uneasy feeling Snake's gonna pop his ugly head around that rock at any moment. So, let,s hit the trail right now."

The little group struck out from the village headed in a northerly direction, away from Washo Land. Noah, who was in the lead, set a steady loping pace which could be maintained for most of the day.

"We'll head for the north end of Pyramid Lake and then cut left toward the upper corner of Washo land," Noah shouted over his shoulder. "Even if Snake does follow us for three or four days, I think he'll give up and go home as soon as we're inside Washo Land."

"I think you're wrong!" stoutly maintained Ai mee, puffing as she jogged. "Snake won't give up just because we're inside our home land. I can assure you he won't. He'll follow us right into Washo Land. Particularly up there in that northeast corner. It's deserted there this time of year. That's Honey Marsh country. The only thing that'd stop him would be if about a hundred heavily armed Washo warriors came to our rescue. That won't happen."

"No such luck!" agreed Bopo. "Right now, all the Washo people are heading into the various hot springs. They always make their winter camps there." "I think our best chance to stay free is head into Honey Marsh," puffed Ai mee. "We can hole up in the marsh for the winter. It'll be very cold this time of year. But, we can survive. Snake won't follow us into the marsh."

"How come?" queried Bopo "That evil Snake fellow didn't look to me like he'd let a little bit of water slow him down."

"It's like this," said Ai mee over her shoulder. "The Paiutes are deathly afraid of the marsh. Because of the quick sand. They're forbidden to go into Honey Marsh. The same sort of taboos that keep the Washos from going out on Da ow aga. Our people fear the horrible Water Baby. The Paiutes are afraid of quick sand. The marsh is completely encircled with pot holes of deadly quick sand. No one can tell where the pot holes are. They're completely hidden in the rushes and cat tails. You can't see 'em!"

"Never saw a quicksand pot hole in my life," grunted Noah.

"Those pot holes are treacherous and deadly," cautioned Aimee. "This is Wel mel ti country, where I was brought up. I know how to avoid the deadly quick sand. I think I know how to live in there. Despite the fearsome winter cold."

Both Noah and Bopo thought they detected a note of uncertainty in her brave little voice.

"You know," puffed Bopo, who was bringing up the rear, "when we were talking back there at the clay pit, I admit I had a few negative thoughts. About whether or not it was a good idea to have some helpless girl along on a trip like this. Sort of hold us back, if you know what I mean. Well, now I'm beginning to sort of have some second thoughts. About having a girl along, if you know what I mean. Sounds like a certain girl is probably going to save our hides. By being very wise about this marsh place."

"Yup!" puffed Noah.

"I'm all for going up there and piling into the middle of that marsh. Just as fast as we can get there. I can get downright enthusiastic about going anywhere that fellow Snake won't go," muttered Bopo.

"Well" puffed Noah "Looks like I'm out-numbered two to one, so the marsh it is . Just as fast as we can get there. Sounds like we've got three or four days of hard trail to cover. Better move a little faster! Concentrate on not letting that bunch of cutthroats overtake us before we get there."

The trio maintained a steady jogging pace throughout the day. Never slowing, they stopped only twice, to gulp down a mouthful of much needed water. The path lay along the hard packed east shore of the desert lake. Brackish water lapped almost at their feet. At times the towering bare mountains paralleling the lake on their right came to the waters edge. On occasion Ai mee would spot an area that looked as if it could be quick sand. She'd suggest they work their way along the steeply

-sloped mountain side until the suspicious spot was passed.

Toward sunset as they were nearing the northern end of the great lake, Ai mee pointed out the huge barren rock islands projecting from the deep blue water. Each one came to a well defined point at the top. These, she said, were the pyramids for which the lake was named. Looking down into the water they could see huge fish, almost as long as a man. They hung motionless in the water, where the green color indicated shallows. At sunset Noah called a halt long enough for them to eat sparingly of their tiny food ration. Climbing part way up the steeply sloping mountain side he could see their back trail. He couldn't detect any sign of pursuit. Jaded, they decided to catch a short nap before pushing on.

Moonrise found them back on the trail again, still northward bound. By sunrise they'd reached the end of the lake. They ascended a high bluff overlooking formidable Smoke Creek and Black Rock deserts. The vast black desert sand extended off into the haze of a distant northern horizon.

From their vantage point the trio could look back down the east shore of Pyramid Lake, along the path they'd followed since escape from the Paiute Village. While the village was hidden in the distance, they could trace most of their route and were unable to detect any movement. There was no apparent pursuit by Snake and the Evil Ten.

"You know, it worries me we can't see any sign of our pursuers. By this time they should be right out there where we can see 'em behind us," puzzled Noah "Do you suppose it's possible they didn't follow us ?"

"I doubt that very much," said Ai mee seriously. "Even if Snake didn't want to bring me back, he isn't going to let Noah off so easily. He hates Noah for ripping his ear off. It didn't look to me like he was exactly fond of Bopo either. I'm sure he's back there some place. Plotting evil against us."

"Well," grunted Bopo, "if he's comin' after us, and I think he is, and if we can't see any sign of him on the east shore of the lake, do you suppose he might be comin' up the west shore? As I remember the lay of the land, he could cut off to the west about halfway up the shore line. There he could cross the mountain. Head directly for Honey Marsh. If he did that, he'd have a shorter route to the marsh than we have. He might even get there before us."

"That's a chilling thought you just had, Bopo," groaned his companion. "It all sounds very logical. I'm afraid you've laid your finger on the truth. I'll bet that's what they did. They started up the west shore of the lake!"

"I'm sure he's right," chimed in Ai mee. "If Snake took that route, he'd place himself between us and Washo Land. That's the way he'd think. Cut us off from home and help."

"If that's the case he may be off there on our left some place. Maybe abreast of us by now. Maybe he can even see us by now. The best thing we can do is get down off this bluff. Out here in this vast open desert you can spot a man or an animal silhouette from a great distance. Right now I'll bet we really stand out against the skyline," reasoned Noah, beating a hasty retreat to the edge of the bluff where he could duck down below the horizon. The others quickly followed.

For the next three days the group pursued a relentless path to the westward. They paused only at night for a little food and a few hours sleep. Usually they resumed flight long before the sun rose. They were constantly on the alert for the murderous band of Paiutes. The enemy were out there in the vast expanse of desert somewhere. Either to the left or, fearfully, ahead of them. There was not a hint of their pursuers anywhere in that great empty space. Snake and his followers had vanished as if into thin air.

At the first light of dawn on the fourth day the trio trotted over the low crest of a sage covered hill. There before them lay a huge mountain meadow. It was bordered on the far side by green forested mountains of Washo Land. The first rays of sunlight bathed the high granite peaks in warmth, while the meadow below still lay in shadow.

As they stood in quiet awe, gazing at their beloved home land, the light slowly crept across the meadow floor. It revealed a thick pasture of golden brown grass. In the center of the meadow, sunlight sparkled on blue water, glinting through dense clumps of cattails. There before them lay the vast expanse of Honey Marsh. A secure haven at last!

Suddenly Noah hissed frantically. "Down, quick, get down! Over there to your left. At the foot of the meadow. There they are! Can you see them? Snake in yellow war paint. All ten of the warriors.

See they're just coming out of the sage brush. Into the grass. I don't think they've seen us. Stay down and be quiet!"

The trio lay motionless, flat in the sand, stretched out on their bellies in the sage brush, hardly daring to breathe. There below them, to the left in the distance, were eleven small dark figures. Carefully, they threaded their way single file into the meadow. While the ant like figures were still quite some distance away, they were drawing nearer to the fugitives hiding place with every step.

"We're gonna have to out run 'em. They're about the same distance from the marsh as we are. Maybe a little closer. Ai mee you know the marsh. What point shall we head for?" hissed Noah with urgency in his voice.

Pointing off toward the north, Ai mee whispered excitedly, "See that flat slab of dark rock near the water. The place without any grass on it. It's right on the marsh. Just beyond that flat slab is where the quick sand pot holes begin. They're all over out there. You can't see them but they're out there! Just beyond that rock! The flat slab tilts up slightly. There's a low cliff-like wall. It runs all along the marsh side of the slab. The wall's about three times as high as a man's head. There's a little cave-like hollow at the foot of the cliff, about halfway down. We can hide there! Nobody can see us from above. I don't think they'll come down there. It's too close to the waters edge. They're really scared to get near the marsh. The place is taboo."

Raising up on his knees and preparing to start running, Bopo grunted. "Let's go right nowwwww!"

The three young Washos broke into a run, pell mell down the sage covered slope with Ai mee in the lead. She hadn't taken more than a few strides before there was a shout from behind. Snake had spotted their movement. He was in hot pursuit. Howling like a hungry pack of wolves, the Paiute band charged after them. Screaming, they waved war axes and bows as they ran. It was a long hard run through the meadow. The Paiutes were beginning to gain on them.

At last Ai mee ducked down into the brush. Disappearing from view, she slipped around the front edge of a rock slab. The cliff face towered above them. They sprinted down a narrow sand corridor formed by the base of the cliff and the edge of the swampy marsh. Gasping for breath the three tumbled into a small cave like opening in the face of the cliff. Crouched on hands and knees, for the cave was quite low, they were completely hidden from the view of any one standing on the rock above.

"Shhhhhhh! Stay back against the wall and don't make a sound," cautioned Ai mee in a whisper.

They panted, catching their breath, waiting, faces toward the marsh just a few strides away. The edge of the marsh was marked by rippling water, from which grew heavily clustered bunches of rushes. If they could just cross that narrow space between cliff and marsh they'd be safe from their murderous pursuers.

The sun was somewhere behind them. The face of the cliff cast a shadow toward the marsh. Suddenly the uniform shadow horizon before them was broken by the shaded silhouettes of eleven tall figures. The evil ones were standing on the edge of the cliff, directly above their hiding place. Disaster, they were cornered.

"Oh noooo!" groaned Ai mee with both hands to her face. "Trapped!"

Snake and his howling band sprinted across the meadow, drawing closer to the three fugitives with each stride. At the very moment when it seemed he could reach out and grasp the long trailing black hair of the racing slave girl, she darted sideways. At the last instant she disappeared behind a high clump of sage. She didn't reappear on the other side.

Dashing out on a large rock slab which slanted gradually upward, Snake raced to the edge of the cliff. Surely from this vantage point he could locate the three fugitives wherever they were hiding in the sage below.

The Evil Ten, panting, joined their leader. They all lined up along the brow of the cliff, gasping for breath as they studied the scene before them. Darting eyes searched for some trace of the prey. Nothing! Nothing moved in the panorama before them. Nothing moved in the sandy sage covered areas to either side. Nothing moved in the huge expanse of water and waving rushes. Snake was furious; the three cringing Washos had disappeared into the marsh. Gone!

"Hear me," Snake screamed, his face distorted with rage, his fists clenched and arms raised to the sky. "Hear me, you have not escaped! You'll never escape from me! Just because you hide in the marsh, like the cowards you are, you'll never get away. My men will circle this marsh! You cannot escape. Soon you'll have to come out. You'll plead with me. Plead to escape that hideous swamp. When you come pleading for mercy, here's what will happen to you. I'll kill those two sniveling Washo pups. I'll do it very slowly. They will wish they were never born. Then I'll come for you, Ai mee! You faithless traitor of a slave. I'll save you for last. I'll use burning embers! I'll put out your eyes! The last thing you'll ever see will be my handsome face. You'll be returned to my lodge. Forever, you'll live there as my slave. Each day I'll make you regret your treachery. I, Snake, swear this before everyone. Snake will have his vengeance. I swear it will be sooooo!" Snake howled like a mad man.

Crouched in their hiding place in the small cave immediately below where Snake stood screaming his threats of vengeance against them, the three fugitives experienced a sickening sense of fear. At length, Noah peered out of the cave, studying the landscape to his right and then to the left. Leaning over, he whispered in Ai mee's ear.

"What does the shore line look like to the north of us? Is there any place up there where I could get into the marsh without being seen?"

Ai mee thought for a moment and then whispered, "For a long ways up that side of the marsh there's nothing but pot holes of quicksand. They run way out into the deep water off shore. Then you come to a finger of land that extends out into the marsh quite a ways. It ends abruptly in deep water. The finger is all covered with sage. At the end of the finger, in the deep water, there aren't any pot holes. A person could slip into the water there. Swim directly out toward the center of the marsh. Out there not very far is a small dry island. It's ringed with rushes and covered with grass. That's the place I'd planned for us to reach as a hiding place. I'd hoped to enter the water here. Work our way up to that little island. I don't think we can do it now. Snake'd fill us full of arrows before we got halfway into the marsh. He's got us cornered here in this cave. I'm really sorry I didn't do better for you. I think he's got us cold."

"Maybe not," whispered Noah. "I've got a plan that just might work. I'm fairly quick on my feet. Got a hunch I can outrun that gang. If I can get lucky. Dodge their arrows for the first few strides. I should be able to draw ahead of 'em. At least, far enough so I'd have time to enter the water. Go in at the end of that finger of land. Hopefully, before they get there. Are you sure they won't follow me? Right into the water?"

"No, they won't get close enough to the water to get their feet wet," whispered Ai mee. "They know how deadly that quicksand can be. They won't get near it. There's a secret to crossing the quicksand. If you don't know the secret or if you forget, you're dead."

"I can't think of a worse way to die," shuddered Bopo.

"Now, both of you listen to me very carefully. Don't ever forget what I tell you," whispered Ai mee, her voice urgent.

"The quicksand usually occurs where the water seems to be about knee deep. If you stand up and try to walk normally you'll get in trouble. You'll be walking along in knee deep water. In one step you'll sink into a deep hole. In the wink of an eye! You'll be in quicksand up to your nose. There's no warning! No way to get out. The more you thrash around the sooner the quicksand will pull you under. The whole marsh, quicksand and hard bottom, is covered with rushes and floating grass. There's no way to tell where the dangerous pot holes are located. It all looks the same." The two fugitives shook their heads. Bad medicine!

"Now, here's the secret. You must never forget it," she admonished seriously. "DON'T EVER STAND UP. It's just that simple. If you ever forget it, even for a moment, you're dead." Ai mee shook her small finger under their noses threateningly, to emphasize her point. "The minute you try to stand up, you'll be sucked under by the quicksand. The secret to survival is, lie down! On your belly in the water. Swim or pull yourself along using the rushes. Just don't stand up," she pleaded.

The young men both nodded their heads vigorously. They understood and would follow the rule.

"You know, Skinny, your plan to decoy those fellows sounds like a real great one," whispered Bopo. "But you know I'm a pretty swift fellow on my feet too. So why don't we just draw straws to see who gets the honor of letting Snake chase him up the shore?" Bopo held out two blades of grass with a grin.

"Nope," muttered Noah. "This is my plan. Besides, it sounds like my job might be safer than yours. You've gotta swim all the way up there without drowning yourself in that quick sand. Just be sure you both get up there safely."

Searching around on the ground, Noah picked up three smooth rounded stones slightly larger in size than a sage hen's egg.

"Lem'me have the two bow covers," he whispered. "I'm gonna make em into a temporary sling. Hope it lasts for at least a few throws. I've spent so much time harvesting sage hens for the family stew basket, I've gotten down right deadly with one of these slings. You never know. My sage hen experience might just come in handy. When I have a bunch of those stupid Paiutes breathing down my neck, I'm gonna need something. " Ai mee shook her head and frowned.

"Now, when I take off will you please throw a hand full of rocks in the opposite direction. It will divert attention, for an instant or two?"

"Sure," said Bopo, holding out his hand. The two boys gripped wrists for a brief moment. "Good luck, Skinny!" whispered Bopo.

Winking at Ai mee at the last moment, Noah turned and sprinted off to the northward, along the shore of the marsh. He dodged from side to side with each step as he went. At the same instant Bopo threw a large handful of pebbles in the opposite direction, as a diversion. However, things didn't work out as Noah had planned. The pebbles hit a mangy coyote who was slinking through the sage. It caused the animal it to erupt into a howling fit of panic.

"Ki Yi-Ki Yi,- Ki Yi!"

Pandemonium broke out above. The Paiutes were startled by the coyote. Noah gained a few precious strides toward safety, before they reacted. For an interval of a few breaths there was a delay as the warriors slapped arrows to bows. The Paiutes launched a flight of deadly missiles after the fleeing figure. None of the arrows caught the weaving runner. Then he was out of range and headed rapidly away.

Howling in surprise, the angry warriors snatched up gear preparing to pursue. Screaming like a hungry pack of wolves they strung out in single file after the rapidly disappearing figure.

"Go, Noah, go!" chanted Bopo, forgetting to whisper.

A few moments later, after the last sound of pursuit had faded into the distance, two figures slipped silently across the opening and entered the great marsh. Stretched out at full length, they quietly slipped into the water and disappeared among the rushes. For a moment it was possible to detect their passage by a slight waving of the dense foliage. Then all was silent. They were gone. A lone red wing black bird flitted from rush to rush. Warm sunlight sparkled across the surface of the quiet water. The swamp appeared deserted.

Meanwhile, Noah ran for his life. He ran as he had never run before. In fact, he had never had quite the same incentive as he now felt. Snake's bellowed threats were all too close behind him. In desperation Noah mouthed a silent prayer to the Maker of All Things.

"Lord, please give me the speed and the strength to outrun those Paiutes."   After a moment's hurried reflection, he added, "And Lord, if you can't help me, please don't you help that fellow Snake."

The sage- covered finger of land turned out to be farther away than Noah expected. He was gasping for breath as he reached the spot and ascended a gentle slope. He'd gained a few precious moments over his pursuers. Sliding to a stop, he flattened himself behind a clump of sage. He was at the point where a finger of land sloped down into deep water. Fumbling at his waist he drew out the makeshift sling. Maybe he could create a slight delay for the enemy.

Frog Face wriggled on his belly. He was hidden behind a rock. He sat up, confident of not being seen by the youth he was pursuing. Snake was crouching down, somewhere slightly ahead of him. The rest straggled behind. Suddenly there was a dreadful howling just the other side of the rock. Without thinking, Frog Face stood upright. Instinct told him to see what was making that awful sound. He was just in time to see a lank gray coyote dash off into the brush. Frog Face had popped upright into view, much as a prairie dog does when it thinks a hawk is approaching.

Noah needed no second invitation. His arm whipped the sling in a blurring arc. Frog Face's usual blank open mouthed expression didn't change a bit. There was a solid Thonk! The round stone stuck the exact center of Frog Face's forehead. His blank face slowly disappeared from view as he sank behind the rock.

CHAPTER 7   The Marsh

A water skater dashed across the smooth surface of the marsh and out of sight into a dense stand of cattails. The sky was sunny and clear, the water a sparkling blue. The air was warm even though the last days of autumn were rapidly passing. Winter lurked just over the horizon. A faint breeze set the tall cattail stalks to swaying, with a dry rustling sound.

Two small brown hands rose silently out of the water, separating the foliage to reveal Ai mee's beautiful little face, with chin just above the water surface. There was a grunting sound and ripples appeared on the quiet surface, as Bopo's dripping face emerged next to hers.

With a roguish smile, Ai mee said, "Why, Bopo, you're becoming a regular marsh otter! You seem to be taking to this traveling on your stomach very well. I'm proud of you for remembering not to stand up. We're making good time. The small island where we meet Noah is just a little ways farther."

"Good! Long swim up here."

"I was just thinking, in case you ever get stuck in the quicksand. In case I'd have to pull you out, that fancy pig tail of yours would make a good handle."

Blowing bubbles in the water as he glided forward, Bopo gurgled, "My father calls that 'pig tail' my Water Baby Handle. Long ago when I was just a little kid he told me never to cut it off. So, I never have. Some time when we aren't so busy, I'll tell you a little story about how it all happened. Some other time when we're in a nice dry spot. By the way, do you ever get dried out when you live in this marsh?"

"Oh sure," laughed Ai mee. "After a while you get things worked out so you travel around in the water during the mornings. Spend the afternoon on some island where you can get dried out before the sun goes down. This marsh is really out in the desert, even though it doesn't look like it. It doesn't snow very often or very heavily here. When it does snow or when the wind blows, it can be freezing cold. That's when you need a nice warm hut with a fire pit in it."

"Yeah! That sounds pretty good."

"I'll get one built first thing, 'cause winter's going to set in any day now. I'll also build a boat later on. Just so you won't get so wet traveling. We can't use a boat in close to shore or we'll be seen. We can use one farther out. In the deep water. Where we're hidden in the rushes.

"I've never heard of a Washo with a boat before. Didn't know they had such things. I've certainly never seen one. Look forward to this boat business. Sounds like fun!" mused Bopo.

The two moved slowly through the rushes talking quietly as they glided along. In the distance a small dry island could now be seen. They worked their way quietly up to the dense stand of rushes surrounding the small sandy hummock. Parting tall marsh grass, Ai mee found herself looking at a level spit of clean dry white sand. And then she gasped. "Oh no, no, no, ohhhh, noooo !"

There on the shoreline of the island lay Noah, partially out of the water. Face down and motionless. His limp figure had the cold clammy look of a drowned rat. From his back protruded a long war arrow, white feathers trembling slightly in the breeze.

"Oh no!" moaned Ai mee, as she kneeled to examine the arrow. "Snake's arrow. One of Snake's poisoned war arrows. Poisoned with rattlesnake venom. Oh, poor Noah! What a horrible end. He was so brave!"

Coming out of the water like an angry young bull, Bopo charged to his friend's side. Gingerly he rolled the inert figure over. Carefully wiping the sand from Noah's ashen face, he placed his ear close to his injured friend's mouth. Could he detect any sign of breathing? Hearing nothing, he placed an ear against the chest. For a very long moment there was total silence. Then ever so slowly, Bopo began to nod his head up and down.

"Yes, it's there, a pulse, ever so faint and awfully slow. But, there is a pulse," sighed Bopo with obvious relief. "Ai mee, help me drag him out of the water and let's get his shirt off. I'll have to cut the buckskin away from the arrow. Let's leave him face down, till we can figure out what to do with this murderous-looking arrow."

"Here Bopo," said Ai mee. She was suddenly all business and taking charge. "I'll take care of the shirt. Unless we act very fast Noah's going to die of shock, from the snake venom. I recognize Snake's arrow! The white snow goose feathers on the shaft. He makes these terrible arrows! Makes 'em with a tuft of rabbit hair lashed right behind the flint arrow head. The rabbit hair's soaked with rattler venom. It acts awfully fast. We may be too late already. Have to hurry!" Together they dragged the inert figure up into the clean white sand.

"Quick, Bopo! I'll get the arrow out of him. Remove as much of the venom as I can. You'll have to find two big pieces of moss. Stuff with the mud still on the back. Look 'till you find some of the bright green kind of moss. It'll be where you see water skaters around it. The moss should have that really black, mucky mud on the back. The kind that's fine. Very sticky stuff! We'll make one of Crow Woman's special poultices out of it. Draw out any poison I can't get out. Oh, I hope we're in time! Poor Noah! He got this trying to save us."

Bopo dashed away to the water's edge, preparing to strike out into the marsh in search of moss.

"Bopo." shouted Ai mee in a small desperate voice. "Don't stand up!" Sheepishly, Bopo parted the rushes and slipped into the water on his stomach, disappearing from view.

The girl deftly cut away Noah's buckskin shirt, from neck opening to a point where the long arrow shaft rigidly projected from his back. Carefully she peeled away the shirt, revealing the spot where the flint arrowhead had entered. The wound was slightly below the junction of left shoulder and neck. The arrow had penetrated almost all the way through the shoulder. It emerging below the collar bone in front. There was very little blood where the arrow head entered. Just a gaping purplish wound. Turning him over partially, Ai mee could see the flint head had not emerged from the front. It made an ugly dark bulge just under the chest skin.

"Noah!" Ai mee said with anguish in her shaking voice. "This is going to hurt something awful! I'm so sorry, but I have to do it. Please forgive me." Thereupon, with a grunt and a hard shove she drove the shaft the rest of the way through his shoulder. The crimson arrowhead protruded from Noah's chest. With a whimper she broke off the arrow head and withdrew the shaft from his back.

"It's going to be all right now, Noah. Honest it is, I promise." Tears rolled softly down her cheek.

Without hesitation, she cleansed the wound and then placing her lips against it, sucked repeatedly and spit away as much of the venom as she could extract. Bopo emerged from the marsh dripping and extended two large clumps of mud-backed moss.

Inspecting the moss closely with a critical, professional air, Ai mee nodded approval and tied the poultice in place, saying, "It's going to take a long time for this to neutralize whatever poison's left in there. All we can do now is hope, say a prayer and keep him warm."

The sun was sinking low in the west, behind the green Washo mountains. They carefully moved Noah's inert body to a more sheltered spot behind a tall clump of cattails. Placing him on a thick bed of rushes the girl covered him with his now-dry shirt. Next they piled on layer after layer of dry rushes, till it looked like a small mountain of foliage. The youth's pale face was barely exposed.

"That'll keep him warm for now," Ai mee mused thoughtfully.

"Yeah, that's all right for now," said Bopo, "but we've gotta get some fire or we'll all freeze before morning." He shivered as the last rays of sunshine disappeared and a cold breath of wind drifted across the water, rustling the sere leaves of cattail stalks.

"Maybe I can find a straight stick and make up some sort of fire drill," he mused, casting about for a stick of any sort. Carefully he searched the entire island, which was quite small and devoid of any thing except rushes and cat tails.

"You know Ai mee, this reminds me of a story my father used to tell about our distant relatives the Yanas. They live to the north of here. Far north where we all came from originally."

"Bopo!" Ai mee exclaimed with some traces of exasperation in her voice. "This is no time for one of your stories; it's cold and it's getting dark and on top of all that, we don't have anything to eat. Except one handful of pine nuts and I'm saving that to make some broth for Noah later on."

"Well, what I was going to say was, the Yanas don't use a bow and a fire drill to make fire, the way we do. They can do the trick just using a straight stick. They turn it by rubbing the stick very fast, between the hands. My dad says it works great when you know how to do it. The turning tip of the stick works around in some tinder on a hard base of bone. The tinder gets hot enough to make a good spark. Now, if I had a stick, maybe I could play Yana and whip up a little fire. What ever happened to that arrow? The one that was sticking in Noah's back. That might make enough of a fire stick to get a blaze started. That's all we need right now."

"I threw it away," said Ai mee "It's out in the water somewhere, over that way." She pointed into the gathering darkness to an open stretch of wind rippled water.

"Great," said Bopo "Just what I need. An invigorating swim before dinner, in that nice cool water." Without another word he assumed the approved horizontal position, slipped into the water and disappeared into the gathering gloom.

The husky young Washo was gone for a very long time as full darkness settled. Ai mee was a small forlorn figure standing at the waters edge peering into the night. At last rushes began to whisper behind the girl. On the opposite side of the island the rushes parted, revealing Bopo's grinning face, distorted by the arrow shaft he carried in his teeth.

"The darn thing drifted around some, but I finally found it."

"I did one good thing while you were gone," said Ai mee who was beginning to shiver in the cold marsh air. "I thought of this," she said, holding out a flat white piece of bone. "It's my comb, made from a piece of deer shoulder blade. Maybe you can use it as a base for your fire drill." In the darkness Bopo's grin spread even wider.

"Ai mee, your a treasure," said he "That's the one thing I didn't have. I'll probably ruin your comb starting a fire on it. I promise I'll make you the finest comb you ever saw, to replace it. Just as soon as I figure out how to get a deer, that is. Come to think of it, that may not be so easy out here in the middle of this damp swamp."

"We still need some tinder and there just isn't anything dry out here," mourned the girl.

"Ah hah," chortled the husky lad. "I thought of just the thing as I was basking out there in the water." So saying, he kneeled beside Noah's pile of rushes and began to dig furiously. In a moment he came up triumphantly clutching the small leather bag in which Noah carried his fire supply.

"Behold!" he gloated. " There may not be a live coal in Noah's little bag, but there sure is plenty of tinder. Good dry incense cedar bark ."

Taking the white feathered arrow shaft, he rounded the broken end with his knife and hollowed out a small depression in the surface of the comb. Kneeling, he placed the comb on the ground and filled the depression with fine red powder from the cedar bark. He applied the rounded end of the arrow to the powdered cedar. Holding the shaft vertically between his palms, he rubbed them together rapidly, turning the arrow shaft in the dry tinder. Glancing up at Ai mee, he smirked.

"Ai mee, my girl, I hope you realize you're dealing with one ingenious fellow here. One who's going to demonstrate how to make fire without a bow. We experts call it the well-known Yana Method."

Bopo ground away with the stick, moving his hands as fast as they would go. Nothing happened! Ai mee bent down. Laying her cheek on the ground she blew softly on the tinder. Nothing happened! Bopo, puffing away at the twirling stick, held a muttered conversation with his totem the chickeree. Nothing happened! Bopo added another pinch of tinder and ground away. Nothing happened!

"You don't suppose, do you, that there was one step in this fire-making process the Yanas forgot to tell my father about?" puffed Bopo. Ai mee muttered a few ladylike prayers to the Maker of All Things, all the while blowing softly on the tinder. Nothing happened!

It was some time after the moon rose, when the little pile of tinder finally gave a faint sputter and a trace of spark appeared. Bopo collapsed on the ground rubbing his aching shoulders. Ai mee took over, blowing gently, while adding blades of dry grass, one blade at a time. At last ! Fire, the friend of man!

That night, it turned much colder. The two fugitive Washos slept fitfully curled up under a monstrous pile of reeds with Noah in the middle. He seemed to be barely breathing. All three pairs of moccasin clad feet were exposed to the warm fire.

During the night the girl arose frequently and stoked the fire with tightly-wrapped bundles of rush leaves, bound together with green roots. She explained this was what was called Wel mel ti fire wood.

No mention of food was made the next morning, for a very good reason. There wasn't any food, except for the tiny supply of pine nuts being held in reserve for Noah. With the morning's first light, Ai mee gave Bopo another lesson in the lore of her native clan, the Wel mel ti. The sky was a sullen gray and a stiff cold wind whipped across the water, causing a steady pattern of waves to splash onto the sandy beach. It looked as though snow was not too far away.

"We need to find a supply of food or we're going to be in trouble soon," admonished the girl. "If we try to go outside the marsh in search of game, Snake'll be on us immediately. So, we'll have to make do with what the marsh will provide. I can gather some of the late roots. Cattail stalks are still tender at the bottom and quite good, but we can't last very long on a slim diet like that. So, let's see if we can borrow some food from the muskrat. He's an industrious little fellow who prepares for winter by gathering grain all during the fall season.

"I don't know much about muskrats," said Bopo dubiously. "Never was around them very much. You don't see 'em in Hung a lil ti country. Are they any good to eat?"

"Some people eat 'em and say they're good, but I don't care for em," said Ai mee. "They call 'em Marsh Rabbit, but I never could get by the fact they're part of the rat family and have those long rat tails. However, there are a lot of them here in the marsh and they all store grain for the winter. So, what say we just borrow a little of that good grain from each muskrat family? We won't take their whole supply, just a small part of it."

"Muskrat food ?" queried a dubious Bopo.

"Sure, you see, they build a winter house that's sort of dome-shaped. It's just above the waterline so it's nice and dry. From the surface, the cave looks like a small mound. They dig an entrance tunnel down under the water. Also, they build several storage tunnels running out from the dome cave. Then ole' Mr. Muskrat goes out in the marsh and finds a nice ripe stand of wild grain. He shakes the stalks 'till the fat kernels fall off. Then he gathers his mouth so full of grain his cheeks swell out like bubbles. He goes through the cave into the storage tunnel where he packs the grain in tight. He keeps doing that 'till the whole storage tunnel is filled full. Then he goes to another storage tunnel and starts in again. Now, if you were to go out and spot one of those mounds, you would know it was a muskrat cave with grain-packed tunnels radiating out from it. You could dig down and get all the grain from one of those tunnels. We won't take more than one tunnel from each cave and we'll cover the hole when we're through. Got it?"

"That all sounds pretty logical," admitted Bopo, "But, why is it I'm beginning to get the feeling that I'm the fellow who's supposed to go out and dig into those caves? Steal food from these poor muskrats?"

"Well," said Ai mee thoughtfully, "we need both food and warm clothing, and if you wouldn't mind gathering the food, I'll stay here and get to work on some woven clothing for us. It won't be very handsome with the materials we've got, but it will keep out the cold better than what we have."

"All right, I'm your man," said a reluctant Bopo. "But, there's just one condition. I don't want this to get out. Not even to a close friend like Noah. What would people back home think? My father, for instance. If they found out that Bopo, that well-known Almost Warrior, was seen out digging in the ground? Trying to steal seeds from a muskrat? I'd be the laughingstock of the whole Washo Tribe. Think about it. Now, I want you to promise this isn't gonna get out. Cross your heart, Ai mee."

Hiding a smile behind a small brown hand, Ai mee said very seriously, "Bopo, your secret's safe with me. I promise." There was a roguish grin on her pretty face as she made a cross over her heart. The Washo sign for truth!

After Bopo departed to hunt for muskrats and grain, Ai mee immediately got to work at weaving. Washo women have always been excellent at weaving, particularly such things as clothing and utensils. Ai mee was well trained at the art and her fingers fairly flew as she started work. First, they needed a little cooking basket. It could be made quite small. She didn't think they were going to have very much food to prepare. Next she started a cloak of woven rushes. A big ungainly thing but surprisingly effective against the cold marsh winds.

As she worked, the girl thought of all the fine materials normally available to her people when they prepared for the onset of winter. Soft suede leather from deer and sheep hides for clothing. Rich, warm rabbit furs for cloaks. Yes, she thought, lots of nice warm winter clothing. When the winds were cold at the family's winter camp, one could slip down to a nearby hot spring. Soak one's self in the steaming sulfur water. And food, this year there'd be plenty of rich pine nuts, rabbits and sage hens, a good supply for the whole winter. Well, life here in the marsh this winter wouldn't be nearly as good as it will be at the family's winter camp, near the hot springs in the Truckee meadows. They'd just have to make do with what they had till spring. Then, hopefully, it might be possible to escape.

Continuing to let her memory rove through the past while she worked, Ai mee's thoughts returned to the previous winter at the family camp. She'd wandered away from the lodges while at her daily task of collecting fire wood. Suddenly, a grinning yellow-faced Snake appeared out of no-where and she found herself a captive, to be dragged off to the village of the Paiutes. She would never forget the scene at night in front of a roaring fire. She was dragged by the hair, before the elders of the village. Snake towered over the four old men who were leaders of the tribe and addressed them abruptly, without the customary polite salutation.

"At great risk to myself, I have taken this slave captive. She is the fairest of all the Washo maidens.   She shall be my personal slave and will not be sold, but will remain in my lodge. No young man of this village may look upon her or speak to her, lest they will feel my wrath. My men will watch her night and day. She'll never be allowed to escape. My number one wife, Night Bird, will train her to be an obedient Paiute woman. In one season she will complete the ceremony of puberty. On that day she shall have the honor of becoming my number two wife. Snake the greatest of the Paiute has spoken. It shall be so. Let no one interfere!"

Ai mee shuddered as she recalled the ensuing year as a slave in the evil man's lodge. Shaking her head to clear her mind of the frightening thoughts, she set aside her weaving and went to check on the condition of the injured Noah. He was still unconscious, looking pale and drawn with dark shadows beneath his eyes. Forcing his mouth open slightly, she dribbled a few drops of water down his throat, said a silent little prayer to the Maker of All Things and returned to her weaving chores. Next she'd begin work on a cloak for him.

Throughout the day the gathering clouds became darker and darker. As the light began to fail at dusk, the first fat flakes of white snow drifted silently by. The small figure stood at the water's edge, carefully searching the darkening marsh for some sign of the returning hunter. Wind rustled the tall rushes around her. Ai mee's brow furrowed with worry as she peered into the flurries of snow. A small fire popped noisily near Noah's motionless moccasin-clad feet. The darkness became more intense and still there was no sign of the missing Bopo.

At last, Ai mee heard a splash from somewhere out there in the darkness. Across the water a deep voice whispered "Ho ho ho, what do I spy but a fire and friends. Ho ho ho, hello, the island."

Shortly Bopo rose up out of the water dripping and shivering in the snowy darkness, as he picked his way ashore through the rushes. In each hand he carried a bulging leather sack. The same sacks they'd used for supplies at the time of escape. They'd been limp and empty at his departure that morning. Holding the dripping sacks on high, he said with a spreading grin. "Behold! Genuine muskrat grain. Tonight we eat!"

Ai mee clapped her hands in delight and gave the dripping Bopo a big friendly hug.

"Food, food, food," she chortled, breaking into a dance of celebration around Bopo.

"Tonight we will have a wonderful feed of nice hot gruel, compliments of Bopo, the great provider of grain!"

Bopo said seriously, "You know, it worked just like you said. There're all sorts of muskrat caves out there. All over the place. We're going to have all the grain we need. We may not have anything else out here in this marsh, but we sure won't starve. Of course it takes a lot of time to dig the grain out. But then, I spent quite a bit of time repairing the damage I did to the caves."

"It's good that you took the time to repair the cave," said Ai mee with a smile. "We want to keep those little fellows healthy. We may need 'em again."

"Used rushes and mud to repair the tunnels, so the ole' muskrat family wouldn't be out in the cold, so to speak," he chuckled.

" Bopo, that's a wonderful surprise to get all this food. Now I have a surprise for you," laughed Ai mee, with her roguish grin. She produced a large cloak of woven rush leaves, on which she'd worked for a good part of the day. The cloak was huge and enveloped him from head to foot. He stood there trembling with the cold while the snow flakes drifted down around them.

" Ai mee, this is great; warm, too." He grinned as he danced around the fire.

CHAPTER 8 The Big Island

Bopo wriggled his buttocks around in the sand, forming a comfortable depression. His back was rested nicely against a thick stand of rushes. He had some serious thinking to do. The spot was sheltered with a clear view of sky, marsh and the forested mountains behind. The sky looked gloomy, scudding gray clouds raced from the west into the deserts of the east.

(Bopo didn't think in terms of east and west: his directions were defined as New Sea or Pacific Ocean to the West, Old Sea or Great Basin Sea to the East, Cold Land to the north, Warm Land to the south.)

A cold wind caused the surface of the marsh to roughen into brooding blue gray water. The air was chilled and he shivered slightly despite the reassurance of his bulky rush cloak. Winter was approaching quickly now. His mind was busily at work, trying to sort out all of the problems. Bopo thought to himself.

"Thanks to Ai mee and her Wel mel ti know-how, we've got an adequate source of grain for the time being. But, we need more than grain if we're going to winter in this place. Besides, I don't know how hard this swamp will freeze up when the real cold arrives. If the place freezes over deep, we may not be able to dig out the grain caves. I'd better plan to get a big supply of muskrat grain stored first thing. Guess that'll be first priority."

"It's going to take many days. I don't know how much time I've got. Now, the ice forms every morning in the sheltered coves around our island. Spending every day immersed in that cold water really saps your strength. The water gets a little colder every day now. We've just gotta get some meat in our diet soon. Can't resist the cold in here without some meat. Maybe finding a source of meat should be first priority. I guess the best thing I can do right now is to try my luck at hunting those big speckled geese flying overhead in large flocks. They're one of the toughest kinds of game to hunt. Awfully smart birds. Real spooky!

"I haven't got any arrows so maybe I can fashion a snare with some kind of string. Maybe use the bow strings from the two hunting bows. Speaking of bows, what we really need now is a big fat buck deer. Takes a bow and arrows to get a deer. That kind of meat we could dry and keep through the whole winter. But I can't even think about deer. Not 'til I can make arrows to hunt with. Maybe the real first priority is to get the stuff to make arrows.

"The heck with arrows, how about Noah? He really looks bad with all that snake venom in him. Suppose old Noah doesn't make it. What would I do then?"

Problems, nothing but problems. Bopo's mind wandered back to their warm winter lodge, at the fork of the river in Hung a lil ti country. Winter time, night time. All of the other family members asleep around the glowing coals in the fire pit. Bopo and his father stretched out with moccasins facing the fire. Toasting their feet. His father, a wise man, said in a kindly voice. "You know, son, there comes a time in every kid's life when all of a sudden, without any warning, out of the clear blue sky, something comes up. Something no one ever expected. That kid, the one who has been having all the fun without a care in the world, he's called on to Stand Up and be Counted. Doesn't have any choice. It's Stand Up and Be Counted Time. That's when that kid grows up. Right then! That's when he becomes a man."

Bopo murmured softly to himself, "This man stuff may be a little tougher than I thought."

Carefully, the young Washo formed a hangman's noose from one end of the bow string. This should make a good snare. Next he set out to find a likely looking spot to hunt the big birds. After swimming from one clump of rushes to another for some time he located a large island near the center of the marsh. He emerged from the cold water, shaking. The island appeared to be a good spot to attract the wary prey. There were numerous shallow pools studded with thick growths of standing grain. Perfect bait to attract the big gray honkers.

Laying flat on his stomach in the tall grass at the waters edge, he stretched the bow string out into the shallows. The hangman's noose was supported on the surface by a series of tiny sticks. In the center of the noose he formed an inviting pile of grain. Just the bait needed to entice some unwary goose. All that goose needed to do was stick his head into the looped bow string. Of course, the other end of the bow string was grasped in Bopo's hand. He lay hidden in the tall grass. He planned to jerk the noose tight around the bird's neck as soon as it started to eat. He shivered in the cold, waiting.

The hungry Washo hunter spent the entire day, patiently trying to snare one of the big speckled honkers. As any fool could plainly see, he'd devised an excellent snare. But, there was one little problem. The snare didn't work. In fact, on two occasions during the long day, a big honker poked his head into the noose and greedily devoured Bopo's hard earned grain. When the lad tightened the noose with a jerk, it wasn't limber enough to close quickly. The frightened goose thrashed away, squawking loudly in indignation. The bow string was just a bit too stiff to work properly.

Discouraged, cold and hungry, the empty-handed hunter moved homeward at sundown. He was disappointed and resigned to another dinner of gruel. As he pulled himself along through the cold water, he noticed some long green strings of what appeared to be milkweed. It peeked out from under a cover of fresh snow on the bank. Now, milkweed stems are made of long flexible fibers which are very tough and can be woven into excellent string or rope. With a tired smile Bopo shook his head and thanked his totem. Here was the answer to the problem. He'd make the noose out of heavy string fashioned from milkweed. Without delay, he gathered a large supply of the supple fiber and headed for home. Maybe a nice hot serving of gruel would taste pretty good after all.

That night after dinner, while seated before the small fire, Ai mee stranded several limber pieces of heavy string from the milkweed. Bopo fashioned it into a noose, to be attached to the bow string.

The sun was high overhead as Bopo, whose muscles were aching violently from laying in one position for hours, heard the telltale Swish, Swish, of wind on heavy wings, immediately above him. Resisting the urgent desire to twist his head around and look up, he remained motionless, not even shifting his eyes. A flash of white from a man's eye was enough to spook the big birds. Shadows cast by the geese passed over him. They sailed majestically across the water. Finally the flight came into his field of view. The huge birds were going away from him across the water as dark silhouettes. Giant wings set, at the far end of the marsh they wheeled and returned low across the water. Heads turned slowly from side to side, as they suspiciously looked for some sign of danger. Seeing nothing alarming they dropped slowly lower, only to flare at the last moment, frightened by some suspicious shadow.

Three times the flock of cautious birds worked over the marsh with wings set, looking for just the right spot to land. At last the leader dropped low, set his wings, honking loudly. He extended large black webbed feet and settled lower. At the last second he leaned back and dropped his feathered rump into the water with a plop. Directly in front of Bopo, almost close enough to touch. Then suddenly there were scores of birds in the water all around him, chuckling softly, searching for grain.

The new milkweed noose worked just fine. In fact, it worked so well, the Washo youth was able to snare two of the huge birds before they took alarm and rose in flight with an urgent cackling. The young hunter gave thanks to his maker and ask to be forgiven for taking the lives of the magnificent birds. He prayed their spirits be allowed to fly on into the beautiful sunset sky over Honey Marsh.

Ai mee stood at the waters edge, expectantly looking out over the quiet expanse. The sky was clear after a rapidly-moving storm. It was sunset and the heavens were aflame. The marsh surface was blazing with reflected color, as Bopo rose up out of the water. Rivulets of moisture ran down his grinning face. He clutched a huge honker in either hand.

With a pleased little smile on her small brown face, Ai mee said, "Bopo, you did it, congratulations! Speckled Goose stew for dinner tonight!"

Later, Ai mee placed a small steaming basket of delicious goose stew on the ground between them. They sat crosslegged before the fire. The aroma wafted up around them. Both inhaled deeply in contented anticipation. The fire light danced across two expectant faces. A slight rustling of leaves could be heard in the background and a quavering voice said,

"That goose stew sure does smell good! Seems like people would invite a fellow to dinner at a time like this!"

"Noah, Noah, you're alive, you're talking, you're all right," shouted two happy voices.

That night the three Washos talked far into the hours of darkness. There were so many things to tell Noah. He in turn recalled all the details of his desperate run before the screaming pack of murderous Paiute warriors. He explained, "Some crazy coyote unexpectedly started to yap at just the opportune moment and inquisitive old Frog Face was stupid enough to stand up. Just had to see what was happening. For him, it was just the wrong thing to do, at just the wrong time. Stood up just like a prairie dog." Noah chuckled.

"Just at that moment I released the stone from my sling. It was a good shot and it nailed ole Frog Face right in the middle of the forehead. The only trouble was, Snake was somewhere behind me and he released a poison arrow. It hurt some and I remember dragging myself down to the water. My legs wouldn't work right and I couldn't swim very well. After that nothing! Nothing until the delicious smell of goose stew wafted into my nostrils."

Ai mee proudly produced the fine new cloak she'd woven and draped it over Noah's shoulders. Then she sat back and quietly listened as the two friends talked. They sounded as if they'd been separated for an eternity. Bopo related his adventures in collecting grain and snaring geese. He went on to say, "I've been keeping my eye out for materials, for making arrows. We really need arrows badly. We need 'em before we can lay in any sort of food supply, anything other than grain and a few birds. Several times, I've seen a good sized herd of deer feeding far out in the meadow. They probably come over to the marsh to drink at night. I'd sure like to find a way to get several of those big bucks. We could really use the hides as well as the venison."

"Yeah, but Snake's watching that same herd of deer, too," Noah pointed out.

"I've seen Snake and the Evil Nine several times. Those fellows are all over the place. Seems like they must be patrolling all around the perimeter of the marsh. Saw 'em one time when I was first trying to snare geese. I was laying in the shallow water hidden in the rushes. Two of them came this close to me." Bopo indicated the distance with outstretched hands.

"Maybe you think I wasn't holding my breath about then. They almost stepped on me. There's a trail runs clear around the marsh. Right along the edge. About as close to the pot holes as they dare to go, I guess."

"What do you think about making some arrow shafts?" queried Noah. "We sure need some. You've got the goose feathers now."

"Well," said Bopo, "I've been looking for a good place to cut some willow shafts. They aren't nearly as good as rose wood shafts. But willow is all we can get here. Just have to make do. The other day I spotted a place where a stream flows into the marsh. There's a very large, good-looking stand of willows there. Right close to the water. I started to cut a few nice straight shafts, while I was laying on my back in the water, next to the shore. Guess I was shaking the tops of the willows. One of Snake's fellows must have seen them moving. All of a sudden, before I realized there was anyone around, an arrow slapped into the water. Right alongside my head. Somebody on shore started to yell like crazy. The fellow must have thought he'd hit me. He was making quite a commotion. Any way, I got outta there in a great hurry."

"You're lucky you didn't end up with one of Snake's fancy arrows stuck in you." murmured Noah. " Maybe we can go back there later on. When there's no one around. Finish collecting those shafts."

Nodding his head in the affirmative Bopo said, "There were some nice ones I was working on before I was interrupted."

"We need willow shafts for a number of things besides arrows," chimed in Ai mee. "If I had a good supply of willows I could make strips from the bark. Use it for tying the frame of a lodge. Also, the strips are essential if I'm going to get started on a boat of sorts. Actually, it'd be about half raft and half boat. Not very pretty, but it would serve."

"I agree," said Noah "Willows are the most important need we have right at the moment. We'd better work out a plan to get a lot of 'em, soon as I can get back in a little better shape. I've been thinking. It seems to me we might be smart to move over that big island, in the middle of the marsh. Over where Bopo has been goose hunting. I'd feel safer if we weren't camped so close to the shore. Snake might think of some way to get to us here. He won't ever come out to the middle of the marsh."

"Sounds good to me," said Bopo. "I'll get started on gathering willows as soon as it looks safe. With willows we can make a boat. Then we'll plop ole' Noah on the boat and move him and our camp to the big island. Guess I'll have to go back to the spot where that stream comes into the marsh. That seems to be the only place to cut willows, without going out of the marsh. That's just what Snake and those murderers are waitin' for. One of us to try to leave the marsh and Bang! He'd be on us!"

Ai mee nodded her head. "They'd be on us in a minute."

"There looks to be an awful lot of those pot holes of quicksand. All around that willow clump. We'll have to be careful. I'll go over there tomorrow. If the coast's clear of Paiutes, I'll get started with a willow harvest."

"Please, please be careful, Bopo," pleaded Ai mee. "I'd never forgive myself if you got into the quicksand. There's no getting out. That stuff's awful. Quicksand's really a great big spring in the bottom of a very deep pot hole. The spring is pumping in water so fast it keeps the sand in suspension. The mix is really viscous. It's so heavy and sticky it just sucks you under, when you try to move your arms or legs. Ugh! It's terrible stuff. Please be very careful when you're trying to get willows for us."

Through the next several days the weather was good, with clear skies reaching out toward the desert. Bopo made two successful trips to the willow patch in the quicksand. He was able to secure straight shafts for arrows as well as limber tips and bark to be used as ties. Ai mee cut and bundled large quantities of long rushes for the boat. They began to weave the rushes into a long tube and tie it with willows.

Bopo busied himself around camp. He peeled, fire-hardened and straightened the arrow shafts. Next he split the small ends, preparing to insert arrowheads. He cut notches in the opposite ends to receive a bow string. After that he began the delicate process of splitting the gray goose wing feathers and cutting them to size with his sharp flint blade. When these were carefully lashed to the shafts with strips of gut stolen from his leggings he proudly exhibited ten arrows, complete except for the heads.

Meanwhile Noah's recovery was proceeding slowly. He was anxious that it go faster, but Ai mee was adamant. He must move slowly at first. She produced Noah's bow and ask Bopo to string it for her. The bow was exceedingly stiff and powerful. Then she stood over Noah, insisting he practice drawing and slowly lowering the string. Time after time as an exercise for his wounded shoulder. At first it was quite painful and he could flex it only a few times before resting.

Noah began to pace furiously around the small island to exercise his legs, which had become quite weak. Under Ai mee's stern direction, he took to the cold water and began to swim for exercise. At last he was allowed to follow along behind Bopo on one of the foraging trips to the willow patch. He acted as lookout for the Paiute warriors as Bopo surreptitiously cut willows. Later he helped to push the willow pile through the water on the return to camp.

Both of Noah's companions felt free to order him about during his period of convalescence. They continually instructed him to work harder or not so hard. To go slower or not so slowly. They threatened he'd never get well unless he followed orders. Poor Noah meekly tried to follow every instruction without complaint. However, after one particularly obnoxious order from Ai mee, he quietly decided to go swimming. He disappeared among the rushes, not to return for the rest of the day. The longer he was gone the more worried his companions became. As the sun began to sink low over the mountains to the west, Ai mee pointed toward the water and said in a stern voice,

" Bopo, go seek poor Noah. I can't understand why you abuse him so when you know he's not fully recovered." Bopo was the picture of innocence as he said, "Me, how come you're blaming me? Your the one who's been ordering him around unmercifully." Then, just as Ai mee started to shake her finger at him in mock anger, he backed into the water and disappeared, in search of his friend.

It wasn't too long before Noah found himself and returned to camp. Coming out of the water with a happy smile, he displayed a pouch containing small pieces of slate.

"You two were so busy playing Boss with me as the only warrior, I decided to go for a swim and see if I could find some material for arrowheads. There isn't any flint to be had in this part of Washo Land. The closest supply I know of is down in my home territory, at the flint mine close to Twin Lakes. So, while this stuff isn't nearly as good," he said holding out the pouch of slate, "it'll just have to do for now. It's all right for arrowheads, although they won't be very sharp. No good at all for knives, however."

With a frown crossing her pretty face, Ai mee asked in an ominously quiet voice, "Where did you find that slate? If it came from where I think it came from, you are in trouble, very big trouble, Mister Noah!"

"Well," said Noah, with a shrug of the shoulders and palms held upward, "It came from that little hollow in the face of the cliff. The one where we hid from Snake and that bunch of blood-thirsty warriors. That's the only outcropping of stone in the whole meadow as far as I know. I remember noticing it, as we stood there with Snake screaming away right above us. Remember? Why do you ask?" he inquired innocently.

"I'll remember it as long as I live!   It'll always scare me to death, just to think about it! But that's not the point," hissed Ai mee angrily, her eyes snapping fire. "The point is, you are not to go outside of this marsh. What'd you think you were doing? Walking out there in the open! Don't you know Snake could see you while you were pulling a dumb stunt like that? I'm surprised at how stupid you can be. You just make me so mad. I don't know what to do!"

"Well," said Noah, with another shrug of the shoulders, "we gotta have arrowheads, don't we? There isn't any other place to get 'em, is there?   I can't see why you're so mad about a little thing like that."

"I'm mad because I'm mad, that's why," was Ai mee's angry reply. "I'm mad because you act like you don't have any sense, Noah. What would you do if Snake caught you out there alone? Injured and unarmed. Tell me that, Noah?" Bopo made the mistake of trying to defend his friend in a mild voice.

"Look, Ai mee, those little pieces of stone could be really important to us. Now we can have ten finished arrows. Suppose a big old buck deer got one of those little pieces of stone right through the heart. Or better yet, suppose Snake got one right through the throat. That stone could make the whole difference."

Turning to Bopo, who was doing his best to look innocent, she stamped a small moccasin foot and said, "And you wipe that smirk off your face, Mister Bopo. You act just as stupid as he does. Floating around out there on your back and just inviting them to shoot arrows at you. Do you think that was very smart? It was stupid! Really stupid!"

Turning away from them, the small indignant figure stamped off, her tiny moccasin feet leaving angry puffs of dust as she went.

Noah looked at Bopo, shrugged his shoulders, spread his hands palms up and rolled his eyes. Bopo repeated the gestures. The pair of them were in deep trouble. No goose stew for dinner tonight!

CHAPTER 9   Warriors

With the next storm the last vestiges of autumn disappeared. Winter arrived at Honey Marsh and the vast mountain meadow surrounding it. As darkness settled each evening, the watchfires of Snake and the Evil Nine could be seen extending in a semi circle around the southern end of the marsh.

The three Washo youths could see the fires had been located to form a barrier between them and their home land. If they attempted to make a dash toward home, they'd quickly be captured and Snake would extract his threatened vengeance. Death for the fellows and permanent blindness for their companion.

After a move to the big island they felt more secure. At least the enemy was out of ear shot and arrow range. Tranquillity was restored when the two fellows promised not to venture near the shore. At least, until a council of war had been held. Noah summed up the matter. It was appropriate to hold a Council of War for all major decisions, inasmuch as all three clans of the tribe were represented on their island. Noah's clan was Pa wa lu, Ai mee, Wel mel ti and Bopo, Hung a lil ti.

The big island was a more suitable winter camp site. They built a traditional rush and willow wind fence against the prevailing gusts. Ai mee built a sturdy frame work for the shelter and they thatched it with rushes. The traditional east-facing doorway was covered with a finely woven mat. She produced pliant sleeping mats to cover the floor: her sleeping spot on one side of the fire and the boys on the other. A neat stone-lined fire pit adorned the center. A typical Washo shelter, snug and secure against the winter winds.

As promised, Ai mee produced a boat of sorts. It was ungainly but serviceable. Two long tubes of rushes tied together at the front and topped with a willow grid platform. It was long enough so all three could sit or kneel while poling the craft. Though crude, the boat was better than the alternative, swimming in the   freezing cold marsh water. Now that the problems of secure shelter and transportation were resolved, the three turned attention to the remaining challenge: an adequate food supply for the winter. Bopo called a Council of War to discuss the problem, saying,

"We've been eating pretty well, what with wheat cakes and goose or duck. The last few days I've seen those big Vee-shaped formations of geese. Headed south for the winter. Any day now they'll pull out of here entirely, along with all the ducks. We need to figure out a way to get some of those fat deer. The ones out there in the meadow. Without Snake catching us. The herd will probably winter right here, in the meadow. I think it'd be suicide for any of us to venture out there, though."

"Agreed," nodded Noah. "However, I've got a hunch the herd must graze near one of the streams entering the marsh. They like to drink after it gets dark."

"Mule Tail Deer are creatures of habit." agreed Bopo. "They probably drink at the same spot every night."

"If we can locate the watering spot, maybe we could rig up the boat. Use a flash pot. Bag some of the animals as they water for the night."

Ai mee nodded agreement and said helpfully, "A few fat deer would do wonders for our food supply. Even more important, we must have some hides for clothing. The woven cloaks are a help. Nothing's as warm and serviceable as nice soft tanned deer hide, though. Our buckskins are all in tatters. Beside, if we intend to make a run for it, get out of here next spring, we can't very well do it in those bulky woven rush clothes."

Smacking his lips, Bopo said, "My mouth waters every time I see that herd of fat deer grazing. You can bet Snake's living well. Enjoying a big venison roast for dinner every night. We all agree he'll slaughter us the minute we go after deer in the meadow."

"I don't want any part of going out in that meadow," admonished Noah.

"We can rig a basket full of sand for a flash pot on the front of the boat. Make a screen to hide behind on the deck. Then, we're ready to hunt! Let's go looking for that watering spot, tomorrow night."

"Agreed!" everyone nodded.

The next evening found the three ready to set out on a search for the herd's watering spot. There was a full winter moon overhead. It promised enough light to see tell tale deer tracks along the shore. The boat was equipped with two poles lashed to the bow. They supported a small sand filled basket containing coals. It was covered by a woven lid. A flimsy deck screen   hid the three hunters. Slowly and silently they poled toward the far shore, where a stream entered the marsh. They arrived just as the full moon broke from behind a cloud. It was startling to see how clearly the sudden burst of moonlight illuminated the scene. They cringed behind the screen, expecting a hail of arrows at any moment, signaling they'd been discovered. But, the scene remained tranquil with only the occasional chirp of a cricket to break the silence.

The time had come to take to the water. Go inspect the muddy bank of the stream for tracks. The bank lay in a densely shadowed clump of willows. The water around it was black. It might cover one of the dreaded pot holes of quicksand. Not an inviting place!

"Well" said Bopo, "You two sit tight and I'll go do a little scouting of that mud bank."

"No way!" exclaimed Noah vehemently "This is my show tonight. You gathered willows while I watched! Now it's your turn to watch. Besides, we need someone to cover that wall of shadows, with bow drawn. Just in case one of the Paiutes shows up unexpectedly. I still can't draw a bow well. I'll feel a lot better with you handling the bow and me in the water."

Quietly he slipped into the inky pool and disappeared among the rushes. For what seemed like an eternity the occupants of the boat peered through the leafy screen, straining their eyes in the darkness. Each tried to detect a ripple or a shadow that would indicate the swimmer,s presence. Noah had completely disappeared into the inky blackness.

Without warning a voice from the water behind them whispered. "Nothing, nothing there. Just a few curlew tracks. Not a sign of a deer."

For the next three nights Noah's whispered report was the same: "No deer tracks here." Then, on the fifth night, they returned to the scene of Bopo's willow gathering expeditions. The large willow clump surrounded by quicksand on three sides. Located at the mouth of a swift stream, it was a likely animal grazing site.

Noah's whispered report from the blackness was, "Good Medicine! My totem the coyote must have been listening last night. Deer tracks all over the place. Big ones! We've found the watering hole at last."

The three were jubilant on their return to camp. A fire was built up quickly in order to warm the shivering swimmer. Ai mee produced wheat cakes. They sat down to excitedly plan the next move. A deer hunt! Bopo and Noah's very first deer hunt!

An enthused Bopo said, "At last, Noah, we're going to get our chance to qualify as full fledged big game hunters. No more rabbits and sage hen. Deer hunters! We've been waiting for this a long time. All our lives, in fact. Tomorrow night we try to flash one of those big ole' bucks. Wouldn't it be fine to bag a huge Mule Tail! Our very first big game!"

"There's one little detail you two great hunters might want to consider," said Ai mee impishly, with just a trace of sarcasm in her voice. "It might be nice if you had some arrows. If you're planning to go hunting, that is. So far you haven't got the arrowheads made. The arrows are a long way from ready. Of course, maybe Noah could smack a deer with a rock from his sling. He's pretty good with that thing, I've noticed."

Bopo whacked himself on the forehead dramatically and groaned out loud. "I knew there was some thing I was planning to get done. Arrowheads! Noah got in so much trouble for collecting that shale, I forgot all about trying to make arrow heads out of the stuff. Where's that slate you picked up, Noah? We better get cracking."

Holding up the pouch containing small pieces of shale Noah said. "It's hard to make good arrowheads with this stuff. Mostly, I use obsidian flint. It's easy to chip. Makes a nice sharp point. Shale's a lot harder to work, 'cause it just doesn't chip as well. The edges aren't sharp like flint. There's plenty of pieces of shale here, so let's all try a hand at chipping this stuff."

The three young people hunched down around the fire and went to work at chipping the tough stone. Noah used the bone handle on his hunting knife as a chipping tool. Wrapped a small piece of the stone in his leather shirt tail and tried to flake off small chips. After trying unsuccessfully for some time, he finally gave up in disgust.

Bopo tried the same approach, but was much more patient. He worked methodically for a long time. He too finally gave up and threw the stone away in anger.

It was Ai mee who at last discovered a way to roughly form the tough stone. She used the sharp edge of a larger piece of the same material as a forming tool. Crowing with delight, the girl finally held up a reasonable approximation of a classical Washo hunting point. Although it was not very sharp and was not quite symmetrical, it would serve.

"Ai mee," said Noah, "at least for the time being, I think we need to set aside the old Washo tradition. You know, the one that says only the men can make weapons. I vote we appoint you the official "Maker of All Arrow Heads. At least for our first deer hunting expedition."

"Ai mee, you've got my vote too," said Bopo, holding the point in his hand and admiring it. In the dusky confines of the lodge, the small girl with the startlingly beautiful face arose from her cross-legged position before the glowing fire pit. Drawing her tiny figure to full height, she folded arms ceremoniously across her chest. With a serious expression on her small brown face, she regarded first one of her companions and then the other. As a radiant smile broke across her lips, she said,

"Gentlemen, I accept!"

The following day was filled with activity in preparation for the upcoming hunt. The expectant hunters were goaded on by an empty stomach. They had visions of delicious venison roasting over an open fire. Even more important, they were about to realize an ambition of a lifetime. As long as either could remember they'd dreamed of this day. The day they'd be old enough, and experienced enough, to hunt for big game. They wanted to go out into the world. Prove to every one they were hunters. Adult warriors who could produce the stuff of life, food. Large game, deer, antelope, bighorn sheep.

When a hunter can produce big game he proves himself to the whole tribe. He's declared by the tribal elders to be a warrior. A full fledged Washo Warrior. At long last Bopo and Noah were about to have the cherished opportunity. They were about to qualify themselves as warriors. No more of this humiliating 'Almost Warrior' stuff. Full-fledged Warriors !

Excitement reigned supreme. Ai mee's fingers flew and produced more arrowheads. Noah, using the very last of the twisted goose gut, meticulously lashed the tough points to flame-hardened shafts.

Holding up the finished arrow for inspection, Bopo said, "These arrows aren't the best. We haven't got the right materials. Sure do hope they'll last, for that one important shot. Have to talk to my totem about that."

All the while Noah was busy with preparation of the boat. He attached the small, loosely woven work basket to the front poles. After filling it with sand, he kindled a tiny fire producing glowing coals. These were shielded from view with a lid. When the lid was opened it cast a glow forward, toward the prey. Woe be to our friends if Snake was able to see those glowing coals from afar. That would end the hunt in a hurry!

As dusk settled around the lodge, they huddled near the fire and devoured a sparse dinner of wheat cakes. All the while they dreamed of a fine venison roast slowly turning on a spit, dripping crackling juices into the fire.

The abundant supplies of Tah gum, the pine nut, and the presence of a large Mule Tail deer population, formed two of the most important staples of the Washo diet. Fruits, grains, herbs, acorns and tubers completed nature's menu.

The large deer was an excellent food source. It could be cooked fresh or preserved as jerked venison. The bones, brain, hide, sinew, entrails and horns were a source of clothing, weapons and tools. Not even the tiniest part of the big game animal was wasted. The Washo people lived in perfect harmony with their environment.

Anxiously, they waited to launch the clumsy boat and be off. Noah counseled that they delay till the moon was down and the night at it's darkest. Best to reduce any chance of being detected by the ever-watchful Snake. As the last bright speck of a winter moon flickered out behind the high peaks of the snowy western mountains, the bulky rush boat coasted quietly away from the dark shore. Ai mee in the rear, Noah kneeling in the center and Bopo seated in front. Each fellow was armed with a powerful hunting bow and two arrows.

They glided smoothly across the black waters to a point where a stream flowed into the marsh. Softly, they eased through thick clumps of willows. At last Bopo raised a silent hand indicating they were within bow shot of the muddy stream bank. The night was black and the silence heavy. They sat motionless waiting there in the shadows.

The sand-filled basket of coals before them was completely masked to avoid Snake's prying eyes.

Time stretched on into an eternity as the three dark blobs sat frozen. There was only the hushed gurgle of water. With practiced stealth the tiny figure in the rear maneuvered the craft slightly. She placed both hunters broadside to the shadowed bank, so the powerful bows could bear. Silence, silence.

Then at last, there was the faint sound of a twig snapping. An impatient snort from the black shadows of the shore line. The abrupt crack of a dry branch. Slowly, as if by magic, a faint warm light began to spread. Bopo's silent hand delicately adjusted the mask covering the glowing coals.

The hunters were suspended in a frozen silence, not even daring to breathe as the boat swayed with the shifting of dark water. Three pairs of luminous yellow eyes, huge unblinking eyes, appeared out of the willowy gloom. Staring, staring, staring directly into the burning orange of the glowing coals.

Bopo's hand appeared, raised in black silhouette against the glow. Three fingers extended. Silently Noah nodded in understanding. There were three deer. The hand silhouette changed to a single pointing finger. It indicated the pair of eyes on the right. Again Noah nodded. The deer on the right was the big buck! An eternity of frozen silence. At last Noah hissed, "Now!"

Heavy bow strings twanged and two arrow shafts glinted in the soft light. There was a loud snort and the crash of frantic animals escaping through the brush. Then there was silence. Broken after a moment by Ai mee's softly hissed message.

"You're sitting in the middle of a huge pot hole of quicksand. Don't move. Stay in the boat." Deftly she maneuvered the clumsy craft alongside the muddy stream bank. The hunters started to frantically search through the willows with their hands.

"Over here," gasped Bopo, "I've got him," as the boat lurched heavily, almost overturning. The antlers of a large Mule Tail appeared out of the darkness, followed by a huge carcass. It was draped across the deck with two broken shafted arrows protruding from the broad chest.

"Quick," hissed Ai mee, "Let's get out of here before Snake and the whole Evil Nine show up."

Poling for all they were worth, the three happy hunters made the bulky boat fairly fly across the water toward the big island. It was a jubilant group who embarked as the boat crunched up against the shore. Because the animal was too big to carry, they dragged it up the beach to the waiting lodge, leaving telltale furrows in the sand. Both arrows had pierced the animal's heart. It had died instantly. As they stood there surveying the magnificent animal, each boy silently addressed his maker, asking forgiveness for taking the life of an animal. Each asked that its spirit be admitted to that great meadow where the grass was always green and deep.

Ai mee took out her flint knife and proceeded to demonstrate her skill at preparing game. The men might be the hunters, but it was the Washo women who knew how to make the most of handling a fine animal. Feeling very adult, the two mighty hunters stood about, making sage comments on the excellent condition of the animal. They noted its plumpness and the thick coat of luxurious winter hair, not to mention the strength and spread of the fine three-point horns.

Anyone could see the lads were very proud of this their first big game kill. The fact that the kill was shared between two best friends made it even more special. The moment for which they waited so long was now at hand. Each swelled with pride to think they were now full-fledged Washo Warriors.

As Ai mee worked at skinning the heavy carcass, she talked over her shoulder. She complimented them on the way they'd conducted the hunt and upon their skill with the bow. Puffing up with pride, the two grinned at each other in embarrassed silence. They reveled in all this attention. They were particularly pleased because it came from Ai mee. They'd come to respect the feisty little person mightily. In fact, she'd grown in their eyes to be a very special companion. Besides that, she was pretty, and boy, could that girl skin a deer!

By the time evening came, the warriors had completed a sturdy frame of willows and stretched the fresh hide on it. The hide with hair still attached would now dry, a prelude to tanning. A second frame work was constructed and was now covered with long thin slices of lean venison, drying into jerky. Most of the precious meat would be treated in this fashion, to preserve it. Only a small portion, the most choice cuts, would be kept aside for roasting or cooking in the stew basket.

The two hunters stood idly aside, talking and waving slender cattail branches over the fresh meat, to insure no insect landed on the precious food supply. A delicious aroma began to waft its way out the door of the lodge. Ai mee was at work doing magical things around the fire pit. The lads sniffed the breeze, testing the aroma. An expression of sheer bliss appeared on each brown face.

Ai mee's smiling countenance appeared at the open doorway as announced, "You can come in and eat your evening meal now."

"Well, Ai mee, my girl, what, may I ask, might we be having for dinner on this fine night?" inquired Noah with a look of anticipation spreading across his hungry face.

"Yes, Ai mee" said a grinning Bopo "I too would like to inquire as to what delicacy you've prepared for us this evening ?"

"Well fellows," said Ai mee with a wicked gleam in her smiling eyes, "since you ask, you two are having all the wheat cakes you want to eat tonight. Of course, I'll be having a little of the venison stew myself. Just to test the recipe, you understand."

The two mighty hunters were appalled.

"Wheat cakes" the two groaned in unison. "We bag a fine deer and all you feed us is wheat cakes?"

"Now, see here, fellows," said the girl, adopting a businesslike attitude, with hand on hip. "You know the Washo tribal customs as well as I do. You know when a newly crowned warrior brings in his first big game, it's used to feed everyone in the tribe. Everyone, that is, except the new warrior. It's not polite for him to eat any of his first kill. Certainly not on the first night. anyway. Maybe we could stretch a point on the second, but not on the first night. No way! After all, a custom's a custom, you know."

"Wheat cakes Ai mmmee?" groaned the two.

Ai mee proved to be a typical woman that night. No matter how they pleaded and cajoled. No matter how they flattered her. No matter how woebegone they looked. That hardhearted woman would give them only wheat cakes. Meanwhile, she sipped delicately at the venison stew, commenting philosophically as to the merits of the recipe.

Shaking his head, Noah mused, "You know, Bopo, sometimes a warrior's life isn't all it's cracked up to be."

After the boys bagged their first deer, the Washo manhood ceremony automatically began. The initial part of the ceremony was completed when Ai mee took the first bite of the venison stew. As she reminded the lads, the ceremony did not permit them to partake of their first kill. Both hunters were now considered men and warriors.

The second phase of the ceremony marked the transition to manhood. The antlers of their first deer were placed on the ground with points down. If the horns were large enough so the hunter could crawl through the antlers without touching them, he was considered an exceptional hunter. He was assured of good medicine on all future hunts.

Noah, who was tall and slender with wide muscular shoulders, slithered through the antlers on his back without touching and therefore passed the test with ease. He received his friends' congratulations with a shy grin.

Next it was Bopo's turn and things didn't work out so well. Bopo was about half a head shorter than his friend and considerably wider, especially through the shoulders. Bopo didn't come anywhere near being able to slide under those three point horns. No matter how he squirmed and wriggled he just couldn't get through without touching. He was terribly crest-fallen.

"I guess that guarantees I'll always be a second-rate hunter and have bad luck," groaned the unfortunate fellow.

"Now, don't you say that" said the girl loyally. "The rules for that old ceremony don't say anything about the situation where you have a shared first kill. I think the rules should say you're entitled to a second chance under the condition of a shared kill. That way you could try for another deer. After all, it isn't your fault your shoulders are so big. I think they're nice shoulders, Bopo."

"I agree with Ai mee," said Noah. "I move we hold a Council of War right now and pass a law that says you get a second chance."

And so it came to pass, the Washo Manhood Ceremony was officially modified by a unanimous vote of all three clans of the tribe, at a special Council of War held deep in Honey Marsh.

As dusk settled upon the little Washo camp that night, Bopo quietly disappeared in the boat alone. Neither of his companions took notice of his absence. They were aware he was gone, of course. There wasn't much question about where he'd gone. Noah and Ai mee sat on the beach talking quietly far into the night. Anxiously they waited for the boat's return. Never was a hunter accompanied by warmer wishes for success.

The two on the beach talked of many things that night. Noah said, "Ai mee, I've wondered many times, what would have happened to Bopo and me if you hadn't come along with us. I remember being really shaken when I looked over my shoulder. You weren't there as we started to run away, from the Paiute village. Just couldn't understand why you didn't want to escape with us."

"It wasn't that I didn't want to escape. I wanted to be free more than anything," said Ai mee, with a pensive look in her lovely dark eyes. "It was just, I thought it unfair to saddle you with a girl. I knew Snake would never let me go. I still wonder sometimes, if you two wouldn't be better off without me. Maybe Snake would have given up by now, if I weren't here. Sometimes, I get to feeling that we'll never again see our families in Washo Land," she said in a gloomily voice.

"Well, Ai me," said Noah in a calm and thoughtful voice. "I'm going back to Washo Land. I'm planning on Bopo and I both going back. I'm planning on all three of us going back. What's more, I'm planning on taking you right up to the door of your lodge and telling your momma, 'Here's that nice Ai mee girl of yours, come home to see you.' " His words had a firm ring to them. His voice took on the cold hard edge of flint on flint.

"Noah" said Ai mee with a curious little catch in her throat, "That's a beautiful plan."

As night ended, the water of the marsh was a motionless black surface. The silent rushes were faintly silhouetted against the sky. In the far distance a single file flight of ducks twisted its way above the meadow in a threadlike fashion. In the hushed stillness there was a gurgle of water. Bopo's usually booming voice, now suppressed to a whisper, floated out of the shadows.

"Ho ho hooo. Hello, the camp! Ho Ho! What do I see at the camp, but two dark blobs sitting on the beach! Ho ho hooo Hello blobs on the beach."

With a sigh of relief the two dark blobs stood up and prepared to welcome the returning hunter. The ungainly boat appeared out of the darkness as Noah waded into the water to drag it ashore. There seated on the deck with legs dangling in the water was Bopo. A wide grin stretched across his usually stoical face. On the deck was stretched the largest deer any of them had ever seen. The massive rump protruded with heavy rear quarters trailing in the water on one side of the boat. The head and great horns hung in the water on the other side.

"Ugh" gasped Ai mee, "That's one big deer."

"I just got lucky." smiled Bopo. "Went back to the same place and when I flashed the coals he was standing there looking right at me. I got off a lucky shot. It was almost too easy. Got him right in the heart and he never moved a step. Just dropped right where he stood. Of course, after that things got a little messy."

"What do you mean, a little messy?" asked Ai mee in an ominously quiet voice.

"Now, Ai mee, don't go giving me a lecture," said Bopo defensively. "I didn't do anything wrong. Not one thing. Just had a small unavoidable problem, that's all. I didn't see that darn Paiute standing back there in the willows. It was that fellow Weasel, I think. Anyhow, about the time I finished rolling this big deer onto the deck, he hauled off and nailed me with this arrow in the calf."

Bopo raised his leg from the water and his companions saw a white feathered arrow impaling his sturdy calf. As they looked, a trickle of bright blood rolled down and dripped from his toes.

In a hurried moment, Ai mee dragged the protesting hunter up onto the beach and was examining his wound.

"At least," she said severely, "it wasn't one of Snakes poison arrows."

Indeed, the next morning a stiff and badly limping Bopo did complete the deer horn ceremony, without too many problems from his sore leg. At last the little party contained two fully qualified warriors who were destined to become great hunters.

CHAPTER 10   The Trap

It was one of those cold, slate gray mornings when the wind swept down from the desert mountains in the east. An east wind always means cold weather without any snow. As was the daily custom, each of the youths had, upon rising, gone to his personal place for a swim and bath. As it was so cold, each returned to the warm lodge rather quickly. Bopo, limping badly and walking painfully with the aid of a willow crutch, was the last to return. Noah was already at work beside the fire, finishing new arrows. Ai mee was busily preparing tasty brown wheat cakes for baking on a flat piece of shale.

As Bopo limped painfully into the lodge, Ai mee looked up in sympathy and said, "Bopo, I'm sorry your leg is hurting you so. Come sit by the fire and prop it up in a nice warm spot. I'll braid that clean, long hair of yours, as soon as it dries. How would you like that?"

"That'd be just great," said the lad. "I enjoy all the attention I can get. Back home my little sister braids my pig tail almost every morning. She does it a lot better than I can do it for myself."

Ai mee sat down crosslegged behind him and began to comb out his waist-length shiny black hair with her firscarred bone comb.

"Remember when we were swimming up here the day we arrived at the marsh?" asked the girl. "You said you'd tell me the story of your pig tail some day. Well, it's a cold winter day and we're snug inside with a nice warm fire and plenty of deer meat to eat. So it should be a good story telling time. How about the pig tail story today?"

Bopo needed no further encouragement. Leaning back on his elbows and propping up his sore leg before the fire, Bopo began to tell his tale.

"Now remember, this is a true story. This is just exactly the way it happened. Well, when I was a little fellow, a very little fellow in fact, I used to follow my father around every place he went. Try to do every thing he did. Our family had just arrived at Da ow aga, for the summer. As usual, my folks set up our summer camp on the west shore. Right at the point where Emerald Bay empties into the lake. The entrance to the bay is quite narrow. There are big rocks located in the deep water at either side of the entrance."

"That's supposed to be one of the best fishing holes on the lake, I've heard. Is it really all that good?"

Nodding his head, Bopo went on. "It's a great place to fish because the big ole' lake trout lay in the shadows of those rocks. Sometimes my father would use a bone hook and crawfish tails for bait. But mostly he used a forked spear attached to a hand line to retrieve the fish. Some of the big ole' lake trout he pulled outta there were bigger than I was.

"Now, there was just one problem with fishing in this place. It was such a problem, that hardly anyone else ever came near. Much less ever thought of camping or fishing there, even though fishing was really good. In fact, no one but our family ever camped there. When you stood on top of one of those big rocks and looked over your shoulder into Emerald Bay, you could see a small island. It had steep sides rising out of the deepest water in the center of the bay. It was bare black rock rising up out of the water. It was a really cold and lonely looking place. I used to call it Old Ominous Island!"

"I've seen the place," said Ai mee with a shudder. 'Ominous Island', that's a good name." She held up Bopo's long black pig tail to admire her work.

"Now, under that evil-looking island," continued Bopo, "Deep, deep down at the very bottom of the Bay, where never a ray of light penetrates, there's a huge gloomy cave. It's got moss and slimy stuff all over the walls. At the back in a huge dark crack lives the Water Baby."

(The Water Baby is a figure of Washo legend handed down over the centuries. It was without a doubt the worst of all monsters in Washo Land, with the possible exception of that awful ONG bird. But that thing is so dreadful it's best not to even talk about it here. That's another story and a horrible one at that. Anyway, the Water Baby is even worse than Snake, who is the most evil of the Paiute. The Water Baby is so bad, none of the Washo people go out on the surface of the big lake because he lives there. They won't even bathe in the lake's waters; it's taboo. At night the

Water Baby comes out of its cave and swims silently all along the shore of the lake. It's looking for humans to eat. If ever that thing came to a place where a child was sitting close to the water, it would sneak right up on the shore after that little kid. Grab him and carry him back to that dark cave under the water and eat him. Pick all his bones clean.)

"I can remember some of the worst spankings I ever got were because I forgot and went close to the water after dark," continued Bopo.

"The Water Baby is a repulsive-looking monster. I can tell you because I've seen it with my own eyes. Up close, too close! It's a great big thing, far too big to fit in this lodge, even if it were to curl up. It's half grizzly Bear and half Great White Shark, and it's all mean! Right down to the soles of its huge grizzly bear feet. He has huge, long black claws as big around as Ai mee's wrist. The thing has this immense grizzly's head. Except, when it opens those huge jaws it has teeth just like the shark. Those cold round fish eyes don't blink, they just stare into you like a shark. The thing's all covered with shaggy blackish gray hair like a grizzly. Except, where the grizzly has a hump, this thing has a great white fin sticking out between the shoulder blades. He can swim faster than a frightened trout and bite a man's head off clean, with those gaping jaws. I know because I've seen him up close," said Bopo with a shudder.

"Are you serious about all of this, really serious?" asked Noah doubtfully.

Choosing to ignore his cousin, Bopo went on,

"So anyhow, my father was going fishing out on the rocks, to catch a lake trout for our dinner. As usual I followed right along behind him. Everything was fine except when we got out on the rocks. I stubbed my toe and fell in the deep water. Boy, was I scared. My father let out a big yell, "Water Baby!" and pointed at the deep water right behind me. I started to swim like mad toward my father. He reached way out and grabbed me by the little pig tail growing at the back of my head. Lifted me right out of the water quick as a wink. But it wasn't quite quick enough. I looked down and saw this horrible thing right below me in the water. It had the great big shark mouth open. It was all hollow and bright red with rows of long sharp white teeth. The smell from inside was all putrid and rotten. Then that awful mouth closed with a crunch. Off went my moccasin and two toes."

Gingerly, Bopo leaned forward and peeled off the moccasin from his injured foot. There was a fine looking broad brown foot with three toes. The smaller two toes had been neatly snapped off.

"Whewww Wheeeee!" exclaimed Noah "I've always thought your stories were a little too colorful, Bopo. But you've sure made a believer out of me!"

"To finish the story," continued Bopo, "When my father got me back to camp and my mother had me all patched up and my tears dried, I got quite a lecture from both of them, about the Water Baby. My father ended the lecture by giving my pig tail a pat and saying, "Son, don't ever cut off that Water Baby handle!"

Ai mee held up Bopo's neatly plaited black pig tail and gave it a loving pat.

The two Washo lads sat concealed in a stand of cattails. A rim of ice circled the clumps around them. The sky above was leaden gray. They crouched waiting for a flight of geese or a flock of ducks to alight. Hunting was very slow, most of the game birds having migrated to the south as winter wore on toward spring. At the shore nearby, was the spot where Bopo bagged the huge mule tail deer, weeks before. A large clump of willows surrounded the spot where a swift stream entered the marsh.

To the left of the stream the ground rose sharply to form a small bluff which overhung deep pools of open marsh water. A faint line in the grass indicated the presence of a trail close to the margin of the marsh. The trail emerged atop the bluff and meandered dangerously close to a spot overhanging the deep pools.

Noah studied the small bluff silently for a long time. At last he pointed at the trail atop the knoll and mused thoughtfully.

"You know, Bopo, up there on top of the little bluff, that trail comes a lot closer to the edge than is safe. It looks to me like a person might fall right into that deep pool if he lost his footing. Would you think that pool has quick sand beneath it?"

"More than a possibility," agreed Bopo. "I paddled right through the middle of that pool with my feet hanging down in the water the night I bagged that big deer. I could feel the quicksand sucking at my feet as I went over. It really felt spooky, knowing all that quicksand was right there under me, pulling away at my feet. I wouldn't even go back there in the boat again. That's a good place to stay away from if you ask me. Ugh! Bad medicine," he shivered.

"Yeah, I think you're right," agreed Noah. "A fellow could get in big trouble in there. Now Bopo, would you say that a fellow coming down that trail and going right up to the edge would land in that pool of quick sand, if the trail just happened to collapse under him as he went by?"

"Well," said Bopo, his forehead wrinkled in deep thought, "if all those supposes and maybes came to pass, I figure any fellow stupid enough to get that close to the edge would end up head first in that old pool of quicksand. It would have to be one mighty stupid Paiute, though. You know, come to think of it, who would be stupid enough? That fellow Weasel. I'll tell you why. He's the one assigned to patrol this section of the trail. I've seen him snooping around more than once, when I was here gathering willows. I'm sure he was the one who was hiding up there on top of that little bluff, the night I came across that pool hunting deer. He's the one who put the arrow through my leg, while I was gettin' that big ole' deer loaded onto the boat. Think that must be his favorite ambush spot. Up there on the trail atop the bluff."

"It looks to me like the rock in that overhang is some of that soft granite. The stuff that's decomposed and crumbles easily. Now, if a fellow was to go over there with a strong sharp stick, I'll bet he could dig away enough of that crumbling rock so there's a sort of cave right under the trail. The roof would be so thin, the first person to walk down that trail would cave it in. Take a header into the pool."

Nodding his head in agreement, Noah said, "Bopo, you've got a good plan there. I just happen to have a couple of blades of grass here. What say we draw to see who goes over there and hollows out a cave under that trail? Whoever wins has got to be real careful, however. He's got to hang onto the face of that rock with one hand and dig with the other. If he slips he's sure to end up in the quicksand. By the way, who ever loses has to sit here with an arrow ready. It would be sort of embarrassing if Weasel or worse yet, Snake, were to show up at the wrong time."

Noah was the winner and spent the entire afternoon clinging to the face of the rock while hollowing out a cave under the trail. Just as the sun was setting he completed his job. Carefully he removed any signs of his labor.

The two young men returned to the camp on the big island, with tales of discouragement over the poor bird hunting. They forgot to mention anything about their cave-digging activities to a sympathetic Ai mee.

That night, as the wind howled outside the snug lodge and the three sat munching the evening meal, Noah broached a subject which had come to mind more and more frequently in the last few days.

"This morning," he reflected, "while bathing, I smelled something new in the air. You have any idea what it was?"

"Sure," said Ai mee enthusiastically, "I know what it was. It was spring wasn't it?"

"Right you are, Ai mee my girl," smiled Noah. "Spring time, the time when all good Washo people sniff the breeze and begin to think about packing the burden baskets. They're ready to move out after a long hard winter. Back home the supply of pine nuts is depleted and everyone has a big appetite for fresh food. They're tired of the hot springs and sulfur water. Ready for a trek up into the mountain country. Ai mee, I imagine all of the people in your family's winter camp, except maybe a few of the very old folks, will be ready to start moving up the Truckee River. Probably find a few deer in the lower meadows. Mostly they'll be fishing in the river all the way. They'll be using spears and building willow fish traps. Catch the spring spawning run of Cutthroat trout. They'll feast on baked fish. They'll also dry most of those fine big trout for later eating."

Smacking her lips, Ai mee said, "I can taste those fresh trout now."

Nodding his head in agreement, Noah continued. "Finally they'll arrive at Da ow aga, where the main summer camp for the whole clan's located. On the west bank of the river, right where the water flows in from the big lake. Where the Truckee is born!"

"Of all the camps, of all the clans, of all the Washo people, I think that's the most beautiful campsite of all," sighed Ai mee. The girl wistfully explained, "Our family usually times their travels so they arrive just before the first new moon of summer. The first new moon marks the beginning of the Womanhood Ceremony. It's the most important date in the life of any young Washo girl. The time when she discards her childhood. Becomes a young woman."

With a most serious expression on her small brown face, Ai mee continued. " When I finally get back, if I ever do get back to my family, I know my mother is going to be shocked at first. Then she'll be delighted to see me alive. But, her next reaction will be to insist I immediately enter into the Womanhood Ceremony. I've already been through the training for the dance. It depicts all the tasks that are important to Washo women. Also, I'll have to go through a strict four-day fast before the ceremony. That's very important and affects your whole later life. You also must keep busy with chores through the whole fast."

With a dreamy look in her eyes, Ai mee continued. "Then I'll climb to the top of Rubicon Peak and light four fires. They can be seen from far away. Tells everyone to come to the ceremony. I'll carry a very special red elderberry pole called a Dance Stick. I'll hide the red pole up there, in some hard-to-find secret place. Later, if some very special fellow finds it and returns it to our lodge, he's the one you marry. Of course, that last part is sort of wishful thinking. Isn't really part of the ceremony," she giggled.

"On the morning of the ceremony, your grandmother gives you a bath in the stream. Right there in front of everybody," she laughed. "In the end you throw the bathwater basket into the crowd, for one of the other girls to catch."

"Whew!" she concluded seriously, "I just have to get back in time for that ceremony. Getting to be a woman is just as important to a girl as getting to be a warrior is to you fellows!"

The fire sputtered and burned low, as Bopo rose to gather an armful of rush logs. It was time to rebuild the glowing coals.

"Any way you look at it," concluded Noah seriously, "if we hope to get back to the head waters of the Truckee by the first new moon of summer, we've got a little less than four moons time. We've gotta get moving out of Honey Marsh, in the next few days. That means outrunning Snake and the Evil Nine. That means we need to be well equipped. How long before each of you can be ready?"

"Three days!" said Ai mee, "I've got to make an extra set of moccasins for each of us. Pack all the jerked venison and grain. Also some clothing and tanned hides and herbs and spices. I'll need some time to clean up the campsite. Always leave a spotless campsite, my mother taught me."

"I'll use the next three days to borrow a big supply of grain from our friends the muskrats," grinned Bopo.

" I'll spend some time scouting Snake's camp and refining the plan for how we escape from the

marsh. So, we're agreed?   The time has come?
Three nights from now we depart the marsh!"
crowed Noah triumphantly.

"Here's the beginning of a plan. See what
you two think. I don't believe there's any way we can
break out of here by going south toward our home-
land. We'd have to go right through Snake's camp.
That bunch is too well-armed. On the alert, for us to
make a move." said Noah, kneeling down to draw a
map on the ground before the flickering fire.

"We want to end up at Da ow aga four
moons from now. We'll trick Snake by heading out in
the opposite direction. Go due north. Directly away
from Washo Land. We break out of here. Make one
full day's hard march as fast as we can go. Due
north! Then we hide our trail. Make a sharp turn to
the west. Just outside the northern border of Washo
Land. For the next five days or so we head straight
west. Straight up the mountain. Over the crest and
down the other side. It's going to be mighty tough
going. The country's rugged. The spring snow pack
will be deep. That part of the trip won't be any fun
at all. If we hit a spring blizzard, it'll be tough.
Anyhow, at this point we hide our trail again. Make a
turn due south.   Right down the crest of the
mountains. Follow the western boundary of Washo
Land. Take the lost trail of the Ancients. It'll take
many days travel to reach Desolation valley, where
we come to Rubicon Peak. From there we turn east.
Head down into Ai mee's folks, summer camp.   In
other words, we just circle around outside the
borders of our country.   Reenter just above the
camp at Da ow aga ."

"Sounds good to me," agreed Bopo, "If Snake isn't too close behind us, maybe we can stop on Rubicon Peak. Ai mee can go hide that little ole' red elderberry dance stick of hers."

CHAPTER 11   The Exit

Snake sat before a crude shelter of drift wood limbs, roughly lashed together at the top and covered with sage brush. There was an ugly scowl on his dirty face. He glared into the roaring fire before him. His war paint was reduced to a series of dirty yellow smudges. His tattered ear glowed an angry red in the flickering fire light. The cloak of black bearskin draped across his shoulders was coated with grime. The black hair was eaten away by rodents in several places, exposing the bare hide beneath. His buckskins were dirty, ragged and unkempt.

Snake was in an evil mood. All winter long reports drifted into camp. Reports carried by Paiute travelers. Whispers and rumors of the gossip going back and forth in the lodges and before the council fires across the land. Slowly, stories were spreading from one end of Paiute territory to the other. Whispered rumors repeated over and over again. Each time repeated, the rumors were a little more distorted. A little more twisted.

There were stories about a great battle. A conflict between Snake, the mighty Paiute, and a lowly Washo youth named Noah. A great battle which raged across the vast desert from sunrise to sunset. A hand-to-hand battle in which the mighty Paiute was armed with his writhing snakes as well as a war ax and a knife. The youth, who was very agile, was armed only with his teeth. The sly story tellers whispered lies behind Snake's back. They related with a smirk how, when the sun finally set on the great battle, Snake lay on the ground frothing at the mouth. Unable to fight longer. They related how the youth ripped an ear from Snake's head and fed it to his writhing serpent pet. Right before the once-great, but now humbled, Paiute warrior. The whispered stories didn't stop. Stories that went on to tell how the Washo youth and his husky friend stole Snake's most prized slave. A beautiful Washo girl child named Ai mee. How they stole the girl from Snake's lodge right before his helpless eyes and ran off into the desert laughing merrily.

Snake exuded malevolence as he plotted vengeance against the three Washos. With relish he planned how he'd drag both Washo dogs before the council fire and torture them. He'd reduce them to near death, screaming pleas for mercy. His face was distorted with a fiendish glee as he thought how he would blind the helpless slave girl's eyes with glowing coals. He'd confine the blind girl to his lodge to serve him for ever more.

Snake smacked his lips with a snarl, and shouted to the wind. "They'll pay for their insolence, I'll show them. Drive them out of the marsh. Drive them out into the open. Use fire, that's it, fire! That's what those three Washo dogs need, is a little fire. When they see the marsh ablaze, how they'll cringe!"

The wind rose in pitch gusting across the darkened meadow, causing Snakes dirty black hair to stream out behind him in flapping strings. He was a grotesque figure with the wild eyes of a madman as he stood before the spark strewn fire. Ancient bearskin robe flapping in the gale, arms waving, he screamed commands at his cowering followers,

" Fire, I want fire! I want the whole marsh afire. Each of you, take a brand from this fire. Go to your sentry post. Go! When I signal, fire the grass and the rushes, fire everything! " Snake was a wild man, gone completely mad!

Ai mee slipped out of the door of the snug lodge and carefully knotted the woven door covering for the last time. The entire camp had served them so well. It was now as neat as could be. Even the earth around the shelter was swept clean to remove all traces of the occupants.

(Washo people took pride in leaving a clean camp!)

At sunset the wind began to blow gently, increasing gradually. At full darkness it was whipping in great gusts. A dry wind moved in from the desert. A wind bearing the first hint of spring, but still a cold wind with memories of the winter now passing. The gale spoke in a mournful voice. Ai mee looked slowly around in the gathering darkness. This had been a good camp through a brutally cold winter. A snug camp, she reminisced with a gentle smile. But now it was time to go. At the darkened beach she climbed onto the waiting boat. The cumbersome contraption silently moved off into the darkness.

Water from the swift stream gurgled in the night. This was the spot where Bopo gathered willows and both hunters made their first deer kill. The bulky rush boat drifted silently out of the darkness and crunched softly against a mud bank. Three dark figures loaded bulky burden baskets onshore. Noah backed the boat away and disappeared into the darkness. He returned a few moments later, swimming easily through the black water. His voice hissed across the marsh.

"Bopo, I notice a portion of the trail's caved in. Over there on top of that little bluff. Any idea what happened?"

" I can't imagine what could have caused a cave in like that," was the husky lads innocent reply. "Possibly a deer ran down the trail! Who knows, it could have been that some innocent but not very smart Paiute ventured too near the edge."

Without another word all three of the silent figures began fastidiously obliterating every trace of their passage. Not so much as a grain of sand nor a blade of grass was out of place as they departed.

The long awaited exit from Honey Marsh was at last underway! Noah led the silent procession northward, followed by Ai mee, with a limping Bopo bringing up the rear. Slowly they worked their way across the damp grass of the meadow, taking care to leave as little sign of passage as possible. It was a night devoid of moon light. Three silent figures quickly faded into the dark shadows.

Leaving the meadow, they followed the sage-covered upward slope to a crest overlooking the marsh. They turned for one last look at the expanse of water and rushes. Their home throughout the winter. Pausing and then hurrying on into the night, bulging burden baskets bobbed at their shoulders.

A strong cold wind whistled about them. Abruptly, a pinpoint of bright yellow light flashed in the blackness, far away along the marsh's southern shore. A sense of alarm swept through the trio. Activity, a fire near Snake's main camp! The light flickered for a moment, then spread quickly into a leaping flame. It invaded the dense dry rushes, as if the flash of fire were a signal. Another flame appeared at some distance to the left. Seconds later, another flash to the right. In the space of a very few breaths the pinpoints of flame completely encircled the marsh.

With a wind-driven roar, the pinpoints erupted into violent flames. Feathers of gray ash and tiny glowing coals floated upon the searing air. The inferno spread across the meadow. The gleaming black surface of the marsh danced in reflected flame. Standing spellbound on the crest of a hill overlooking the marsh, three youths cast black silhouettes against the flame-filled sky. Speechless, they witnessed the wanton destruction of the beautiful mountain meadow.

Shaking his head in disbelief, Noah turned to his companions and said, "We're being pursued by a madman. Let's get out of here!" In panic the three turned in unison and fled toward the north.

Throughout the rest of the night and far into the next day they maintained a jogging pace to the north. Their trail led through broad meadows, over low rolling sage-covered hills, in what seemed an endless chain. The fast pace ate up great chunks of distance. On several occasions they paused beside a clear stream long enough to consume a hasty handful of jerked venison washed down with water. Immediately they resumed the urgent journey. Toward dusk the sky cleared and the cold desert wind abated, hinting of a fair day on the morrow.

With a grunt Bopo collapsed. "Sorry about this, but I'm in need of rest for a spell. The old leg is about to give out," he groaned.

"Don't worry," Ai mee said in sympathy. "You've got a rest coming. We've been pushing the trail pretty hard. But then, Snake's probably discovered we've gotten away and he's sure to be pushing just as hard as we are." Rolling up her sleeves, she began to massage Bopo's injured calf with vigor.

"See that outcrop of pines over there on top the knoll, against the mountain base?" said Noah, pointing off to the west. "What say we head for there and see if we can find a hiding place to camp for the night. We'll have a good view of the back trail, just in case Snake's close behind.'

"That sure does look good to me," grunted Bopo.

"I'll lug a couple of the burden baskets over there. Find a camp site. I'll come back and help get Bopo moved over. He looks all in. Ai mee, you tell

Bopo some funny stories to make him feel good. I'll be back in a little while."

With that, Noah struck off laboring under the weight of two burden baskets while dragging the third. As dark was beginning to set in he returned with a cheery smile on his face. "I've found a nice clear stream and a good camp spot," he said. The three set off immediately, Bopo in the middle supported by one of his companions on either side.

"You know," said Bopo, limping badly but enjoying himself tremendously. "I sure do like all this sympathy! If I'd known I was going to get all this help, I'd have gotten sick a lot sooner. Do you suppose we could talk about building a stretcher out of willows? Maybe you two wouldn't mind carrying me for the next few days. Just till I heal up you understand."

"Be quiet Bopo," said Ai mee, puffing heavily "or we'll drop you right here and you can crawl the rest of the way to camp."

The night was cold as the three fugitives huddled around a tiny flicker of flame, carefully screened from view. Their simple meal consisted of wheat cakes and jerked venison. As night fell Bopo was in a good mood despite his painful injury. He leaned back on his elbows and proceeded to tell one of his father's favorite stories. He thought it might divert his companions attention from Snake, the madman on the trail behind them.

"Long ago, very long ago, our people were all gathered together as Hokan speakers and there weren't separate clans. We lived in a land far away to the north. Actually, we were trying to escape that land, because it was so cold. So we moved southward continuously. Always on the move. Never stopping very long in one place. Always searching for the perfect land where it was warm and there was plenty of food. During that time long ago our people were mostly hunters. While they ate what vegetables and herbs they could get along the way, they were always on the move. It was a lot easier to get food by hunting. Mostly they hunted large animals like deer or elk. The people didn't know about Tah gum yet. They hadn't reached the place where the pine nuts grew."

Noah yawned and stretched his arms wide. Ai mee batted her eyes in an effort to stay awake.

"Now, one of the things that was very different in those days was the shelter we lived in. It was much better than the thatched lodges we have now. It could go right along with us as we moved continuously southward. The lodge of the ancients used a willow frame. It was covered with animal hides, usually deer hides. It took nine deer hides sewn together to form a half circle. It covered half of the shelter. The man carried one of these covers rolled up across the top of his burden basket. The woman carried the other cover. If the family was on the move and only camped for a single night, they didn't put up a shelter. Just slept on one half and used the other half as a cover against cold or moisture. When they wanted a permanent shelter, they erected a simple set of poles and put the cover halves over them. That made a really serviceable lodge, summer or winter. In the winter the shelter was covered with a thick layer of sage to provide insulation against cold."

"Hmmmm- is that so?" said Noah.   Ai mee was silent, stifling a yawn.

"Now, if we had a couple of those shelter halves with us tonight," continued Bopo. "We'd sleep a lot warmer. My father says the reason we don't use the ancient's shelter today, even though it's better, is because we stopped traveling south when we finally came to what's now called Washo Land. Deer hides weren't as plentiful because we were now harvesting from just one herd. Also when we settled here we found the nut pine tree and discovered what wonderful food it bore, so we didn't eat as much venison. As we weren't traveling south any longer we took to building our lodges with grass thatching. Not as weatherproof and it doesn't move with us when traveling. But the materials are a lot easier to get."

As Bopo finally finished his story about the deer hide shelters of the ancient people who came from the north, he became aware his audience was no longer listening. Both Ai mee and Noah were snoring softly. Shrugging his shoulders the lad curled up and soon joined his companions in sleep. None of the tired young Washos noticed the tiny flash of fire that flickered faintly in the distance along their back trail. Snake!

Bopo struggled valiantly to return through a deep ocean of heavy slumber, up out of the depths to consciousness. Slowly he became aware his shoulder was being shaken by an urgent Noah who hissed in his ear.

"Wake up! They're here. Back there in the shadows at the edge of the meadow! On our back trail! At the spot where we stopped to rest yesterday. Snake and the Evil Eight. They're camped there. I just saw the sparks from a camp fire. It must be them. I had a bad dream and woke up. Saw the sparks for just a moment. I dreamed my totem the coyote howled right in my ear. It was so real it woke me up and I saw the sparks. Come to think of it, maybe that was a real coyote howling in my ear."

Both Ai mee and Bopo mumbled a sleepy response, indicating they were at last awake. The three huddled together as Noah whispered. "Snake's so close we've got to leave this instant. With Bopo's leg in bad condition he can't move fast enough to escape. I'm going to see if I can lead them northward, on a false trail. Make 'em think it's all three of us they're chasing. Bopo, you and Ai mee head west. Follow the creek straight up the mountain. I'll double back in a day or so, soon as I can lose Snake. I'll meet you two along the creek wherever you are. I'll find you."

His two companions nodded agreement, realizing the situation was desperate and there was no time for argument.

"Ai mee, let me have the new moccasins you made for yourself and Bopo. I'll stuff em with grass. Make it look like the trail of three persons headed north. I just hope they don't have a good tracker with 'em. One who can tell I'm laying a fake trail," continued Noah in a worried voice.

"Now Bopo, listen closely. I'm beginning to put together a plan. It depends on whether or not we have snow. If we do, the plan might have a chance of working. Bopo concentrate," whispered Noah urgently. "Smell the air. Smell it carefully. Can you smell snow coming? Before I went to sleep, I thought I could smell the last big storm of the year, blowing toward us from the west. Now I can't be sure. Tell me. Can you smell anything? It's important. What do you smell?"

Sniffing the air as he rubbed the sleep from his eyes, Bopo said indifferently, "I can't smell a darn thing in the air."

He sniffed again dutifully and said, "Well skinny, I can't smell any snow. I never could tell if it was going to snow by smelling the air. I think that's just an old wive's tale. That snow smelling business. It just doesn't work. But, if you're really interested, I can tell you this. It's going to snow! Hard and soon! It is going to snow! No question about it. Probably start some time after noon. Be a big storm too! What's so important about an old snow storm?"

"Bopo, how do you know it's going to snow?" whispered Noah frantically.

"Because," said Bopo belligerently, "my toes itch."

In disgust Noah slapped himself on the forehead and said, "Here we are with Snake closing in on us, getting ready to slaughter us. I'm doin' my best to make a plan for our escape. It depends on snow. I ask for your help. What do you do? You tell us your toes itch. Honestly, Bopo!"

"Well" said Bopo defiantly, "my toes do itch, and it never fails. Absolutely never. My toes, or at least the place where my toes used to be before the

Water Baby bit 'em off, always itches like crazy, just before a snow storm! It's about to snow. So there!"

Shaking his head in relieved amazement, Noah said, "Look, this is the place where we planned to hide our trail. Make a sharp turn to the west. Follow the stream. Go straight up the mountain to the crest, over the top. I'd sort of counted on having a couple of days' lead over Snake at this point, but he's right on our heels. Here's what we're gonna do. Bopo and Ai mee head west. Follow the creek straight up the mountain. Before you go very far you'll hit a heavy accumulation of last winter's snow. It'll stay frozen hard on the surface 'till about noon. You'll be able to move fast. By noon it'll begin to melt. You'll slow to a crawl. When the new snow falls on top of the old snow pack, it'll be hard to move without snow shoes. If we have snow shoes, we can keep right on moving up the mountain. Meanwhile, Snake and the Evil Eight won't have any snow shoes. Their being desert people, they probably don't know how to make 'em. You see, every thing hinges on you two finding the right materials and getting three pairs of snow shoes made quick. Do you think you can do it?"

Scratching his head where the que sprouted from his skull, Bopo said, "Sure, there should be both Red Bud and willow growing along the creek. It'll take at least a day to get three pairs of shoes and six poles made. Can you keep Snake busy following you for that long?"

"I can sure try," was Noah's reply as he glanced worriedly over his shoulder.

CHAPTER 12   The Storm

"You know," said Bopo, gazing up into the sky which was beginning to lighten with the first hint of dawn, "Snake's going to get here before we know it. He'll find our camp right off. No use our trying to hide the camp. He'd find it anyway. First thing he's going to do is scout up that creek. See if we've gone that way. If we start out up the creek we'll hit snow right away. There's no way we can keep from making tracks in the snow."

Ai mee nodded her head. "Yeah, but Noah said we should go up the stream."

"If Snake comes along and there aren't any tracks in the snow, he'll be sure we are with Noah heading north," continued Bopo. "So, we won't make any tracks in the snow. We'll just hide right here near camp. Wait for Snake to find the camp. Let him scout around until he convinces himself all three of us are headed north. Then, he'll follow the trail north. That will allow us to proceed up the creek and get some snow shoes made. We'll wait for Noah to double back to meet us. What do you think of that idea, Ai mee?"

While the girl was terribly frightened at the prospect of the evil Paiute getting any closer to them, she couldn't argue with the logic of what Bopo planned. She agreed. The two began frantically searching for a likely hiding place near the campsite.

Bopo reasoned the most promising place to hide would be somewhere in the direction from which the enemy would approach their camp. Backtracking along their trail of the previous night, they came to a small grass covered meadow within sight of the camp. The grassy spot was surrounded by fir trees with a cluster of large rocks at the edge of the grass. Ai mee pointed to the rocks as a likely place to conceal themselves, but Bopo shook his head in rejection, saying,

" Those rocks are too obvious. First place I'd look if I were Snake." Walking carefully so as not to disturb the grass, he moved to the center of the clearing, to a spot where there was a slight depression in the ground, washed out by the melting snows of another spring. The depression was heavily overgrown with knee high grass.

The spot where Bopo stood looked exactly like any other spot in the clearing. It was completely inconspicuous. Taking two of the woven grass sleeping mats from the burden baskets, he laid them end to end along the depression in the ground. Ai mee carefully worked the mats under the grass and rearranged the thick golden brown foliage over the top. The mats would be invisible to a casual observer.

Bopo took the two burden baskets into the forest and carefully concealed them in the top of a thickly covered fir. Standing back to survey their handiwork, they were pleased to see the open patch of grass looked just as it had before. The meadow appeared completely undisturbed.

At the lads' instruction Ai mee wriggled head first on her stomach under the concealed sleeping mat. Her face was toward the camp, which was barely visible through the protruding clumps of grass.

"Don't breath or you'll make the grass shake," whispered Bopo before he crawled under the other sleeping mat. His face was toward the soles of Ai mee's small moccasins.

The two young Washos lay flat against the ground, trying desperately to sink into the earth. They hardly daring to breathe for fear the grass above them would quiver and give away their shallow hiding place. The first pale streaks of a rising sun raced across the silent grassy opening. The fir trees surrounding the spot were still shrouded in deep shadow. The total silence of dawn prevailed. Deathly silence!

They hadn't long to wait. The first dark ominous figure, running low to the ground, bent forward at the waist, detached itself from the deep shadow beneath the firs. It slipped toward the camp only to disappear immediately back into the shadow. Far to the right another silent figure appeared momentarily, moving with a sinister stealth toward the camp. Yet a third form darted out of the forest and then a fourth. In the space of a breath, all eight of them grew out of the deep shadows surrounding the camp. They moved ominously toward the spot beside the stream, where the three refugees had slumbered but a short time before.

Silently, majestically, the tall threatening figure of Snake, the worst of the Paiute, strode from the forest. He marched into the little meadow, which overlooked the recently deserted campsite of the three fugitive Washos. His eyes glittered above an evil mouth twisted in an ugly sneer, his face painted a hideous yellow. The tattered black bearskin robe hung from his shoulders displaying a deep muscular chest, upon which was painted his totem, a coiled rattler. In his right hand he carried a heavy lance tipped with a large black obsidian point. His burning eyes never leaving the deserted campsite, he strode out into the center of the clearing and came to a dramatic halt with heavy arms folded across his chest. One large moccasin was planted on either side of a slight depression in the earth, washed out by the thawing snow of another spring.

Snake, with arm outstretched, pointed a bony finger at a tall, ugly Paiute warrior named One Eye. In a guttural voice he commanded the man to take three warriors and scour the land to the north. Search for tracks of the missing Washos. He turned to a heavyset warrior with bowed legs. "Skunk, take three men. Search up the creek. Look all along where it flows down from the mountain. If there's snow, look for tracks."

Silently, Snake continued to stand and study the empty campsite with an evil scowl etched across his face. The eight warriors trotted away with nose to the ground like a pack of famished wolves searching for sign or scent.

(Have you ever smelled the scent of a rattle snake? If you have, you will never forget that smell, that awful pervading odor. If you've ever been exposed to that odor, or worse yet, smelled the lair of a rattler or a nest full of writhing baby snakes, you will never again be able to erase that horrible stench from your awareness. The scent of the rattler is, in the author's opinion, the most offensive of all odors.)

Snake, through his long and intimate association with pet rattlers, absorbed that awful scent into his very being. He exuded the aroma of the rattler wherever he went. Even his eight warriors, who were with him constantly, preferred to stand back away from him a slight distance. They always arranged to eat and sleep in a spot which was upwind from their noxious leader.

Ai mee was stretched out on her stomach with chin resting on the damp ground. With all her being she concentrated on looking very small and flat and invisible, not breathing or moving a muscle. Bopo took hold of both her moccasin clad feet and squeezed them silently, to let her know he was in position under the mat behind hers. It was reassuring to know he was there, but she was still panic stricken.

The silence was interminable. Waiting, waiting! Rolling her eyes upward to the extreme, Ai mee peered out from under her eyebrows. Immediately before her nose a clump of yellow-brown grass erupted from the ground. From a distance she could see the camp, peaceful in the early morning sunlight. It was partially obscured by the grass before her face.

All was silence. Then there was the faintest of sounds, the rustling of tall grass. Rustling, rustling! The picture before the frightened girl's eyes dimmed and suddenly she became aware of a shadow. A very long shadow. It engulfed her and stretched out toward the camp.

Ai mee's fingers clenched. She knew the answer, but she couldn't bring herself to accept it. With mind spinning she thought, "No, no! It can't be, it just can't be!" In horror her eyes refused to leave the scene of the peaceful camp. Suddenly the picture was framed on either side by the dark leather-clad heels of two high-topped moccasins, spread some distance apart and just a fingers length before her face.

A scream welled up in the girl's throat, but she clenched her teeth in silent agony. Slowly, slowly, a realization began to wash over Ai mee. The terrible truth! No, no, it wasn't realization. It was scent, that awful odor. It could only be Snake! He was standing directly over her, casting his long shadow toward the camp.

Was he looking down at her or was he studying the camp? Agony! Waiting in the silence was unbearable. The moccasins before her eyes didn't move. Not a blade of grass quivered as time stretched on endlessly. Then at last, just when it seemed she couldn't take another breath without screaming, the warriors appeared.

Silently, eight sinister dark figures glided into the camp, surrounding the cold gray ashes of the fire. Above the cringing girl, sharp guttural orders rattled out in the Paiute tongue. As a result of her year-long captivity, Ai mee could understand the language and speak it fluently. Four of the warriors led by One Eye had scouted the trail to the north. One Eye motioned Snake to come, pointing first to the north and then to the ground at his feet. They'd found tracks of the refugees.

Still the moccasins before Ai mee's face were motionless, but only for a moment. Skunk was shaking his head, indicating his group had not found any sign. There were no tracks in the snow upstream. The girl's aching lungs collapsed in a great sigh of relief. Suddenly the moccasins before her face were gone, along with the dark shadow. The campsite was again deserted and peaceful. Snake and his ugly band had taken Noah's bait. They were in hot pursuit along the trail to the northward.

Two young people moved briskly westward under a cloudless blue sky. The air was warm and it was a beautiful spring morning. Bopo's injured leg was on the mend, but he still limped slightly. They trotted along the creek, up a sage-covered grade, coming to the point where dense pine forests covered the steep lower slopes of the mountain.

As Noah had predicted, patches of snow soon appeared in the shadowed areas among the trees. Shortly, the snow became a solid blanket covering the forest floor. In the cool shadows of the forest the snow still retained its frozen crust, allowing the two to make excellent progress over the hard surface. Soon they found themselves on a steep wooded hill side, looking down on the stream winding its way along the bottom of a canyon. Pointing down at the stream Ai mee said,

"There's a patch of willow as well as some red bud. Do you think we should climb down there and collect some for snowshoes ?"

"Not yet," counseled her husky companion. "There will be plenty more material higher up. Let's keep going and cover as much distance as possible before the crust on this ice begins to melt. As soon as that happens we'll be in soft snow up to our waist. Then the going will be very slow. Plenty of time then to dig in near one of those clumps of bushes and get to work on the snow shoes."

Forging ahead at an urgent pace, they made good progress up the steep mountain slope as the morning wore away. When the sun was at last directly overhead they found the air warmed considerably. Without warning, they began to break through the icy snow crust with each step. Thrashing slowly and painfully along in the now chest deep snow, they came to an outlook. There it was possible to see some distance ahead. The canyon below came to an end at a point where a cascading waterfall dropped from the hanging meadow above. Atop the waterfall, a stream emerged from a shoulder-high stand of red bud and willow.

"There's our snow shoe material," gasped a panting Bopo, "Can you keep going in this deep snow for a while longer? It's going to be a tough climb. That clump of bushes looks like just the place to hide while we make snow shoes."

"Bet I beat you there, Bopo!" panted the tiny girl, shifting her heavy burden basket and setting off uphill through the deep snow. At times, as she fought her way through the drifts, the snow was actually over her head. With a rueful grin Bopo limped along behind her.

The two finally arrived at the clump of bushes atop the waterfall in a dead heat, gasping and exhausted. They cleared away the snow in an area near the stream. There was an abundance of willow shoots no larger than the little finger. With their flint knives they nicked and broke off straight shoots, measured to be the length of Bopo's arm with fingers extended. Next, they collected somewhat larger shoots of red bud, which were as tall as the girl. Sitting crosslegged before the pile of red bud, they stripped off lengths of the bright bark to be used in binding the willow shoots.

While Bopo held a bundle of four shoots in a flexed position, forming the rounded nose of a snow shoe, the girl deftly lashed the assembly together with long narrow bark strips. Next a similar assembly was lashed to either side, forming the body and tail of the shoe. Ai mee produced tough thongs of thick twisted deer hide from her burden basket and the laced webbing for each shoe was woven into place.

Holding up the first completed snow shoe, Bopo crowed triumphantly, "Just look at that, the famous Washo Snow Shoe. No one else in this whole range of mountains has the snow shoe. Only the Washo. This is pure magic, a secret handed down to us from our ancient ancestors!"

As the two worked at the willow patch near the stream, they frequently glanced down the long slope of glistening white, to a point where the snow disappeared from view at the forest's edge. A deep furrow clearly marked their path from the time they exited the forest till they reached their present position. Snake would have little trouble in finding their hiding place. Hopefully, they watched the edge of the dense pine forest. Noah might appear at any moment. At least he wouldn't have any trouble in finding them, with their path so clearly marked.

The first stiff breeze swept across the vast white slope. The first gray clouds appeared, tumbling over the bare granite peaks looming high above them. Shadows of the clouds raced across the glittering white snow field and suddenly there was a chill to the air. The two shivered with the cold as the sun disappeared. The sky became a gray expanse of racing clouds.

The wind had a thousand quiet voices. Bopo paused and laid aside the snow shoe on which he was working. He held out a hand, palm upward. A large white snowflake appeared in the brown palm. It had the delicate blue-white tracings of a fairy crystal. Slowly it disappeared, leaving a single large drop of water.

"Yup," muttered Bopo, studying the palm of his hand. "Snow! Just about noon, too! It's sad, sometimes people just won't believe you, even when you tell 'em the truth."

Ai mee smiled, shaking her head in amazement as she returned to work on a snow pole.

Silently the big fat white flakes drifted by on the breeze, as the storm quietly increased in intensity. A white mantle began to build on the crown of the girl's shiny black hair. She hunched forward over her work, skilled fingers flying.

The silent world closed in around the two. The clump of willows nearby became a dark brown blur in the whirling maelstrom of drifting white flakes. In the total, whirling white silence of the storm, it was no longer possible to see the dark green forest from which Noah must emerge.

The two huddled figures repeatedly paused at their work to peer off into the twisting white haze, eyes anxiously searching in the direction of the forest. They strained to hear the first sound or see the first blurred image of their friend. Silence, nothing but silence, as the fluffy white snow grew all around them. Relentlessly it continued building, building, all around. Busy hands moving quickly in the cold, numbed fingers working urgently to accomplish their task. The two completed work on the last pair of snow shoes. Now, they turned to finishing the snow poles. Unspoken concern for Noah grew with each passing moment.

As the tension became unbearable, the wind slowly began to abate. The falling flakes subsided momentarily. Briefly the scene cleared down the long sloping snow field and dark green of the forest slowly crept into view. The trail in the snow, which a short time before had been so sharply defined in bright sun light, was now but a faint line of blue shadow stretching out of the distance toward them. Freshly fallen snow was quickly blotting out the sign of their passage. Maybe Noah could no longer find them.

At that moment, as they stared out into the vast empty world of white, there was absolute, total silence. Then faintly, faintly, came a trace, a tiny thread of sound. A thread of sound from very far away in the dark sinister forest shadows. Just one tiny thread of sound, and then, stark silence.

"That could have been a wolf, or even a pack of them a long ways away," whispered Bopo anxiously, his head tilted sideways to catch even the faintest murmur of sound. Then the sound drifted in again. It was very faint and just for an instant, somewhere far to their right and deep in the forest. And then, the sound came again, faint and distant, but this time it came from the left.

"Wolves," hissed Bopo, "They're talking to each other. Probably a hungry pack. Spread out across the forest, hunting." He shuddered involuntarily.

Shaking off a feeling of dread and of impending disaster the two turned back to their work. It was completed, but now needed to be tested. Each donned a pair of the fine new snow shoes and experimented in the newly fallen snow. The formula of the ancients still worked. The new snow shoes were a complete success!

Turning back toward the forest below, Ai mee said with worry in her voice, "Maybe we should go back and look for him. Maybe he's been hurt and needs help."

"Wait a little while longer," counseled Bopo. "Let's figure out what those sounds mean first. Something's not quite right about them."

At last the noise to the right was repeated. This time the sound was a little closer and it still seemed like the howl of a lone wolf. An answering howl floated out of the deep woods to the left and then a moment later another sound. A long, agonizing drawn out wail of urgency.

" Those aren't wolves," whispered the lad with a haunted look on his usually stoic face. "Those noises are human. They're out there hunting like a pack of wolves. That's Snake and the Evil Eight. They're out there hunting Noah. Closing in on him. Tracking him. Each time one of 'em finds his sign, they howl for the rest of the pack. UGH! Bad Medicine! They must be a lot closer to Noah than he intended. Sounds like they're closing in on him now. He must still be a little bit ahead of them. Headed this way. Noah must be following our tracks through the forest. About all we can do is wait, Until we see where he comes out of the forest down there below us."

Bopo took up his powerful bow and laid out all of his arrows in preparation for a last stand. All the while he kept eyes glued to a spot where he expected to see his friend's figure burst into the open. The excited yelping rapidly grew in intensity. Waiting was unbearable, and yet, there was nothing else they could do. Bopo spoke quietly, but with great sincerity, to his totem the chickeree. Ai mee called fervently upon the Maker of All Things. Bopo concluded by muttering out loud, "Totem, if you can't help Noah, don't you help those Paiutes!"

At that very instant the weary figure of Noah appeared at a spot where the two young people first emerged from the forest. Stumbling and staggering with fatigue, in the deep new snow, Noah tottered along the partially buried trail toward them. They watched in frozen fascination, expecting the pursuing Paiutes to appear at any instant.

Noah staggered closer and closer, his breath coming in great steaming gasps. Snowshoe clad, the two Washos raced across the surface of fresh snow toward him, shouting encouragement at every step. At that point, Noah's legs collapsed and he disappeared in a cloud of fresh snow.

Noah's friends wasted no time on greetings. Turning the gasping figure over on his back, each grasped one of his feet. Together they dragged him down the trail to the clearing beside the willows.

It was at that instant, which seemed frozen in time, the hideous screaming figure of a yellow-faced Snake emerged from the forest. Shortly he was followed by the eight cutthroats, howling like mad-men at the sight of all three fugitives. They plunged into the deep new snow and began to break trail. Frantically they pursued the fleeing Washos.

Working like a well trained team over the gasping Noah, Bopo lifted one leg and Ai mee the other. Quickly they fitted snow shoes to his feet. With arms spread wide, Noah lay wheezing for breath, like a fish tossed up on the bank. Bopo glanced at the slow progress of the screaming Snake, who was brandishing a war ax over his head. Ai mee took a long strip of jerked venison from the burden basket. She folded it neatly and pressed it into the spent warriors open mouth, with orders to, "Suck on this, it'll give you some strength."

Still keeping an eye on Snake's frantic but slow progress toward them, the two began to massage the spent runner's legs vigorously. At last the youth's heavy breathing began to subside. The color returned to his face. He made an attempt to sit up.

"Time to go," Bopo said calmly "Snake'll be within bow shot in a moment. Ai mee, you move out first. Straight up the mountain. Noah, you're in the middle. I'll bring up the rear. Let's go. Now!"

Three dark figures emerged from behind the willow clump and moved away up the steeply sloping field of snow. They were rapidly disappearing into a renewed flurry of flakes. The smallest of the figures led the way, breaking trail, as the three moved with the fast shuffling gait of experienced mountaineers.

At the same instant, the murderous group of howling savages broke out of the deep snow and into the trampled clearing by the willows.

Screaming in rage with foam dripping from his cruel mouth, Snake lunged after the three. He threw himself full length in the snow at Bopo's rapidly retreating figure. His outstretched hand grasped a rear tip of the fleeing snow shoe. Clawing fingers sank into the webbing. For an awful instant Bopo became a frozen thing, with one leg drawn back, unable to move. Gritting his teeth, a roar of anger erupted from Bopo's barrel chest. His thigh muscles bunched and he tore the snow shoe free from Snake's frantic grasp.

Screaming curses, Snake pounded his hands in the powdery snow, as the three young Washos dissolved into a world of swirling white flakes.

CHAPTER   13   Straight Up The Mountain

(About three million years ago, the area in which our story takes place was very different.   The surface was a flat rolling plain at an elevation of about 6000 feet above sea level. One day the earth began to shake. Suddenly a great zigzag crack in the ground began to form. It was just as though mother nature had opened an immense zipper running from north to south for many hundreds of miles.

The crack was many miles deep. With a great roar, the earth trembled. The entire plain on the east side of the crack began to slowly sink, until the elevation was only 4500 feet.   At the same time, west of the crack the ground began to rise with a series of groans. Creeping up and up and up, the ground on the west side finally came to rest. Some of the peaks were almost 14,000 feet high. As the ground crept upward it slowly exposed   an   immense,   sheer   granite   face. A towering wall of smooth stone.

If you were to stand at the edge looking down that bare granite face, you would see the sunken eastern plain almost 10,000 feet below.

Of course, there weren't any people around at that time to witness this great event; the people came eons later.

This tremendous crack in the surface of the earth was softened over the years by weathering and erosion and finally became known as The Sierra Nevada Mountain Range. When our friends, the three Washos, decided to head 'Straight Up the Mountain' in the face of a howling blizzard, they were in fact starting to climb that sheer wall of bare granite.)

The snow storm was intense and continued throughout the night. Noah recovered from his exhaustion and assumed the lead in their upward journey through the darkness. By dawn a waist deep deposit of fresh snow surrounded them. The first faint light found the three Washos still moving upward with the same steady shuffling gate. Covering the ground at a rapid rate, they far outdistanced their pursuers, who were forced to break trail through deep fresh snow.

Dawn broke revealing a cloudless blue sky overhead. The world around them was perfect in its gleaming expanses of pure white snow and bright blue shadow. It was a world fresh and new, reborn throughout the night. Clean, pure and white. Flawless in the bright morning sunlight!

The three shuffled quickly across the vast white expanse of the steeply sloped snow field, moving with little effort across the top of soft new snow. Relentlessly they moved toward a dense grove of Lodge Pole pine. Behind and above the pine forest the immense face of a clean granite headwall erupted upward. It towered out of sight into the deep blue sky. The huge old pines dwarfed three tiny figures approaching the trees. The pines were themselves dwarfed at the foot of that solid upward thrusting face of granite. It was impossible to comprehend the size of the great monolith.

A large gray and white Nutcracker perched precariously atop the tallest pine at the edge of the forest. His raucous cry defying the approaching Washos, he declared the tall pine to be his personal kingdom. Silently, the three figures slipped into the shadows of his towering tree and disappeared from view.

They paused in the sheltering roots of a huge pine, overturned in some recent gale. Noah lowered his burden basket to the ground and heaved a great sigh of relief.

"This looks like a sheltered spot. What say we take a little rest? I haven't been on snow shoes since last winter. Don't mind admitting that all-night walk got me a little tuckered out."

"I've been ready for this rest for quite a while," sighed Ai mee, sinking to the ground into a snug pocket formed by the protecting tree roots. Slowly, she began to unlace her snow shoes.

"Let's take a little nap for a while. We can eat something when we all wake up."

"Good idea," said Bopo, "You know, this is the first time I've felt a little bit secure in weeks. Guess my totem the Chickeree must be out there doing some work after all. At least we know where Snake is. He's back there plodding along in the deep snow. We must have a fair lead on those Paiutes at the moment. At least enough so we can catch a few winks of sleep. You two get some sleep. I'll do lookout duty for a while."

And so the three Washo youths curled up for some much needed rest beneath the Nutcracker's personal tree. They were secure in the knowledge he would challenge any unwanted visitors, with his raucous cry.

Silently the gray clouds drifted in, bring with them huge white snow flakes. The wind died out completely. The forest silence was intense as soft white flakes drifted down steadily. A blanket covered the three slumbering figures crouched in the sheltering tree roots. Sleeping quietly, they were completely buried beneath fresh snow, all traces of their camp obliterated.

Hours later, Ai mee was the first to awaken. She sat up with a shout of laughter at the discovery of a deep blanket of soft new snow.

"Noah, Bopo," she laughed, "wake up you lazy fellows. Look at all this beautiful snow. It's a whole new world out there!"

Grumbling, while they sleepily rubbed their eyes, the two slowly emerged from beneath the deep blanket. They surveyed the sparkling new world around them.

"Ho Ho Ho," chortled Bopo "Old Snake's going to be buried up to his eyeballs in this new snow. We're just going to scoot off on top of it, while he flounders around in the stuff!"

Rubbing his ribs and stretching luxuriously, Noah said, "Ai mee, I'm hungry as a bear. How about we have a big meal before we start out this morning?" So saying, the three set about building a fire; the boys collected wood and Ai mee, produced her fire drill. Soon a cheerful flame blazed. She got out the little cooking basket and prepared a delicious stew of venison, flavored with herbs and dried greens from the marsh. Meanwhile, the warriors toasted biscuits at the end of a stick held over the fire.

It was late in the day when they finally emerged from the lodge pole pine forest. They found themselves nose to nose with a towering wall of granite. The head wall covered the entire end of the canyon up which they had been traveling. It projected straight up to the sky, where it vanished into the distance. From where they stood, with hands touching the smooth granite, it was impossible to guess the size of the huge face. It looked as though the wall might extend to the end of the earth or beyond.

Scratching his head so that his pigtail bounced up and down, Bopo said, "Noah, I know your plan is to 'Turn to the West and go straight up the mountain.' I admit that sounds like a good plan. But I think we have a little bit of a problem here. I'm not just sure how we're going to get up this rock. The going does look a little bit steep from here on, wouldn't you say?"

Nodding his head reflectively, Noah said, "Bopo, my friend, Lump. There are times when what you say does make some sense. Maybe we should reconsider our plans slightly."

In exasperation, Ai mee said, "Look, you two clowns. We're stuck. There isn't much we can do but turn north and crawl up the side of this canyon, 'till we get to the top of the head wall."

Turning to face Noah, Bopo bowed majestically from the waist and said, "Skinny, my friend. you've heard the wisdom of the Great Woman. May I suggest, in all humility, that you act as our leader and proceed up the side of this steep canyon."

With a grin Noah shook his head and said, "Sounds like a good plan. Let's go." Turning back toward his companions, he adopted a more sober air and said, "You know, we could get in some serious trouble, going up this steep hillside in such soft snow. It's built up awfully deep through this storm. The new snow under our feet must be as high as my head. It's resting on a surface of solid ice that's probably just as thick. The solid ice is really slippery. That new snow could slide down the steep hillside in a big block. All it needs is some slight movement to start the whole hillside going. I've seen it happen. The whole thing takes off with a great roar. Just happens. For no reason at all. It takes every thing with it when it goes. Big trees, boulders, the whole hill! It's just an awesome amount of power, released all at once. The destruction is really terrible! Just awful! My father calls those things an avalanche They're bad!"

"My father's gotten into these avalanche things too. On winter trading trips. They go back and forth over the top of the mountain in winter as well as summer. Guess they must be really devastating," agreed Bopo.

"We could start one going up this steep hillside, so move very carefully. Don't start any snow sliding. It'll flow just like water. Another thing, don't make any unnecessary noise. Just a loud sound or even an echo is enough to set off one of those avalanches."

Facing the granite headwall, Noah started a gingerly ascent of the steep side hill. He'd raise one snow shoe up hill and set it down in the snow. Then lift the other snow shoe, placing it in the track of the first. Very slow going, but it was the only way to ascend such a steep hill. The three laboriously made their way up the bare slope. The deep snow was heavily drifted in some places and in others there were deep crevasses to negotiate. Darkness found them only a third of the way up the slope. It was obvious they would spend the night on a steep side hill. As they bedded down for a cold sleep in the snow, they thought fondly of their camp of the previous night beneath the roots of that fallen tree.

Noah's Totem, the shaggy old gray coyote, curled up with his bushy tail covering the tip of his nose. To protect it against the winter night cold. He was burrowed into the snow under a sheltering bush, on a knoll overlooking the roots of a huge old fallen pine. As he dreamed of the tasty mice one could find just about anywhere around Honey Marsh, he kept one eye open. Furtively, he was watching the occupants of a sheltered spot beneath the roots of a fallen tree. The same sheltered spot where just hours before three young Washos had slumbered blissfully.

Just as darkness   settled upon the forest they   appeared, silent as death. They slipped from tree to tree, running low, bent forward at the waist, dark, stealthy, evil figures, moving furtively.   They clustered about the recently abandoned campsite, studying every trace left by the Washo fugitives.

"Good thing!" thought Old Mr. Coyote to himself. "Good thing that foolish Noah couldn't see the old campsite right now. Might just shake him up a little bit, that's what!"

At that very moment Noah was otherwise engaged. He was trying to figure out how to go to sleep on an empty stomach while stretched out on a steeply sloping hill side in the snow. If one stretched out with both head and feet at the same level, one started to roll downhill, as soon as he dosed off. If one stretched out with feet down hill, he didn't roll. He just couldn't seem to fall asleep. Finally, Noah curled up in a tight ball and burrowed into the snow, just as a coyote would do. He dropped off to sleep immediately and began to dream of the delicious food Ai mee used to prepare in the comfort of the Honey Marsh camp.

With the first faint light of dawn our three Washo friends were up and away. Resuming their agonizingly slow sideways ascent, they gradually crept toward a small exposed clump of Fox Tail Pine. The trees grew like a little island oasis sheltered by the towering granite headwall.

Puffing mightily with exertion they finally entered the small level cluster. They found a sheltered spot where the weathered old pines emerged from a jumble of jagged boulders. Pausing briefly, the climbers consumed a   midday meal of wheat cakes and jerked venison.   Shortly the trio resumed their grueling upward journey through the vast field of snow.

The air was cold and clear. The altitude had a noticeable effect, causing all three to puff with shortened breath. On and on they plodded, upward ever upward. They were near exhaustion as the shadow of the towering headwall lengthened and night began to creep forward. Full darkness descended on the tired Washo youths and still they labored upward.

At last, a gasping Noah called back to the other two, encouraging them with news that the top was near. The snow surface was gradually becoming more and more level. Finally, his head hanging in exhaustion, Noah gasped, "This must be near the top. This is where we camp for the night."

Bopo and Ai mee stood transfixed, gazing at the panoramic view before them. Exhausted by a long hard climb, they slept soundly, and awoke to find Noah already departed. The two followed his trail in the snow for a short distance to where they now stood, at the very edge of a granite headwall. High winds swept the rock. They could look straight down past their toes, to the green forest of tiny lodge pole pine they'd traversed two days before. It was far below them. It was a dizzying spectacle. This must be the way the world looked to an eagle as he soared on high.

Snow crunched under Noah's snow shoes as he shuffled up behind the two, carrying a pair of large white snow shoe rabbits.

"I decided to do a little scouting this morning before you two woke up. Just happened to spot these two plump hares. Had my trusty sling along. Time for a good breakfast."

"Ho Ho ho," chortled Bopo, thinking about a big breakfast and how hungry he was. Ho, Ho, Ho,! echoed the mountain, the sound reflecting off granite walls.

"Bopo, do that again, that Ho Ho Ho business. Do it one more time," said Noah, as an idea began to form in his mind.

" Ho Ho Ho, I'm hungry as a bear," said Bopo dutifully.

"I'm Hungry As A Bear" echoed the mountain. Noah's busy mind was hatching a plan to use echos and so he began to experiment. For the next few minutes the three took turns shouting to create echo's, marveling at the clarity and intensity of the reflected sound.

"This gives me an idea," said Noah thoughtfully. "You know, my father always told me loud sounds can start an avalanche. Maybe we should see what we can do about starting an avalanche with echoes. Just in case ol'e Snake gets too close to us."

Snake appeared in the distance at the same instant his name was mentioned, almost as if by magic. The Evil Eight emerged, following behind in single file. Of course, they were a very long ways away from our friends, so far they looked like ants, in the distance. Bopo was the first to see them. A horrified look crossed his face as he pointed, speechless, off toward the east.

"Gulp," he said, "You had to go and mention Snake, that did it. There he is!"

There, very far below, the procession of nine tiny figures emerged from the forest onto a vast white field of snow.   Instinctively, the three youths crouched down to avoid detection, even though it was probable the Paiutes couldn't spot them from such a distance. They watched in silent horrified fascination, as the procession moved diagonally across the snow field toward their hiding place.

Slowly, the line of Paiute warriors moved upward toward a small oasis of Fox Tail pine, Toward the very spot where the three Washos had eaten a noon time meal the day before. The progress of the ant like figures across the steep slope was painfully slow. They labored upward in the waist deep drifts. Their leader was mindless of the hazard in moving across a great unstable expanse of newly fallen snow. They plodded onward, sinking into the new snow with every step. As time ground agonizingly forward, the column moved imperceptibly closer and closer. Now it was possible to identify Snake from his followers by the dirty yellow smudge across his face.

"Come on you lazy dogs. March! Forward! Hurry! The Washos are getting away." Frantically he urged his men on through the deep snow. He pleaded with them, commanding them, bullying them to move forward.

"What do we do now? The Paiutes are much closer than I thought."

Noah had a sinking feeling in the pit of his stomach as he lay stretched out on the smooth granite head wall, peering downward at the approaching war party. What should they do, run for it or stay where they were and fight? After all, they were above the enemy, which was always an advantage. Noah's thoughts flowed.

Let the Paiutes move in close, within bow shot. They should each be able to put two of the enemy warriors out of action as they closed in. Certainly, they we're well equipped with powerful new hunting bows. But then, up close it would be five of them against two Washos. The Paiutes all carry murderous looking war axes. We Washos have only flint hunting knives. Not very good odds. Then too, how about Ai mee? How safe would she be in such a skirmish?

What would his father tell him to do at a time like this? He always knew best, particularly when it came to handling dangerous devils like the Paiutes. Reflecting, Noah was pretty sure what his father's advise would be. When the odds are against you, use surprise. Strike unexpectedly. Then disappear quickly before the enemy can recover.

Good advice thought the hard-pressed leader, now how do I use it? Screwing up his face and closing one eye, Noah watched the enemy approaching. He searched his mind for the right idea. What would his old friend tell him to do at a time like this, with all those angry enemies so close? And then he had it!

Out there on the horizon drifted the answer. A long white string of puffy little lenticular clouds. Small white clouds that looked like a tear drop flattened out into a smooth shape. Flattened by violent winds sweeping through the upper sky. Lenticular clouds!

Those puffy white little clouds indicated ONG was hungry and on the prowl. The sign every Washo knew and feared. ONG had left his nest in the middle of the big lake and was hunting for human food. Slowly a smile spread across Noah's worried face.

(For those of you who don't know about ONG, it's time to learn what every Washo child is taught early in life. ONG is a figure of Washo legend. For generation after generation, down through time, the old women of the tribe have recounted his story to their grandchildren. ONG is a monstrous evil bird who lives in a nest in the center of Da ow aga, the big lake in the middle of Washo Land. ONG is the only creature as fearsome and as awful as the Water Baby. No one really knows, but ONG might even be worse, and that's pretty bad! The Washo people are the favorite food of the terrible raptor. Man, woman and child. ONG hunts 'em continuously and when he finds 'em, he eats 'em!

ONG is so huge and powerful his wings create a great wind as he passes over head. When he flies over the mountain passes the wind from his wings is so strong it breaks the tops right out of huge old Red Fir trees. Next time you're in the high forest and see a great big fir tree with the top snapped right out of it, remember, ONG did it.

You might see ONG hiding in one of those lenticular clouds anywhere over Washo Land and sometimes way out over the desert. He likes the taste of Washo people best of all, but sometimes when there aren't any to be found he'll settle for a tough old Paiute, although everyone knows they don't taste very good.

Sometimes, when ONG is very hungry and also angry, he carries a powerful bolt of lightning in his long hooked talons. He uses it to stun his prey. Just as he strikes an innocent victim with his great cruel beak, a tremendous roar of thunder erupts within him. All the Washo people know, when you're out in the open, you must always keep one eye on the sky. Beware the ONG!

This is a true story. I heard it straight from the mouth of Grandma Noah as she puffed on her stone pipe, one stormy night on the ranch in Long Valley. She says the story was told to her by a spirit of the Ancients who came to her in a dream when she was a little girl.)

CHAPTER 14   Avalanche

Noah continued to mull over his options as the file of angry Paiutes moved slowly toward them. The three sat cross legged at the very edge of the towering granite cliff, looking down upon their pursuers. Bopo in the middle, Ai mee on his left and Noah on his right. To himself Noah thought, loud sounds are supposed to start avalanches. First we'll try to call down an avalanche on the Paiutes. If that doesn't work we can try to call ONG down on them.

Turning to Bopo, he said, "Lump, how about you demonstrating your talents for us? Sound's supposed to start avalanches. How about you doing a little of that Ho Ho stuff against that big snow field out there? Point your Ho-Ho's right in the middle. Sort of up at the top. Right above Snake and the Evil Eight. Make 'em good and loud and keep 'em coming. Let's see if you're warrior enough to call down a first class avalanche. No little avalanches. We need a big avalanche. A really biiiiiggg avalanche!"

Sticking out his lower lip, Bopo said, "Skinny, my friend, I want you to know you've come to the right man. You're dealing with a fellow who may just become the foremost avalanche caller of all time. It's a highly specialized talent, you know."

So saying, Bopo proceeded to make quite a show of preparing for the feat. He wriggled his hips around to make sure his buckskin clad bottom was firmly planted on the smooth granite surface. A position of great power. Next he ceremoniously drew a huge breath into his barrel chest. Clearing his throat with a loud growl and placing hands on either side of his mouth, he emitted quite a respectable "Ho Ho Ho Hooooo!"

Nothing happened! There was silence across the vast snow field below. Then, as the sound traveled across space and reached their pursuers, something did occur. Snake who was still a considerable distance away and far below them, heard the faint "ho ho ho hooooo!"

His eyes darted across the landscape, searching for a source of the sound, ranging out across the field of smooth white snow. Piercing eyes traversed up the slope, to where the oasis of Fox Tail pine stood out as a single dark point in a vast expanse of nothing. They ranged beyond the oasis, to a point where the massive granite monolith erupted from the snow and climbed up, up into the sky. There he spotted three tiny silhouetted figures, seated cross legged, peering down at him.

The sneering yellow face erupted in an angry roar as Snake pointed an accusing finger at the three, commanding his followers to charge ahead.

" There they are, at last we have 'em! After em. Quick, before they get away!"

Our friends recoiled in horror at being discovered. Bopo and Ai mee, acting instinctively, drew back out of sight and began to rise in preparation for a hasty departure. Run, escape! Placing a restraining hand on Bopo's shoulder, Noah hissed,

"Bopo, for a fellow who's going to become the foremost caller of avalanches, you certainly didn't make much noise. Can't you get your Ho Ho Ho working any louder than that?"

Momentarily nonplused, Bopo settled back into place and accepted Noah's challenge, saying "Well, I might just give it another try. I wasn't really warmed up last time, you know. Just start up slowly and build up to a big finish, that's my motto."

Puffing up like a blue grouse at mating time, Bopo bellowed out a resounding "Ho Ho Ho" followed by another great breath and a thundering "Ho Ho Hooooo! Come to Bopo little avalanche. Come to Bopo!"

The last faint echo rolled back to the three listening Washos: "come to bopooooo." Then total silence. Nothing happened!

Ai mee, who was listening intently, regarded Bopo's apoplectic face which had turned bright red with the exertion of shouting. She could contain herself no longer, despite the seriousness of the situation, she burst out in uncontrolled laughter. Bopo, chagrined at his failure to produce an avalanche, drew another deep breath and emitted an ear splitting challenge to the mountain. When this attempt failed, Noah, despite a manly effort to maintain a straight face, broke out into great peals of laughter, as well.

At the very top of the huge expanse of snow, a shelf of bare rock projected upward through the white surface. A row of tiny icicles clung to the lower edge of the shelf. A single ray of sunlight played on the last icicle in the row. After several moments, a tiny drop of moisture began to slowly form at the tip of the icicle. Gradually the drop increased in size, growing longer and longer with time. At last the drop detached itself, falling to the surface of the snow below, where it formed a tiny blue crater. Some time later another drop of moisture formed on the tip of the icicle. In time it too fell, enlarging the crater ever so slightly. Over time the drops of moisture formed the crater into a crevasse. It extended in blue shadow down the slope of soft unstable snow. The crevasse was aimed exactly at the column of Paiutes, as they plunged frantically upward.

A tiny crystal of ice detached itself from the blue shadowed wall of the crevasse and clung precariously to another crystal. The two crystals were top-heavy and leaned forward, quivering. A faint vibration from a stray Ho ho hooo sound impinged upon the unstable crystals. They toppled. Joining with a third crystal they formed a tiny sphere. It rolled ever so slowly down the bottom of the crevasse. It became slightly larger and turned faster as it emerged from the shadows into the sunlight. The sphere gathered speed and grew in size, 'till it was as big as a clenched fist. Still it grew and began to emit a low rumbling sound. The sphere became a giant ball roaring down the mountain. The giant ball was absorbed as the entire side of the mountain ground into movement and churned downward, like a huge raging river of snow. It flowed like water. A last faint echo of sound "come to bopoooooo" was drowned in the raging river.

Abruptly, the Washos laughter died as they detected the first movement of a surging river of snow. In horror they watched as the wide river divided itself into two roaring walls of snow and debris. The right side turned directly toward the three youths, raging through the oasis, snapping the Fox Tail pines like twigs. It crashed against the foot of the solid granite head wall with a sound like thunder, throwing a spray of snow, rock and splinters high into the air. With a groan it piled up against the head wall, coming to rest at their very feet.

The left side of the avalanche swept down the hillside, curving slightly past the frantically scrambling Paiutes. A tiny dark figure at the rear of the column could be seen for an instant clawing madly at the moving surface. Slowly, the helpless Paiute Warrior disappeared into the maelstrom. Raging down the mountain, a great rumbling wall slammed into the forest, tearing a wide swath of destruction before it. The immense mass of ice, snow, splintered trees and rock slowly ground to a stop. And then at last there was total silence.

ONG the monstrous bird hung motionless in the air, soaring in a great river of wind blowing over the surface of the earth far below.

(ONG's color is dark brown almost black, with long needle-like talons of dark amber color. His burning yellow eyes are the only thing that moves. They dart back and forth searching every nook and cranny of the earth far below. His eyes are unusual because they change depending upon the condition of his stomach. When he's hungry, as he is now, his eyesight is very sharp. From a great height those fierce eyes can spot the smallest object. For example they can detect a spider as he walks along the ground and even see the footprints the spider leaves behind him. Nothing escapes detection when he's hungry and out hunting for human food. Now, when ONG has just finished eating it's a different story. His eyesight is all blurry and he can't see at all well.)

At the moment ONG hung motionless, far above our three friends and the band of Paiutes. He's wondering which of the humans far below will be the most tasty. No need to hurry, he can sink his cruel talons into which ever one he chooses. Mentally he licks his chop's and begins to drool, as his empty stomach growls like thunder. He assumes all those figures down there are Washos and every one knows they're tasty. Must be all those pine nuts they eat!

Unaware of the ONG over head, Bopo says thoughtfully "How about Ai mee and I scout downhill to the west. See if we can find a hiding place. Just disappear for a while. Maybe we could loose Snake that way. I don't think he's gonna give up the chase."

Shaking his head in agreement Noah said, "He seems to have lost another of his warriors to the avalanche. Even that won't stop him."

"Noah, you could sit here in plain sight of the Paiutes below. Play decoy. That would buy Ai mee and I time to scout the country ahead. Then one of us'll duck back here and pick you up."

"All right with me, just don't waste any time getting back here."

As the two small dark figures set out over the snow to look for a hiding place, Noah called after them and pointed toward the sky.

"Don't forget the ONG. See those little flat clouds drifting in? ONGs out hunting right now. Watch yourselves. Good Luck! Don't forget to come back and pick me up."

Snake sat hunched forward in his bear skin robe, a forlorn figure in a desolate setting. The Evil Seven were clustered a short way up wind from him. They were not speaking, just sitting and glaring in a sullen fashion at the leader who brought them to this awful place of destruction. There was no fire, they were afraid to light one for fear the heat would be enough to send another avalanche crashing down upon them. They spoke in whispers, the smell of fear was everywhere.

The forlorn group sat in the center of a long strip of snow, ignoring the two arms of the avalanche. On either side of them , almost close enough to touch, lay the avalanches path of total destruction. The force of the thing was incredible; it ripped apart huge trees, snapping them like twigs and scattering jagged splinters every where. Great granite rocks were fractured and spread at random through the tumbled dirty snow. Huge piles of dirt and mud were extruded from beneath the path of the avalanche. A mixture of snow and debris was piled up against the face of the granite cliff, reaching almost to the top.

Snake could see the seated figure of his enemy. With seething anger he reflected, "Here I am at the foot of this awful cliff , within sight of that Washo dog and I can't reach him. I'm afraid to move for fear of starting another snow-slide. My men, the lazy dog's, are sullen and angry, near revolt. They are frightened by the fact their comrades have been swallowed by the avalanche."

Bopo and Ai mee traveled at a fast shuffling clip down the gently sloping west face of the great mountain. The sky was a cloudless blue, the altitude very high. The air was crisp, thin and cold. Their breath came in white puffs. No trees grew at this altitude. Before them stretched a vast granite monolith, swept bare of snow in places by the whistling winds. They traveled rapidly down the slope a considerable distance before encountering the first tip of a Fox Tail pine, peeking above the smooth white expanse of snow. Later, twisted clumps of stunted Limber Pine came into sight. The tracks of a single coyote approached the trees, stopping at each one to search for a stray mouse or chipmunk, then fading off into the distance.

As the two traveled through that beautiful, pristine wilderness of glistening white, they came to a small high mountain meadow. Twisted bare aspen trees projected through the snow, announcing the presence of a stream below. One could hear the soft gurgling of water beneath the deep cover of spring snow. On their left a long finger of granite formed the face of a cliff rising out of the snow. It ran along the margin of the meadow. They seated themselves on the shattered trunk of a huge Red Fir, laying at the base of the low cliff.

"ONG's been at work here," said Bopo, tapping the trunk of the tree on which they sat. "This is going to be a beautiful mountain meadow when the snow melts and the grass turns green. A beautiful place to camp, beside the stream, later on. What say we separate and search both sides of this meadow? See if we can find any sort of suitable hiding place."

Bopo proceeded to explore the cliff on one side of the little valley. Ai mee crossed the meadow to examine the trees lining the other side.

Bopo was thorough in his search, looking carefully along the top of the cliff, crawling into every crack and opening. But, he could find nothing that would serve as a hiding place. At last he returned dejectedly, to the meeting place at the shattered tree trunk. Finding no sign of Ai mee, he decided to explore the base of the cliff. The snow, which was higher than his head, had drifted against the wall and melted, forming a fissure.

Bopo lay flat on his stomach and dropped feet first to the bottom of a passage, which was several feet wide. It extended along the stone cliff face. Standing upright, with one hand against the wall and the other against an icy surface of the fissure, he inspected the length of the passage. Nearing the end he came upon a shoulder high bush growing against the wall and shrouded with ice. Exploring behind the bush, with the palm of his hand he encountered an opening at ground level. Kneeling, he used his flint hunting knife to cut away ice laden branches, exposing an opening.

Very carefully, Bopo slithered on his stomach into the narrow opening. He twisting his broad shoulders through the cramped space, until the soles of his moccasin feet disappeared from view into the darkness.

Ai mee sat on the tree trunk glumly waiting for her companion to reappear. Behind her she heard a loud grunt coming from the snowy fissure. Turning in surprise, she saw a large brown hand reaching up out of the passage. It clawed at the surface of the snow. Springing to her feet, she rushed to Bopo's assistance. Grasping him by the arm, she dragging him to the surface.

"Thanks," gasped Bopo "I was climbing out of that place by cutting foot holes in the snow with my knife. One of the holes collapsed. I was about to fall back in."

"What, in heavens name, were you doing in that deep fissure?" quizzed the girl "It looks as though it would be dangerous, if the snow caved in on you."

"Nope," grinned Bopo, "I walked the whole length of the fissure. It's pretty safe down there. Besides, you should see what I found. You'd never believe it, but, there's a little tunnel behind a bush. When you get inside, there are stairs carved out of stone. They lead up to a cave. It's a great place to hide. Only thing is though, we aren't the first ones to be here. It's sort of spooky! Looks like some one lived in there. A very long time ago. Really ancient people, maybe. Lots of paintings of things on the walls. People and animals and stuff. Kind of eyrie like! I expected someone to step out of the shadows at any minute."

The two discussed Bopo's find excitedly for some time. At length they decided it was late in the day, time to return and pick up Noah. The wind was rising and shadows lengthening by the time they finally reached the spot. Their friend was waiting, at the edge of the great granite head wall. They stopped, in shocked amazement at what they found.

Noah was standing at the very edge of the precipice, overlooking the avalanche. He presented a stark, solitary figure. With arms outstretched to the heavens, long black hair streaming in the wind, he was shouting like a madman.

After his two companions departed to search for a hiding place, Noah proceeded to carry out his assignment of acting as a decoy. He seated himself in plain view of the enemy, at the edge of the cliff. Nearby was a large crack in the rock. There, one could hide quickly in the event of an attack by ONG.

He reflected, "It's going to be a long day,

just sitting here, where Snake can watch me." Glancing up at the sky he started to speculate as to which of those flat little lenticular clouds ONG might be using, as a hiding place. He mentally urged one of those nice flat clouds to drift over his way.

"Drift over here, where old Mr. ONG can swoop right down and gobble up that whole band of Paiutes," he murmured to himself.

Of course, the monster raptor might take it into his head to gobble up Noah. Everyone knew the murderous bird preferred the taste of Washos, to Paiutes. What to do? There must be some way to lure the great bird over here, convince him to attack the Paiutes.

Slowly, an idea began to formulate. How to get ONG to eat the Paiutes and not Noah? It might just take a little lie. Not a very big one, just a little one. Now, Noah's parents didn't approve of a lie. In his younger years Noah received several spankings for stretching the truth. But, in this case maybe they'd agree. Just one small lie might be overlooked. After all, he only needed to convince ONG that Noah was a Paiute and all those fellows down there were Washos.

Abruptly, ONG accepted Noah's unspoken invitation. A long thin cloud detached itself from the cluster floating lazily over Washo Land. The wind began to moan. Noah's long black hair streamed out behind him. He watched in fascination, as the cloud streaked directly toward him. It focused on the exact spot where he stood, poised on the brink of the precipice. The shadow of the cloud raced across the landscape at an amazing speed, drawing closer, ever closer. In panic Noah waved his arms and shouted, his voice almost drowned in the wind's rising roar.

"Hear me, Mr. ONG! Those are the fellows you want, down there! Nice tasty Washos, every one of 'em. Especially, that one with the yellow face. Be sure you get him! You'll find him the most tasty."

Noah screeched at the top of his lungs, "Leave me alone! I'm a Paiute. I'd taste very bad. Very, very, baaaadddddd."

Suddenly, the sun was blotted out, an ominous thunder rumbled in the distance. The wind reached gale force and streaks of distant lightning flickered. Summoning all his courage, Noah stood defiantly at the edge of the cliff, with arm outstretched. He pointed downward at Snake, and the Evil Seven. At first, only the great amber beak emerged from the cloud. It opened wide, emitting screams of fury. It was followed by a huge head, with glaring yellow eyes and a long black body. The great wings were set. A blast of thunder, so loud it seemed to shake the ground, erupted from the open beak. Lightning flashed from the tips of the gleaming talons, as they struck at Snake's yellow face.

Snake's reactions matched those of the flashing talons. He had lived too long among his rattle snake friends. He'd inherited their lightning fast movements. The snarling leader drew his head away from the reaching talons. The drew only a red slash, across his yellow cheek. The claws went on, to sink deep into the exposed chest of a terrified One Eye, cowering behind his leader.

Abruptly, the great wings began to thrash. One Eye, an amazed expression on his face, disappeared, snatched away by the hungry ONG. The great bird quickly faded into the distance, bound for Da ow aga and his nest. One huge black leg hung down, the claw clutching a feebly struggling human figure.

CHAPTER 15   The Cave

Ai mee gazed in wonder at the interior of the cave. After crawling through the bush covered entrance, she found herself standing in a shoulder wide corridor. Before her a set of stairs ascended into darkness. She was standing in a natural fault, separating two immense pieces of granite. The stairs were neatly carved into solid rock. As there was nowhere else to go, she began to climb upward into darkness. She held her breath and carefully placed her moccasin clad feet so as not to make a sound.

Up and up she went, with finger tips touching the smooth granite walls. Ai mee climbed in the darkness for what seemed like ages, following the walls upward. Just as she was about to turn in panic and flee back to freedom, a faint hint of light crept along the wall above her. Quickly, she dashed up the remaining stairs and burst into an open cave.

Bright sunlight poured through a large window like opening in the south wall. Approaching the opening timidly, she peered put and found herself looking down on the meadow.

Heaving a sigh of relief, she said to herself, "Well at least I know where I am now."

Turning, Ai mee inspected the walls of the cave, her curiosity aroused. It was unlike anything she'd seen before. Most of the wall was covered with a long colorful, panoramic mural. "My oh my!" she mused in awe, turning slowly as her eyes traversed the mural.

The colors were fantastic browns, oranges and yellows fading into reds with patches of bright copper blue. Marching along the length of the painting were small stick figures done in dense black. The colors were dulled by layers of smoky stain which must have accumulated over the ages. The stick figures consisted of rectangular bodies with round heads, and protruding arms and legs. Also depicted were curious animals, who dwarfed the humans hunting them. One of the animals had a strange humped back, while another had an unusual snout like nose that curled up at the end. It also had great curling tusks.

The most successful of the depicted hunters appeared to be a fellow who carried a strange weapon. It seemed to be an extension of his arm. Apparently, it was used for throwing a large spear.

Turning away from the mural, Ai mee noticed a substantial fire pit, against a smoke blackened wall. A fresh fire of sticks was laid neatly, waiting to be ignited by the next user.

"That was thoughtful of some one," the girl mused. "Left a fire all set, for the next person who comes along. Maybe someone was just here, and expected me to come along at any minute."

Curiously, the girl touched one of the sticks with a finger tip, only to have it disintegrate into dust.

"That fire was laid ages and ages ago." Ai mee shuddered, looking over her shoulder apprehensively.   "I hope there's no one here now, watching me."

Behind the fire pit was a narrow opening in the wall. Entering, she found a trickle of cold clear water collecting in a pool in the stone floor.

Returning to the cave, Ai mee shivered, realizing as had Bopo, "The Ancient Ones must have inhabited this place.   Their spirits must still be here."

Maybe they were watching at this very moment. She turned, hearing a scuffling sound and saw her two companions emerging from the blackness of the stairwell. They were carrying the burden baskets, which contained the Washos every possession.

"What do you think Ai mee? Doesn't this look like a safe place to hide for awhile? I think we ought'a settle down here. At least for a few days."

Noah nodded his head in agreement, and camp was established. Our friends had a hiding place, temporary though it might be.

The three young Washos found their new home to be quite comfortable and it certainly seemed to be secure. As long as they remained hidden within the cave they could be reasonably sure Snake wouldn't find them.

Food supplies diminished rapidly.   It was necessary to begin a hunt for deer or other game. Without saying as much, the two boys adopted an unwritten rule. Only one of them would be absent from the cave, at any time. The obvious purpose being, they didn't want Ai mee to be left alone, as long as there was any possibility Snake might be near.

There were no deer to be had in the meadow as the snow was too deep. The hunters traveled some distance to a lower elevation. There forage was plentiful. As Noah was about to set out on the first hunt, Ai mee admonished him,

"Now, if you do get a deer, don't forget to bring the brain back with you. So I'll be able to tan the hide. We need a new supply of leather." Extending a small wrapped pack of food, she said,

"Here's a little lunch for you in case you get hungry. Oh, don't forget to take a small coal from the fire, before you go, for your fire-pouch. Just in case you run into trouble and need to start one."

Looking at a grinning Bopo, Noah spread his hands palms up and rolled his eyes, "Just like a mother," he groaned.

It was a long day. The shadows were lengthening into evening by the time the young hunter returned. His burden basket was heavily loaded with the carefully butchered meat of two deer, wrapped in fresh hides. Meanwhile, Bopo had located a supply of milkweed, under the snow. He'd produced a length of twisted rope. Fashioning it into a ladder, he suspended it from the cave window. Finding the ladder, upon his return, Noah used it to ascend to the cave. "The hunter returns," he said with a grin.

During the next few days, life settled into a routine of preparing to resume the journey homeward. Hunting, tanning hides, drying venison jerky, cutting and sewing moccasins, breech clouts, leggings and shirts, consumed their time.

One day Bopo returned from a successful hunt, a big smile stretched across his usually expressionless face. Bursting with enthusiasm he rushed up to the girl and said, "Ai mee, do you suppose you'd weave another cooking basket for us? I know we already have one, but we need another. You see, today I made a big discovery. You'll never believe this, but I found a nice warm spot where the snow was melted out. There was the best supply of Violet Mushrooms I've seen in a long time. They're quite a delicacy, you know. Haven't seen any of them for a very long time. They taste just wonderful, when you cook 'em in my Auntie Blossom's Two Basket Stew. What do you think? Do you suppose you could find the red bud to make one more basket?"

"Well," said Ai mee skeptically, "I've never heard of Violet Mushrooms before. Never ever heard Crow Woman mention them. She knows about everything that grows. But, if you're sure it's all right to eat 'em, I'll make up a new basket. You have to be very careful about what kind of mushrooms you eat, you know. The wrong kind can poison you, or even worse, make you hallucinate something awful. You sure this Auntie Blossom of yours knows what she's doin'?"

"No problem." assured the lad seriously. "Auntie Blossom is one of the last of the great mushroom cooks. Really knows what she's doin'. Tomorrow, I'll use her recipe and cook up the finest stew you ever tasted. No problem !"

The next evening Ai mee and Noah stretched out before the fire at supper time. They were prepared to watch Bopo demonstrate his skill as a cook, by creating Violet Mushroom stew. The husky fellow laid out all the necessary ingredients. He assembled select pieces of fresh venison, a large pile of Violet Mushrooms sliced in thin purple strips along with a number of herbs and dried onions from the marsh. He chopped things in little pieces. He created numerous piles, which he divided and combined with other little piles, very methodically. He placed one basket on his right side, the other on the left. It was obvious, he was following a precise ritual. All the time he worked, he talked over his shoulder to his companions, saying,

"I guess I oughta tell you a little bit about my Aunt Blossom. She's the one who invented Violet Mushroom stew. Auntie Blossom is married to Uncle Put. She's a really nice, friendly person. Smiles a lot and talks a lot. In fact, she talks almost all the time. Seldom quits talking, if the truth were known. Also, she's a little on the plump side. Actually, she's short and very much on the plump side. But, she's a great cook. Cooks all sorts of good stuff, she's invented herself. Oh Yeah! There's one other little thing about Aunt Blossom. She's cross-eyed. That is, her eyes are crossed most of the time. But then, the rest of the time her eyes look out sideways. Each eye in a different direction. It's kind of disconcerting, when you're trying to follow what she's doing, like when she's making two basket stew. Because, you're never sure which basket she's looking at when she starts to put the different piles of ingredients in.   It's quite important, you know! Because, both baskets taste great when finished. However, one of them contains the good stuff, and the other contains the poison stuff.   That causes people to have these weird hallucinations."

"Well, make sure you get the right basket," said Ai mee dubiously.

Bopo talked on as he worked, deftly placing a pile of purple mushroom strips in the left basket and a smaller pile of onions in the right basket. "You see, you need to be careful not to put Violet Mushrooms and onions in the same basket or you get a violent sort of reaction," he said, adding a little water to each basket.

"Any how," he went on, "I've watched Auntie Blossom make Two Basket stew so many times, I've got the formula all set in my mind, memorized it exactly. So, there's nothing to worry about. Ole' Bopo's going to turn out a superb dish here. Just you wait! I can just see the expressions on your faces, when you wrap a lip around this delicious stew. Guess I oughta tell you about Uncle Put as well," Bopo went on,

"Uncle Put is a skinny little old fellow. Short and all sort of wizened up. He always has a worried expression on his face. Comes from trying to figure out which way his wife is looking at the moment, I guess.   He's a quiet little old fellow. Doesn't say much. In fact he hardly ever talks. Just looks worried. Of course, the reason he never talks is because he never gets a chance. He doesn't like to interrupt Auntie Blossom. She talks all the time. I'll tell you though, there's one time when ole Uncle Put really does shine. That's when he's had a big feed of Violet Mushroom stew. That stuff really makes a changed man out of him. He doesn't say a word, just puffs up his chest and puts on his new pair of moccasins, goes out into the forest and kicks rocks. Man, you never saw any thing like the way that little fellow can kick rocks! Big Rocks!"

In the beginning, Bopo placed six of Ai mee's clean cooking stones on the fire pit hearth. They were now blazing hot. Using a reed holder, he dropped three of them into a liquid filled basket, beging the cooking process. In a short time those stones, now cooled, were replaced with three others. This process continued until the stew was thoroughly cooked and steaming hot. Finally, he dipped a wooden ladle into the basket and took an exploratory sip. Smacking his lips, he declared the stew finished.

The three seated themselves cross legged around the basket and sampled the first steaming bite. Both Ai mee and Noah registered surprise, and then pleasure. The Violet Mushroom stew was a success !

The fire burned low. There was no breeze outside the quiet cave. The air within began to cloud with smoke. Our three friends slept soundly around the fire pit. They lay flat on their backs, arms spread wide, open mouthed, they snoring loudly.

Silently, a tall ghostly figure began to materialize in the shadowy gloom at the back of the darkened cave. Long gray hair surrounded a narrow aristocratic face, devoid of expression. In the smoky gloom, next to the face, sat a large jet black crow. It's piercing scarlet eyes never blinked. Slowly the figure drifted forward, through the smoky air, without ever giving the impression of moving a limb. It seated it's self, with hands on knees in a regal position behind the fire pit. The wraith looked down, upon three sleeping figures.

A hollow voice echoed softly, down through the centuries, saying, "Bopo, Awake! Rebuild the fire."

Immediately, the sleeping lad began to stir, shaking his head with groggy motions, rubbing at his eyes. He attempted to rise, only to collapse on hands and knees. He crawled with a staggering motion toward the wood pile. Gathering an arm full of wood, he lurched back to rebuild the smoking fire. Slowly, the flames kindled, filling the cave with a dim flickering light. First Ai mee, and then Noah, struggled awake. Groggy, with faces slack, they assumed a sitting position before the regal figure cloaked in shadows. They slouched, open mouthed with vacant eyes, regarding the figure before them.

There was a long period of silence as the stately wraith studied the three. Finally a hollow voice reverberated through the cave, saying with authority, "Bopo, what are you and these slack faced strangers doing in this sacred place? Why have you come here to disturb us? Do you wish to incur the wrath of the Ancient Ones?   Speak!"

Bopo's head rolled from side to side. He spoke in a weak and empty voice, as though hypnotized.

"These are my Washo friends, Noah and Ai mee. We're hiding here. Hiding from Snake, the worst of the Paiute, and his band, the Evil Six. He wants to kill Noah and I. He has sworn to blind Ai mee and take her back to his village. To serve the rest of her life as his slave. We meant no harm. All we want is to escape. Return to our home in Washo Land."

The great black crow puffed out his chest, arched his back, spread his wings and ruffled the tip feathers. Standing rigidly, he fixed gleaming eyes on the slumped figure of Bopo and began a loud, raucous cawing. He went on for some time, giving the impression an oration was being delivered. At length, he paused. He placed the tip of his cruel beak at the ear of the regal figure. He muttered at length in her ear. She nodded her head, indicating she understood the message, and said,

"Crow says, you're arrival in this meadow and this cave is not an accident. Crow is very old and very wise! Crow knows how the Ancient Ones think. Crow says the spirit of the Ancient Ones led you to this cave. You've been brought to this sacred place! You've been chosen by the Ancient Ones! Chosen to save the Washo people, from a terrible scourge that has befallen them. Crow says, you are to be given the precious secret of the lost Atl-Atl. Crow says you will use the deadly Atl-Atl in a great battle. You will defeat the enemies of Washo Land. Crow says, I am to reveal to you the secrets of this sacred place. He says, you are to be given the scroll that tells how to construct the lost Atl-Atl. Crow has spoken, for the first time in many, many centuries."

Shaking his head in bewilderment, Bopo said, "Crow Woman, I just don't understand what this is all about. You're the one who's always brought medicines to my family when some one was ill. You're the one who's taught my sisters the secrets of all herbs and foods that grow. You're the one my father always consults, when there's some question about the fairness of a trade. Now, you're telling me all this wild stuff about the Ancient Ones, who are my ancestors. I just don't understand what you're talking about."

The barest trace of a smile flitted across Crow Woman's shadowy features. Dense smoke from the fire billowed in and out around her, adding a ghostly element to the gloomy cave. Quietly, she said,

"I'm not surprised that you're confused. I'll tell you all. First, I am not the person you think I am. I'm a shadow, a shade, a ghost from the past. I'm the grandmother of the person you know as Crow Woman. The grandmother a thousand times removed. I come from the time of the beginning. The beginning, a time when the Maker of All Things created the people who are now known as Washo. The Maker of All Things was counting out the seeds that were to become the different tribes. He counted them out on a big winnowing basket in equal numbers. West wind, the mischievous wind, watched until the Maker divided the seeds into equal piles on the tray. Then he blew a gust of wind that scattered the seed to the east. Most of the seeds that were to be the Washo people were blown away and lost. A very few seed drifted into a crack in the rock. That rock was in the cold land very far to the north. Moss covered the crack and kept the seeds warm until it was time for them to sprout. The sprouts grew up through the warm moss and became the Ancient Ones, only then they were Young Ones.

The Maker addressed them. He told them they were Hokan Speakers. They were to leave the cold land and search until they found a warm place. That was to be their own land. They were to follow the caribou to the east, crossing the dry floor of a narrow sea, where the water had disappeared. They were to continue toward the rising sun, until they reached the high mountains. Then, they were to turn right and travel to the warm lands.

Many generations later, they came to the summit of a beautiful mountain where there was a meadow overlooked by a secure cave. The elders of the group gathered in the cave, drawing pictures telling the story of their long travels. They believed they had arrived at a place that was to be their home land. Part of the group wished to live on the west slope of the mountain, and so they departed and went that way. The others wished to make the east slope their home, and so they went to what was to become Washo Land. They wished to remain hunters and the land was plentiful with animals.

Later they explored the lands along the edge of Old Sea and found a wonderful new food they called Tah gum. The two groups remained friends, the western tribe was called the Yana. The eastern tribe became the Washos. There were no other peoples in the land. They were the first, the Hokan Speakers.

Bopo listened spellbound as Crow Woman continued her story. "When the Hokan Speakers began their journey in search of a home land, they obtained their food by hunting the huge animals of ancient times. The Maker gave them the secret of a mighty weapon called the Atl-Atl. It was so powerful they became very successful hunters. But then, not long before they reached this hidden cave, they became careless. They lost the secret of the Atl-Atl. It remains lost, until this day." Bopo shook his head.

"The mighty weapon extended the length of a hunters arm. It allowed him to throw a dart tipped spear with tremendous force and accuracy. Now, upon Crow's command, I give to you this soft leather scroll. On it is the long lost secret of the Atl-Atl. The great weapon must be made exactly according to the secret. It must be fashioned only from the wood of a sacred Yew tree. There is no Yew tree that grows in Washo Land. You must travel for three suns to the northward, until you come to a great mountain, whose top is always hidden in clouds. Climb that mountain to it's highest peak. You will find a great Yew tree. Cut a single living branch from that tree. Fashion it into the mighty Atl-Atl." Bopo shook his head.

"You must teach yourself to use the powers of the great weapon. Then, bring all of it's awesome force against the scourge of your people. Now, go forth and hunt the evil Snake, worst of all the Paiute people." Bopo shook his head.

Drawing herself to full height, the shadowy Crow Woman wrapped the gray cloak around herself with a swirling stroke. She glared down at the befuddled Bopo. The great black crow with the glittering scarlet eyes glared down at Bopo.

"The Ancient People have spoken. ATTEND!" she hissed.

There was a great puff of smoke and the three trembling Washos were alone in the silent cave.

CHAPTER 16   Mountain Of Clouds

Noah awoke the next morning shaking his head, "Ugh! Bad medicine! My mouth tastes like a pack rat's nest. Can't understand it. I had nightmares all night long. My totem must be acting up again. I never know what that pesky coyote is up to! I feel so bad! Guess I might as well go out in the forest and kick some rocks. Ugh !"   Walking over to the window Noah tossed out the rope ladder and climbed down out of sight.

Ai mee and Bopo also awakened feeling strange. Rubbing the sleep from her eyes, Ai mee said, "My what a night that was. I had weird dreams all night long. Kept seeing Crow Woman in my dreams. She was giving someone I couldn't see a big lecture. Seems like she kept at it all night long. What a night that was !"

With a grimace, Bopo shook his head from side to side to clear his mind. "You know, I think I must have gotten some bad mushrooms in that stew. It sure did give me some weird dreams, too. Man, I don't wanta go through a night like that again. I'd like to think the whole thing never happened. Except for this!" Grimacing, he held up a small scroll of soft sheep skin.

"What's that thing?"   asked the girl, a puzzled expression on her face.

"This little old thing just happens to be the lost secret of the Ancient One's mighty weapon the Atl-Atl. I just happen to have been assigned to build one of the darn things out of special yew wood. Go out and make war on Snake with it. Nothing to it. Just like that. Nothing to it," said the lad shaking his head in resignation.

"Just go out and pop off old Snake." He then went on, to tell Ai mee in detail about his meeting with the ghost of Crow Woman's grandmother a thousand times removed. He repeated his assignment from Crow. He was to go far to the north and find the only yew tree in the area.

"Ugh." said Ai mee. "If it takes three days to go up there to get your yew wood and three days to get back, I hope that won't make us late getting to Washo Land. We need to be there by the first new moon of summer. If I'm not back in time for the Womanhood Ceremonies, that means I'll be just a little kid for another whole year. Do you know what I'm going to do? I'm going to make up some time sticks, so you fellows don't forget about the first new moon of summer."

"What's a time stick?" was Bopo's question.

Ai mee picked three green willow sticks from the wood pile. "Well Bopo, you wouldn't have much luck making a time stick, cause you don't have enough toes. But, I have all my toes, so I'll do it. A time stick is a way of counting the days until some special event. Like the first new moon of summer. Last night was a new moon. I'll take my knife and carve a notch in the bark on this willow stick for each sunrise until the next new moon. The way I know how many notches to carve, is to make one for each of my toes and one for each of my fingers, and then, one for each of my toes again. There are that many suns for each new moon. Almost always seems to work out that way, or close enough anyhow. So I'll make up three notched time sticks, because there are three new moons until the Womanhood Ceremony. I'll scrape off one notch from the stick every morning at sun rise. When there are no more notches, we'd better be home, or I'm stuck to be a little kid for another whole year." grumbled the girl.

"That's pretty complicated stuff." said Bopo skeptically. "Why don't you tell Noah about all those notches and getting home by a certain time, all that stuff. I'm sure he knows how important it is to you. I'll bet he has a good plan, to get us there on time. Besides, I'll be pretty busy making one of those Atl-Atl things. Have to learn how to blow ole' Snake away with it. By the way, Noah's gone out to scout Snake's position, so we know which way to run next."

It was after dark that night before the young warrior returned. Ai mee was anxiously peering out the window opening into the darkness. The rope ladder began to creak and Noah's head appeared over the threshold. With a serious look on his face Noah said, "Well, I finally found them. They're out there still searching for us, hunting along the main trail. That's the one that runs from Cold land to Warm land, along the crest of the mountains. Snake's sure he's between us and Washo Land. It'll be hard to head down trail and sneak by that bunch. They know that's the shortest way home for us."

Nodding his head in agreement, Bopo went on to explain about the assignment from Crow Woman, to travel for three suns toward the Mountain of Clouds. Noah thought the trip was a good idea, as Snake was expecting them to head in the opposite direction. All three agreed it was best to leave the cave the next morning, and head for the Mountain of Clouds. They were now rested and well provisioned.

"Oh, by the way," said Bopo, with a wicked grin, "Ai mee has a new trick with some willow sticks, she's anxious to show you. I'm sure you're going to get a thrill out of this."

The first rays of sun light were just creeping over the great granite head wall as the trio left the secret cave of the Ancient Ones and began the long trek northward to the Mountain of Clouds. Their burden baskets were loaded to overflowing with food and new buckskin clothing. Bopo's long pig tail was freshly braided and the first rays of sunlight struck blue high lights in Ai mee's neatly parted black hair. The girl upheld the Washo clean camp tradition, by scouring the cave till it was impossible to tell anyone had been there.

The snow melted quickly in the warm spring weather. Golden-brown patches of grass were beginning to appear in the meadow. Looking back over her shoulder Ai mee said regretfully,

"This is such a beautiful place, I hate to leave it. I hope we can all return here someday, when every thing is peaceful."

" By the way," Bopo called to Noah who was in the lead. "According to the sheep skin scroll of the Ancients, we're going to meet a strange member of the Yana tribe, who will be helpful to us when we visit the Mountain of Clouds in search of yew wood. So if you bump into anyone, there's at least a chance he'll be friendly. There is one little problem, however, the scroll was written by a bunch of spooks, you know, Ghosts! Well, these spooks failed to mention, whether or not this Yana fellow we're to meet is a ghost or a real live person. So keep the old eyes open, and don't be surprised at anything you meet. I'll just stay in the back of the procession here, observe how you handle things."

"Thanks a lot," said Noah sarcastically.

The trail they followed led toward Cold land. The snow was melting rapidly, signs of springtime were every where. The snowshoes, which had stood them in such good stead, were no longer needed and so they were concealed in a large White Bark Pine. Moving ever downward, they wound through rocky switch-backs and across great fields of finely shattered talus. At length, they dropped down into a dense forest of pine and fir.

Coming to a rushing stream of icy snow water, they were forced to wade waist-deep in the freezing stuff. Laughing and shivering upon emerging, they broke into a jog, to warm themselves. Coming to a small clearing in the forest they stopped to bask in the warm sunlight for a moment. The golden grassy clearing was surrounded by deep green forest shadows.

With no warning, in complete silence, a dark figure dropped from the high branches of a deeply shadowed tree. Landing behind them like a silent cat, the figure crouched, arms extended forward, hands open, ready to take instant flight. It was a man, small and wiry with shaggy gray streaked black hair. He was clad in a ragged buckskin shirt, breech clout and leggings. At his waist was an obsidian knife and ax. Crouching there, with dark eyes flashing, he gave no sign of being friendly, just wary readiness.

Bopo who was closest to the wild figure was the first to recover his composure. Without moving so much as a hair, he quietly said, "Greetings! We're Washo people. We're Hokan speakers. Do you understand Hokan?" The crouching figure made not a sound, just stared.

Trying another tact Bopo said, "We're very glad to see you're not a ghost. You look just like a living breathing person. Are you a member of the Yana Tribe?"

"Let me try," said Ai mee softly, as she took a step forward, holding out one small hand. "Are you a Yahi?" she queried. This drew an instant response from the unsmiling man, but it was guttural and meaningless to them. Over her shoulder Ai mee explained, "Yahi are the southern clan of the Yana tribe. Their dialect, the Hokan language, is different than ours. I think I can get him to understand us, if I work at it for a while."

Ai mee continued her questioning of the man, gradually they began to understand one another. The warriors resigned themselves to relying upon the girl, as their spokes person. Bopo was particularly interested in this strange fellow, he must be the one sent by the Ancients, to help them. The fellows answers were simple. He knew nothing about the Ancient Ones or of secret caves or Atl-Atl's. He lived to the south. His name was Ishi. He was visiting the land of his northern relatives the Yanas. He had come to dig for flint. He'd climbed the Mountain of Clouds to find a good deposit of fine black obsidian. He had a good supply of the stuff. He was now on his way home. When asked if he'd trade with Bopo, for several large pieces of choice flint for the Atl-Atl missile, he said yes. Not now, however. His obsidian was hidden in the forest. He'd meet them along the trail to home, on the day of the fourth sun. Then they would trade.

Ishi was still unsmiling, but he no longer seemed to be afraid of them, just cautious. Relaxing for a moment in the small clearing, Bopo recalled his disastrous attempt to make fire by the Yana method, rubbing the fire drill between his palms. So he asked Ishi to make a fire for them. Without a change in expression, Ishi produced materials and within moments had a fire blazing.

With a grin and a wistful sigh, Bopo said, "Fellow, I'm really impressed with the way you make a fire!"

Bopo looked closely at Ishi's single stick fire drill. A gleam of understanding crossed his quizzical face, "Now I can see how it's done. No wonder I had such a tough time, making fire by the Yana method. That single stick of yours has a very slight taper to it. Makes all the difference in the world when your trying to hang onto it. Well, thanks a lot Ishi. Glad I bumped into you! Drop in out of the trees any time."

Ai mee broke out some venison jerky and wheat cakes, motioning Ishi to be seated by the fire. As soon as the food appeared, Ishi's personality changed completely. He began to rub his wrinkled hands in anticipation. A big smile spread across his wrinkled brown face. As it turned out, Ishi was one very hungry fellow. He consumed a great deal of good Washo food before signaling he was full, by rubbing his belly with satisfaction. A full stomach made the little fellow talkative. Ai mee began to draw him out about his travels. After a short conversation, the girls face blanched, and putting her hand to mouth, she gasped, "Oh no, oh no!"

Turning to her companions she moaned, "Ishi says he was sleeping in a tree last night. A big man with a yellow face passed beneath his tree. The ugly man had many followers. They were traveling on a trail that led to the top of the Mountain of Clouds. It's a shorter trail than the one we're following. The Paiutes'll arrive at the top of the mountain one day before we do."

Ai mee reacted violently to his news. It frightened Ishi, and he rose abruptly. Saying he would meet our friends as agreed on the fourth day, he unexpectedly swung up into the trees and disappeared as he had come, silently.

Shouldering his burden basket and kicking out the remains of Ishi's fire, Noah said to his two glum companions, "Well there just doesn't seem to be anything else to do but keep on heading northward, to the top of the mountain. We'll just have to go up there and get the yew wood. We'll get there as fast as we can, without lettin' Snake catch sight of us. That's gonna to be a big order. All we can do is try. Better do a lot of serious talking to our good luck totems, in the mean time."

For the next two and a half days our friends moved up the steep mountain slope. They were wary in their movements, with eyes darting from side to side. They glanced back over the shoulder, always expecting Snake or one of the evil six to appear suddenly. Noah in the lead, stopped frequently, with raised hand. He'd slither forward on his belly, to peer out at the horizon. The three moved quietly, conversing only in whispers or with hand signals. At night the camp was cold, no fire to give away their location. One person was always on guard through out the night, to insure against a surprise attack.

They moved up the mountain   skillfully, with out leaving a sign of their passage. A casual foot print, a broken blade of grass, an overturned pebble was deftly replaced to eliminate any sign of their presence. Noah avoided the well marked trail. He traveled alongside, over cover that wouldn't tell of their existence. They moved ever upward, until the sun was blotted out and they found themselves slipping silently through ghostly white clouds. These were so dense they could see only an arms length ahead. Whispered voices were oddly muffled by the swirling mists. They were nearing the summit.

Suddenly, without warning, Noah stepped out into a bright sun light world and was quickly followed by his two companions. Looking around, they were truly at the top of the world, above the clouds. It was as though they occupied a small island in a great sea of floating white. Here and there the tip of a distant mountain peak emerged from the frothy layer. Below them, soaring just above the white layer , were two Bald Eagles. The landscape of decomposed granite was bare, desolate, wind swept and awesomely beautiful.

Before them a long low barrier of granite monolith rose out of the sandy soil and at its very center stood a single tree. It was old, gnarled and wind swept, defying time and the elements. It stood majestic and alone.

"Whew wheeee!" breathed Bopo reverently. "There's my yew tree."

Cautious as ever, Noah beckoned his companions into the shelter of several low bushes. They squatted for some time, studying the landscape around them, searching for any sign the enemy had arrived before them. Thoughtfully, Noah whispered, "Looks deserted! I've been thinking. It's late in the day. Maybe we oughta copy Ishis trick. Sleep in the yew tree tonight. There's better cover in the top of that big tree, than there is out here in the open. Let's go explore the tree."

The massive old Yew tree had several dead branches. They trailed down close to the ground in a tangle of dried foliage. Carefully, the three worked their way through the cluster, without disturbing so much as a twig. Mounting a limb, they disappeared into the dense olive green foliage. Working their way to the very top, they were hidden under an umbrella like canopy. Each seated himself on a limb, with back against the trunk. Bopo whispered over his shoulder,

"This is a comfortable enough spot. I have a limb in front of my face that's about as thick as my wrist. Should be good for the Atl-Atl. The only problem is, it'll be a tough job to cut through this green wood. Only have my flint hunting knife, and a couple pieces of shale."

"Might as well get started," hissed Noah. "I'm going to breath a lot easier when we're headed on our way down hill, out'a here. If your knife chips and gets dull you can borrow mine. I'll try rechipping yours. Remember, be really careful with all the wood shavings. Catch 'em all. Don't let any fall down to the ground, for someone to find. That'd give us away for sure. Snake'd have us dead! Unless you know how to fly, that is."

At the top of the world, Ai mee squirmed around and found enough voids in the foliage so she could peer out, acting as a lookout. While she watched, Bopo sawed away at the tough limb. It wasn't long before he passed his knife to Noah, saying in a disgusted voice, "A flint knife's a great weapon. It's fine for dressing game, but it sure wasn't meant for cutting tough green wood." The youths worked diligently through the after noon. The shadows were beginning to lengthen when at last Bopo gave a grunt of satisfaction. He held up the severed limb.

At that instant Ai mee gasped and whispered in a frightened voice, "Quiet, quiet! There's one of the Paiutes, stepping out of the clouds. Don't move a muscle. He's looking right at us. He's walking this way."

The tension grew, as the tall Paiute warrior moved toward them, carefully placing one foot before the other as if stalking game. He wore leggings and a breech clout, his chest bare. A white stripe of war paint was drawn down the bridge of his nose. Noah clutched his dull knife. Silently, he looked down for an opening through which he could drop on the enemy. The warrior finally halted his stalking stride, as he reached the barrier formed by the monolith. The wall provided a shelter from the wind. The man seemed to select a sheltered spot near the tree, as the best place to set up a camp.

Noah was about to heave a sigh of relief when he felt Ai mee's insistent finger, tapping on his shoulder. Looking around, he could see she was silently pointing at a second figure, approaching from the opposite direction. This warrior was dressed like the first, but with a bright blue cross of war paint on the forehead. As he reached the barrier, he hopped up on it and walked directly under the tree. He glanced up into the dark interior. Noah quivered and prepared to leap, but the warrior apparently satisfied, continued on to the camp site.

As darkness settled down upon the camp with it's flickering fire, the Paiutes emerged from the gloom, one by one. The last to appear was a hulking figure with a permanent scowl, blotched yellow war paint and shredded remains of an ear.

Hunched before the fire in his tattered bearskin robe, Snake issued guttural instructions to his followers. The band seemed to have ample provisions and soon the fragrant aroma of an evening meal wafted up into the yew tree.

In darkness, each of the three youths squirmed on his hard limb, and drooled. Ai mee silently poked each fellow in the ribs, handing him a piece of dry jerked venison.

All night long a lone coyote howled plaintively nearby. Just before dawn the Paiutes arose and moved silently away, down the mountain.

Chapter 17   Step Toward Home

Ai mee regarded Noah's lanky figure jogging down the trail ahead of her, burden basket bouncing. As they left the Yew Tree and started down the Mountain of Clouds they followed a steep western trail, descending quickly. From here on, each step was to be a step toward home. They looked forward to a meeting with Ishi, to trade for flint. Bopo was enthused at the prospect of building the ancient Atl-Atl. He'd would need flint for the missile head.

They traveled at a steady jogging pace throughout the day. Toward evening, as they followed a stream down it's steep slope, it disappeared into a tangle of White Bark Pine. Prying their way through the debris of a windfall, they emerged to see the stream tumble noisily over the edge of a cliff and drop into space. Crawling on hands and knees to the abrupt edge they beheld a spot far below, where the waterfall plunged into a small pristine lake. Standing under an ancient juniper tree at the far end of the lake was none other than Ishi, with a wide grin on his face, motioning for them to join him.

At last they dropped down into soft sand at the foot of a towering cliff. There they were met by an expectant Ishi. His first salutation was to rub his stomach and point to his mouth, indicating he was hungry.

That night the four camped in a thicket at the foot of the lake. They eagerly talked far into the night. Now, they were able to converse in the Washo version of the Hokan language, thanks to Ai mees tutoring of Ishi.

"I need three good blanks of flint, Ishi. I remember, you said you had some really nice pieces you might trade, right?" said Bopo. "Need the stuff for some large points, sorta like a ceremonial point. You have anything that would do?"

Ishi nodded with a grin, and produced three rough blanks of black obsidian, from his basket. "Here's best pieces I have. I think they would make pretty good points."

"Mind if I look at 'em?" questioned Bopo, carefully turning one of the blanks from side to side and holding it up to the light.

After a prolonged session of friendly haggling, Bopo was able to trade quite a bit of venison for the three excellent pieces of obsidian.

As they talked, Ishi explained to his listeners how his family group, the Yahi, had long ago moved far toward Warm land, making their home in an inaccessible place they could defend against enemies. Vast areas of the foothill slopes were covered with dense growths of Mountain Oak, a heavy shrub much like a miniature oak tree. It grew into a closely packed solid cover, no more than twice as high as a man's head.

It was in these dense jungles the Yahis made their homes, where enemies could not penetrate. They were like rabbits in a briar patch. They developed intricate, hard to find passages, through which they could traverse an entire hill-side.

They fished the streams bordering their jungles, using woven nets and spears. They hunted game animals with bows and snares. Much of the foothill country, in which they lived, was cut with deep canyons and towering cliffs. Many of their twisting passages ended abruptly at the edge of a cliff. There, they'd negotiated the cliff face with sturdy ladders of woven milk weed rope, usually hidden nearby.

If an enemy entered the jungle, he invited a disastrous ambush. So, Ishis people lived in comparative safety. They went out of the jungle to hunt deer, wildcats, rabbits and an occasional bear. They collected acorns from the Black Oak tree, which they ground into flour.

Dawn found the four travelers moving swiftly down the mountain with Ishi now in the lead. As they traveled Bopo was on the look out for materials, for his new Atl-Atl. During the day he collected a number of large missile shafts and hard shale for shaping the throwing arm. As the food supply was rapidly being depleted by Ishis voracious appetite, they paused at dusk to stalk a fat barren doe.

It wasn't long before the aroma of delicious roast venison filled the air. After darkness descended, Bopo worked beside the fire far into the night. He meticulously shaped the yew wood throwing arm.

For the next several days our friends pushed rapidly down the mountain, clinging always to the security of the dense green forest shadows. At one point Noah exhibited his skill with the sling, by bagging a large gray goose. Stout gray feathers were added to Bopo's collection of materials.

On the morning of the fourth day, the group crouched shadows, at the edge of a great forest. It looked out over a vast plain of green spring grass. Ishi's Mountain Oak covered foot hills could be seen in the distance. Pointing, he proudly explained,

"This is where my home land begins. Once we reach that dense brush we'll be safe. I know where to find the hidden tunnels. Any stranger who ventures into that maze will be lost. They'll never come out. Many times we find the skeletons of enemies, who have tried to enter and have died without finding a passage that leads out."

"That stuff's really dense, it'd be a long walk to get around it. A mighty long walk." mused Noah.

"I'll show you the way to cross that entire hillside and come out at a deep canyon. There you'll find a stream that flows down to River of the Feather. From there you can follow the waterways 'till you're near your home land."

"That sounds great," enthused Ai mee.

"However, there is one very big problem," cautioned Ishi. "First, we must cross this wide plain of grass. We'll be completely exposed. Your enemy, the ugly man with the yellow face will be able to see us from a great distance. I'll go now to see if I can locate your enemy. Pray to your spirits that he's far behind us. Hide here until I return."

So saying, Ishi reached over his head. Grasping a tree branch he disappeared up into the green shadows above.

Our three friends concealed themselves to await his return. They were surprised when he reappeared almost immediately and hissed,

"Hurry, we must go! The evil one with the yellow face is close by. They will be here any moment. They're hunting through the forest like a pack of hungry wolves. We must run! It's a very long ways before we reach safety in the oak bushes. Come!"

Ishi broke away, running in terror across the plain. He was followed very shortly by three young Washos. At that very moment, a screaming yellow faced madman and his six evil followers erupted from the shadows of the forest, directly behind them. Howling with frenzied anger the hoard took up pursuit, waving battle axes and knives. They were bent upon annihilation of the youths who had alluded them for so long.

Running at top speed, shoulder to shoulder with his friend Bopo, a puffing Noah shouted,

"Let's each take out our last two arrows. When I yell Bopo, one, two, three! Stop and turn. Let off two quick shots. Then we'll both run like crazy. Last man to the bushes has to make new arrows!"

"Your on." shouted Bopo. "Just make sure you yell good and loud, when you come to three !"

For a while it was an even race across the plain. At times the desperate four even appeared to be gaining slightly. But then at last, as the leaders drew close, Snake put on a flashing burst of speed that closed the gap.

Instantly, Noah shouted in a gasping voice, "Bopo, one, two, threeeee!"

Both wheeled, flexing heavy hunting bows and four arrows were in flight instantly. Bopo's first arrow was wide, but the second drove into a fleshy shoulder of the Paiute with a white stripe of war paint down his nose. The man immediately broke stride, grasping his shoulder in agony.

Noah's first arrow was directed at the snarling yellow face of the leader. Snake, with the lightning like reflexes of a striking rattler, twisted his head aside. The arrow only slashed a red cut across his cheek. It whizzed by harmlessly. The second arrow was better placed, penetrating the exact intersection of two crossing blue lines of war paint, on the forehead of the following warrior. He registered a look of shocked surprise and sank from sight. In an instant all was confusion.

Ishi was the first to reach the edge of a dense bank of oak bushes. Frantically clawing open a small entrance in the foliage, he shouted back over his shoulder,

"Take off your burden baskets and shove them in the hole ahead of you. Follow me! Quick now!" He disappeared into the dark shadows, crawling on his stomach like a desperate rodent. In the time it takes to wink an eye, the three Washos disappeared into a tangle of oak brush. Each one anxiously followed the moccasin clad feet of the one before him. Into the shadowy jungle gloom they disappeared. Outside the twisted yellow face of Snake distorted in a scream of frustrated rage.

In the dim interior of the jungle, Ishi finally ceased wriggling on his belly. He sat up, dusting his buckskins. At last, his gasping breath slowed enough for him to speak. He pointed out what appeared to be a narrow passage or tunnel, leading off into the darkness. The passage was quite low. Where Ai mee and Ishi could walk erect, both fellows were forced to stoop. The passage twisted in and out among the heavy oak branches, winding it's torturous way down the hillside. Ishi was anxious to start down this main thoroughfare at once.

Frantically he pointed out. "If it occurs to Snake to set fire to this tinder like oak brush, it's gonna be quite uncomfortable for the occupants of this jungle. Mainly us!"

The group stumbled hastily down the tortuous tunnel of darkness, grasping the massive branches for support. The trail they were descending was a steep one. Occasionally it passed large boulders embedded in the dense foliage. At one point a small spring bubbled up through the rocks into a cave like room. The presence of a blackened fire pit indicated this was a spot frequently used for overnight resting.

Fumbling in the gloom, Ishi produced a long pole. He used it to force aside an overhead branch, allowing a bright shaft of sunlight to enter. Seating himself cross legged on the ground, the wizened little Yahi signaled the others to do the same, and said,

"We rest here for a moment and have a little food, to rebuild our spent energy. For some reason I feel quite hungry."

"All right," said Ai mee.   "We don't have much venison left. Might as well finish it off."

"I'm going to leave you in a short while and take another trail that leads to my lodge. You three will go in the opposite direction, so I'll explain to you, the paths you must follow."

Ai mee, always obliging, withdrew venison jerky and the last of the wheat cakes from her battered burden basket. The four travelers formed a seated circle around the sunlit spot on the ground. As usual Ishi was ravenous and consumed a greater part of the dwindling supply of food.

As he munched away, he drew a map with his finger tip upon the soft dirt, saying to his companions, "You must listen very carefully to what I have to tell you. This is the exact route you must follow. If you miss a single turn you'll be lost, and never find your way out. Remember what I told you about the many skeletons to be found in here. You'll continue down hill. Pass three tunnels which turn off to your left. I'll leave you at the first tunnel. You must continue past two more tunnels, down a very steep path in total darkness. When the path levels you will turn right into another tunnel. Follow for some distance until at last you see the daylight of an entrance. There, you will find yourself standing on a narrow shelf, high on the face of a cliff. There's a stream and dense forest below, at the foot of the cliff. Search and you'll find a hidden rope ladder, at the end of the shelf. Use it to lower yourself to the stream below. Search downstream, you'll find a hidden boat made of rushes. Not a very good boat but it'll float. Take the boat and float down stream through the rapids. The rapids will be a very dangerous place for you. Once you're through the rapids you'll come to a big river. That's the River of the Feather. Float down this river, until you come to an even bigger river. This will be Great River. Float down this river past two big rivers. Go for many suns until you come to a third river. This will be Indian River. Stop and leave your boat. Walk upstream to your home land. At the point where you leave the boat you'll find a mighty Black Oak tree. Climb to the top and you'll see the snow capped mountains of Washo Land in the distance. Do you understand all I've told you?"

Noah nodded his head up and down thoughtfully, memorizing each instruction. Ai mee interjected, asking Ishi, "Can you tell us how many moons it will take to go this way? You see I have it all figured out on my time sticks here. We only have two moons. That's three feet and three hands worth of suns, to get back to Da ow aga. Do you think we can make it, if we go by water?"

Shaking his head, Ishi said. "I have troubles with these numbers things. The fingers and toes games, I just can't understand. I don't know the answer to your question. I just know it's faster to go by boat."

With a suspicious look Bopo said, "Tell us about that little part you skipped over so fast. The part where we might have a little problem at these rapids. Tell us all about that, if you please?"

"Well," said Ishi, with a sly grin. "Those rapids could be a problem all right. You see, the trail leading around this jungle, leads right past this place where the stream goes through a deep and narrow gorge. Lots of white water and sharp rocks in there. It's a perfect place for an ambush. An easy arrow shot from the trail at cliff's edge. Right down into the gorge. Now if that yellow-faced fellow can move as fast as I think he can, he could get to those rapids about the same time as you do. Understand?"

With a shrug of his shoulders Noah said, "Best thing we can do is get started right now. Move fast as we can. Maybe we can beat Snake to the rapids."

At the first turn off to the left Ishi bid our friends goodbye. With a thank you, for all the good food and a jaunty wave of the hand, he disappeared into the gloom.

"Now I don't want anybody to say a word to me until we get to the sunlight and that ledge," said Noah. "I've gotta remember all those directions Ishi gave me. The last thing we want to do is get lost in here. Who wants to be a skeleton, anyway?"

Our three friends spent a stressful time stumbling along in the near darkness. Noah mumbled to himself, repeating Ishi's instructions over and over again. He even repeated the part about the skeletons. After an agonizing period of time, they finally made the last turn and shortly thereafter stumbled out into blinding day light.

Ishi was right about one thing, the ledge was very narrow and it was very high above the forest. With back against the wall, Noahs moccasin toes hung over the edge and the stream below was an awfully long ways down there.

"At least," reflected Noah, "We're out of that spooky oak brush and on our way home. All I have to do now is find that ladder, and crawl down the darned thing without breaking my neck."

CHAPTER 18   The River

Noah hunted up and down the stream bank for some time, before he was able to discover the cleverly hidden rush boat. It was similar to the small boat Ai mee had constructed while in the marsh, but almost twice as large. The construction was the typical long tube of rushes held together with willow tips, folded in the middle to form a prow. It was topped with a laced willow grid that served as a deck. Ai mee surveyed the boat critically, for she considered herself an expert having made the marsh boat.

"Well," she said, "It's not a very handsome thing but it looks strong enough. If it has to go through rapids, maybe I should weave more willows into that deck, strengthen it." Taking out her knife Ai mee went off in search of a willow supply. Noah went back up stream to collect the burden baskets. Bopo began work on new arrows.

Ai mee returned with a willow supply. She carried four well made cedar paddles, which she'd found cached near the boat. In no time at all the three Washo youths had the boat repaired and all of their worldly possessions loaded aboard. They cast off on what was hoped to be a last leg of the journey home.

The stream, though not very wide, was swollen with a springtime flood of snow water. It surged along at an alarming speed. However, Noah who was seated in the stern found the craft quite controllable. No one spoke for some time as they rapidly moved down stream. Finally Noah broke the silence, saying. "I think it's time we had another Council of War. Those rapids can't be too far away. In fact, I'd swear I can begin to hear a roar of water downstream. I've got a question for the council to decide on. What do you think are the chances we'll reach the rapids, before Snake and the Evil Five? You know, get through without any trouble?"

Ai mee, who was seated in the middle, stopped paddling and held out a small brown clenched fist, with thumb extended downward. Bopo glancing around nodded his agreement and repeated the gesture.

"I agree with you two," said Noah. "I've a plan. Lets steer over there toward the shore."

Meanwhile two Paiute warriors, Snake and White Line On The Nose, streaked down the trail circling the huge patch of oak brush. Snake selected White Line to accompany him, even though he had a slight shoulder wound. He was fast of foot, an excellent archer and he had a special reason for hating Bopo, an aching shoulder. There was no doubt about it these two warriors were angry and ready to kill! The rest of the group Snake had dispatched to hunt for food.

The two arrived at a point where the trail ran along the very edge of a narrow gorge, directly above the roaring rapids. Crawling to the brink they peered down. The angry stream crashed through partially submerged rocks, swirling and twisting. It threw spray high into the air. This was the spot they were seeking. This was a perfect place for an ambush. While the gorge was not very long, their victims couldn't escape once they were in it. There'd be plenty of time to pick them off one by one.

Crouching, the man with the sneering face, torn ear and yellow war paint, methodically laid out three arrows in a neat line before him. Each fully recovered his breath, eyes studying the water upstream, waiting for the first sign of their victims. Like wolves waiting for the young of the deer, they were motionless.

The clumsy looking craft moved steadily down the stream. Three forms were crouched low on the deck. "Oh hooooo," laughed Snake, wickedly. "They think to outwit us by covering themselves and crouching low! The time has come, now I have them. The three Washo dogs. Now it's time to kill them. Like the vermin they are. Now it's time for Snake to strike! Now they shall taste my venom."

"Yes," hissed White Line, "we'll shoot 'em down like the rats they are. Shoot 'em while they can't escape. I want the one who's hiding in the front of the boat. He'll be the one who put an arrow in my shoulder. I want him to die slowly."

"I kept that girl against my wish," growled the sneering Snake, grinding his teeth. "Thinking I could make a Paiute out of her. But, it's no good. They never change. Those Washos. They're no good. Wipe 'em out. So, I'll take the girl. She's sure to be in the middle. Leave her to me. You take the dog in the front. Then we will both finish the one in the rear. He's the one who tore my ear off. I hope he screams when he dies. I want to hear the sound of his screams."

By now the rush boat was directly below them in the crashing water of the narrows. The two stealthy men knelt and drew their deadly bows. "Ready." whispered yellow face and the other responded. "Ready, shoot!"

Two arrows flashed and hissed their way downward. Above the roar of the swirling water a sharp cry of agony could be heard. Then another, long drawn out quavering moan that ended in a gurgling hiss. Two more arrows dropped down searching out the stern of the diving craft and a high gasping cry floated back.

Snake chuckled, "I've waited a long time for that. At last, revenge!"

The two watched as a rush boat, bristling with four arrows, exited the swift water of the narrows. It drifted into a broad quiet pool down stream. The boat should drift slowly into shore, where they could reach it easily. Something was wrong, the boat didn't act quite right. Slowly it began to revolve end for end. At first it drifted tantalizingly close to the shore. Snake hurried down the bank, preparing to enter the water. Then it did another complete turn, spinning out of reach and moving slowly toward the other shore. It disappearing out of sight around a bend in the stream. The boat would surely drift into the shore and become lodged in the brush along the bank.

The rush boat circled slowly and lodged against the overhanging grass. Two silent forms glided out of the willows growing along the bank, and crept forward to meet it. If one looked carefully, a single dark object about the size of a human hand could be seen, clinging to the stern. The object detached itself and a dripping head and shoulders emerged from beneath the deck of the boat. One of the figures on the bank spoke in a low voice.

"Good medicine. Well done!" said Ai mee with concern, "Are you hurt?"

"Not a bit." replied the dripping figure of Noah, rising from the water. "I'm just fine, except I swallowed so much water I darned near drowned. Snake was fooled completely. You should'a seen the expression on his face when the boat drifted by, just out of his reach. It's a good thing they were such accurate shots, none of their arrows came close to me. They all stuck in the victims. I shrieked like a mad man when the first arrow hit Bopo. Bopo you really died an agonizing death. Then when the arrow struck Ai mee, I tried to shriek in a high pitched voice like a girl. Got a whole mouth full of water. It sounded so awful, it struck me funny. I started laughing. Almost spoiled the whole thing. Then I sobered up real fast. When the two arrows struck me."

"They'll swim across the river, be here any minute." chuckled Bopo. "Lets take these corpses out of this terrible death boat and be on our way."

Three neat piles of drift wood, each covered with grass and evergreen boughs were quickly unloaded from the deck. From the top of the gorge those three neat piles had looked just like three crouching figures. The protruding arrows bore mute testimony to the evil intent of their assailants.

Holding up a large chunk of wood with a quivering arrow firmly embedded, Bopo said. "Wagh! Here's my death wound. Right in the throat. Whoever shot that arrow wanted me to die slowly."

" Look at mine," exclaimed Ai mee, "Who ever shot that knew it was me, searched me out in particular. Right in the middle of my back. I couldn't have made a sound with a wound like that. Much less do all that gurgling." She shuddered as she held up the piece of wood. A white tufted arrowhead was buried in it. "Ah !" she gasped. "Now I'm sure it was him. I haven't lived with Snake's arrows all that time and had to put the rattler venom on that white tuft of rabbit hair, without knowing one when I see it. I guess his anger finally overcame him and he decided not to settle for just blinding me. He decided to kill me with a poisoned arrow in the back."

"Well." said Noah holding up a piece of wood with two arrows embedded. "I seem to be more popular than either of you. Do you suppose it's maybe that Snake is still a little out of sorts because I chewed on his ear? What ever it is, he's a very evil man. One way or another he's going to come to a bad end. Maybe, something awful will happen to him. Like maybe the ONG will swoop down and eat him. Come to think of it, with all the snake venom that fellow has in him, it'd probably kill ole' ONG too. Wouldn't that be something, get rid of both of 'em at the same time. Good Idea ! They deserve each other."

"Enough of this wishful thinking," said Bopo, "Those fellows may swim faster than you think. Let's get in our little ole' boat and get out of here, just as fast as we can go. Before we get some arrows stuck in us for real."

Meanwhile, back upstream Snake and White Line recovered their arrows from three pieces of drift wood while muttering curses of hatred.

At the same time our three friends were moving down the stream at a dizzy speed. All three paddled frantically in an attempt to avoid capsizing, as they swirled around one boulder after another. By and large the Washo people are not boat people, and this was a rather frightening experience for them. As they swept along they gradually became more proficient at managing the bulky rush boat. It was quite functional, flexing and twisting with the powerful currents. They discovered Ai mee's efforts at paddling, in the middle of the boat, were not very effective. She soon retired, contenting herself with being a passenger.

While the spring air was not frigid, the three were constantly lashed by sprays of ice cold stream water, thrown into the air after crashing on the rocks. They were wet to the bone and shivering in dripping buckskins. Their craft raced madly down the steep twisting surface of the mountain stream at flood stage.

As the day wore on, they became somewhat accustomed to the cold. Gradually they sensed the ungainly craft was coming more and more under their control. Apprehension began to subside. Some how the roar of the crashing water became less frightening. The feeling of being crushed against the jagged protruding rocks no longer reduced them to panic. Suddenly, without anyone realizing what was happening, the wild ride became an exhilarating experience. The three Washos found themselves laughing and cheering with each frantic movement of the boat.

The excitement continued for some time, but came to a sudden sober halt when Ai mee shouted above the roar, "This is a lot of fun, but we'd better head for shore right now. This boat has had all it can take of the rough water. It'll start to fall apart, any minute now! Help! Head for shallow water!"

With that the willow deck beneath Ai mee buckled. It came apart, plunging the screaming girl into water up to her waist. Leaning forward Noah was able to grasp Ai mee's buckskin blouse by the collar, just before the girls head disappeared beneath the boat. With one hand Noah concentrated on keeping the girls nose above water. With the other hand clutching the paddle just above the blade, he attempted to turn the pitching boat toward shore. Sensing the problem, Bopo put his broad back and big arms into a mighty effort with the paddle, and soon had the boat flying toward safety.

Pulling the sodden craft onto the bank the three lay down in the warm grass to let their soaking clothing dry out. They needed time to take stock of the situation, glad to be alive.

Ai mee was the first to recover. Sitting up, the always sensible girl said, "Our poor old boat's just about done for. We've already come a great distance. We've been traveling at high speed. I think we moved a lot faster than a man can run. We just have to be quite a ways ahead of Snake. That is, unless he's found some way to get a boat, as well. If you fellows will start gathering willows, I can begin repairing the deck. Make it last a little longer. I'll need a lot of really slender willow ends. Need to retie the rushes in places."

Fingering the soggy boat, Noah said "Those rushes are in bad shape. The rocks crushed 'em and they're water logged. Won't last very much longer."

"Hopefully they'll last long enough to get us down stream."

Have to find some place where there's a marsh with a new supply of rushes. No rushes around here." added Bopo.

Before too long the warm sun dried our friends wet clothing. The sagging boat was repaired enough so they could continue their journey down the turbulent stream. The shadows were lengthening into dusk as they at last rounded a bend to behold a fairly large meadow of grass. At the far side of the meadow was a large river. It looked less turbulent and two or three times as wide as the stream the were on. Behind the meadow, on all sides stretched dense forests of Lodge Pole pine.

"This must be the river Ishi referred to as the River Of The Feather," said Noah. "According to him this river runs a very long ways, turning slowly toward Warm land, till it finally comes to the Great River. This river looks like it's not moving quite as fast as the one we're on. There doesn't seem to be very many rapids in it. It certainly is at high flood stage and moving mighty fast, even so."

"I'll be glad to get out of this turbulent stream, speaking for myself. That was an exciting ride we just had. But, I for one, will be just as happy to have a little less excitement for a while," agreed Bopo.

"What say we head for the far bank of River Of The Feather. Set up camp back in the trees, out of sight?"

"Sounds great to me!" exclaimed Ai mee enthusiastically. "Do you think we can have a camp fire tonight? I'll bet there are all sorts of good green vegetables and bulbs growing in that beautiful meadow. A hot meal will taste wonderful, after what we've had for the last few days."

"My mouth's watering already," said Bopo. "Come on Noah, lets get over to that far shore. Get camp set up. Then we can do a little hunting. I heard some Blue Grouse talking to each other back there a ways. A little grouse stew would go down mighty easy, right about now."

That night our three friend slept to musical sounds of the gurgling river. It was a warm and happy camp!

The morning sun sparkled on the water. Ai mee sat on a sand bar near the edge of the river. Bopo and Noah returned from the privacy of a morning bath and sat next to her. Noah stretched out at full length, enjoying the warmth of the sun. All eyes were alert, watching for any sign of an approaching enemy. A leisurely Bopo said, "Look at the fine black abrasive sand I found in the bottom of this pool. This stuff will be just the thing, for putting the final finish on my Atl-Atl."

Taking out the piece of yew wood which he'd carefully fashioned to exactly fit his throwing hand, Bopo began to polish it. He used a piece of suede leather dipped in the black sand. Bopo worked away, with head bowed over the missile launcher. Ai mee knelt down, gathering a hand full of his freshly washed long black hair. She began braiding it for him.

Bopo, she said, "You're really lucky to have some one play the part of your little sister. Braid your pig tail for you, I mean. What do you do for your little sister when she braids it?"

"Well," said Bopo over his shoulder, "Sometimes when elderberries are in season, I'll pick her a whole pouch full of berries. She really likes 'em. You know, stuff like that."

"All right Mr. Bopo," smiled Ai mee as she worked busily at weaving the long shiny black hair, "I'll expect a big batch of berries from the first ripe patch we come to."

Pausing to admire her work she mused, "You know, you must have just about the finest pig tail in the whole of the Washo nation. I'll bet all the pretty young girls smile at you when you go by, don't they?"

"Well, not enough of 'em, but some. I'll tell you what," said Bopo, with no sign of modesty, "There is one purty little ole' girl who always smiles very nicely at me. Her name's Magpie and she lives down by where Noah comes from. In Antelope

Valley. You know what? I've been thinking about maybe going down, to sort of call on her. When we get home, that is."

"Bopo, I'll let you in on a little secret." broke in Noah, "Two things you need to know. First, Magpie is very pretty all right. But she talks almost all of the time. Magpie's a good name for her. Second, she has a great big angry father. He doesn't like young sprouts hanging around his daughter. Ugh! He doesn't like 'em at all."

"Now that you mention it," grunted Bopo. "I noticed that man was sort of antagonistic. In fact he scares the moccasins off me."

Holding up the polished Atl-Atl for inspection, he proudly said, "How do you like this, for a fine looking missile launcher. All I have to do is attach a hook to the end. One made of deer horn. The missile body seats against it."

The weapon was indeed a beautiful piece of work. The leather scroll of the ancients described construction of the weapon precisely. It was supposed to be the exact length of the users forearm. Measured from tip of elbow to tip of finger. However, Bopo came from the school of thought, 'If a little is good, a lot is better.' So he made the Atl-Atl half again as long as required. The result was a weapon that would be tremendously powerful. It remained to be seen if Bopo's long muscular young arm was strong enough, to operate it properly.

Just as Noah's long sling greatly increased the speed with which he could throw a stone, the Atl-Atl increased the speed and power of the long missile it propelled. The ancients told glowing stories of the awesome power of the mighty weapon. They'd used it to slay the monstrous beasts of their time, like the Curly Mammoth. Bopo had only to make one of the great missiles. It would stand as tall as he stood. Then the fearsome weapon could at last be tested.

Without farther delay all three set to work to produce one on the required missiles. The end of one long willow pole was hollowed out to form a cup shape. This would anchor it to the deer horn hook on the missile launcher. A set of three gray goose feathers were lashed with sinew to the cupped end of the shaft, to provide stability in flight. Now the missile began to look like a monster arrow. Ai mee, the official arrow head chipper for the expedition, produced a beautiful ceremonial point as long as a mans hand. This was the missile head and was lashed to the feathered shaft. Now, the armed missile was complete.

"I'll bet you can't throw that huge arrow across the river. Much less hit any thing with it," joshed Noah.

Without a word, Bopo fitted the missile launcher comfortably into his hand and slipped the cupped end over the horn hook. He grasped the missile at mid length. With arm outstretched and the feathered tip of the missile almost touching the ground behind him, Bopo gave a grunt. With a mighty heave, he launched the missile. It arched high into the air, still gaining altitude as it crossed River of the Feather. It flashed across the meadow beyond, finally returning to earth, where it impaled the sod at the far edge of the meadow. It stood quivering, at the point where a swift stream emerged from the forest.

"Wow!" said Noah reverently, "This is a new age in fire power!"

The camp at the edge of the forest overlooking River of the Feather was a comfortable one. Our three friends rested there for a while, always keeping a guard on duty, to watch for any sign of Snake and the Evil Five. They feared Snake might pass camp without detecting them, and proceed down river. In that case, they'd always be in danger of another ambush, as they descended.

A Council of War was held and the three decided to tarry in the camp long enough to completely rebuild the weary rush boat. They must be able to depend on it to carry them over a great distance. They still had to travel for many, many suns through unknown waters. Finally, they'd embark and begin the last march toward Washo Land.

As there were plenty of willows near camp, but no rushes, it was decided the young warriors would follow a nearby rivulet to it's source, in hope of finding a meadow and a usable supply of the reeds. Ai mee was to remain hidden at camp and watch the river in case Snake should pass by.

Ai mee secured a supply of small limber willow shoots and concealed herself in the bushes on a sand bar. There, she began work on a new bowl shaped basket. It was coarsely woven and quite strong. When finished, it would be lined with smooth pebbles from the river and covered with a layer of sand. The basket, to be carried on the deck of the boat, would be used to house a small cooking fire. In that way there'd be no need to beach the boat in order to prepare food.

Humming as her busy fingers manipulated the flexible green shoots, Ai mee dreamed of their return to her families summer camp. The camp was a place of great beauty, located back against the forest in a small grass covered meadow at the very spot where the Truckee River was born. There, it flowing smoothly out of the glistening waters of Da ow aga.

The camp was surrounded by huge towering pines with trunks so large three warriors clasping hands were needed to reach around. A number of lodges were sprinkled at random along the edge of the forest, a wisp of smoke drifting from the vent hole of several. Some of the lodges were covered with deer hide tarps like the ancients used. Indicating a family that were primarily hunters who moved constantly, following game herds. Other lodges covered with thatched grass were permanent, housing families that would reside there through out the summer. Ai mee's family were the latter, spending as much time fishing as gathering.

Ai mee's mind drifted, as it did frequently of late. The womanhood ceremony was to be carried out shortly. With a sigh, she laid her basket work aside and brought out the time sticks. Carefully she counted the number of notches remaining in the bark. They represented the number of suns before the first new moon of the summer season. The day the traditional Womanhood Ceremony was to begin.

(The day of the first new moon began a special ceremony marking a young girl's passage to womanhood. At that time her parents held a puberty dance which was one of the most important Washo women's ceremonies. The dance stressed tasks important to the girls life. Each girl fasted strictly, for four days. During the fast, the girl was expected to keep busy with her chores. On the fourth night, she climbed to the top of a mountain, in Ai mees case Rubicon Peak. There she'd light four fires, they could be seen from a great distance. These fires were an invitation to everyone, to attend the dance and share in the ceremony. During the dance the girl carried an elderberry dance stick painted red. Later she would hide it atop Rubicon Peak. At sunrise the following morning the girl, facing east, was blessed, prayed for and given a ritual bath in the Truckee River by her grandmother. The basket used to contain the ritual water was later thrown to the crowd for some lucky person to catch. After that the girl was recognized as an adult and it was possible for her to marry. If some handsome (and responsible) young man should find her hidden red elderberry dance stick and return it to her door with a gift, it was considered as a proposal of marriage.)

Aimees day dreams were harshly interrupted by the raucous cry of a Nut Cracker. Quickly the girl turned to study the treetops, in the direction from which the cry came. She could detect no sign of the large gray, white and brown bird and turned back to check the direction from which they expected Snake to appear. There was no sign of the enemy and so she turned back toward the forest, standing up and revealing her hiding place for the first time.

Immediately, a great bristling pile of brush emerged from the forest and lumbered toward her. On closer inspection the brush pile grew feet and legs at the bottom. Bopo's grinning face could be detected among the shadows in the middle of the pile. A second lumbering stack of reeds hid all but Noah's Moccasins. A grumbling voice whispered, "Bopo, I can't see a thing. Are we about there?"

"Ho, ho, ho!" was Bopo's reply, " Materials for the new boat have arrived."

CHAPTER 19   Searching for Indian River

The comfortable forest camp was the scene of many days of activity. Preparations were underway for the forth coming trip down river. All three of our friends worked at rebuilding the rush boat, with Ai mee, the boat expert, generally in charge. The long tube of reeds was dismantled and all of the battered members discarded. The woven deck was reassembled with fresh willows, till it was more durable than the original. A new fire basket was lashed in place amid ship, next to Ai mee's seat.

It was necessary for the warriors to make two additional trips to a small marsh for more reeds. At last, the boat was pronounced complete and the three laboriously dragged it through the meadow grass to the water.

At every opportunity, Bopo retreated to the forest where he could practice throwing the Atl-Atl missile. With each practice session he became more proficient. He hoped the trip down river would turn up some sort of large game, allowing him to finally try out the new device. It was just too powerful to be used on the Mule Tail deer, which abounded around camp.

The hunters had been successful in bagging two deer, with bow and arrow. They built drying frames to stretch and cure hides, as well as smoke meat. With forked willow spears, they gathered quite a number of large trout, which they filleted and smoked. Concerned that Snake might appear, the smoking of meat was done at night over a small concealed fire.

The burden baskets had been so thoroughly shredded on the trip through the oak brush tunnels, Ai mee declared them no longer usable. She set about producing three new ones. This was a time consuming chore, but the baskets were an intimate part of Washo life. They were considered indispensable when one was traveling.

To let your men folks appear with a torn and shabby burden basket was not only unthinkable, it reflected very badly on the person taking care of them. If Ai mee's mother could see them at the moment, she would have some very pointed comments to make, about a girl who allowed her companions to travel with worn out baskets.

Ai mee consulted her time sticks and was apprehensive about investing so much precious time in the weaving work. In the end, her conscience and the mental image of a scolding mother overcame her concern. Besides, the fellows were busy building a supply of food for the forthcoming trip. It would be difficult to get them to depart until the smoking of meat was complete.

The first light of dawn stole across the dew drenched grass of the meadow. The River of the Feather gurgled quietly as light drifted down the swiftly moving water. An early morning bird chirped softly, flitting from twig to twig along the streams edge. A dark slate gray Water Ousel hopped out of a swiftly moving riffle to shake his feathers and preen for a moment, while uttering a series of short calls bzeet - bzeet - bzeet, before he plunged head first into a pool. The bird walked along the river bottom consuming his breakfast of insects. It seemed ages and ages before his head again appeared above the water's surface and he flitted away to sit atop a wet moss covered rock, enjoying the morning sunlight.

Noah watched the little creature with an all consuming interest. The Ouzel was among his favorite bird friends. He greatly admired its ability to hold its breath under water, for such a long period of time. A remarkable little fellow who was at home in the air, on the surface of the land or under water!

Noah's two friends joined him at the waters edge, throwing long black shadows across the swift river surface. Before boarding their strange craft, all three cast a fond glance over their shoulder. It'd been a comfortable camp, a happy camp. Now it was impossible to tell that the spot had ever been occupied by humans. Ai mee had done her usual job of leaving a tidy camp site.

Shoving the laden craft out into the current, Noah hopped atop the rear seat, deftly avoiding so much as a damp moccasin. The appearance of the craft was even more strange than usual, as Ai mee had carefully packed the new burden baskets and then upended them on the deck to form a back rest for each of the voyagers. Securely lashed in place they proved to be quite comfortable during the long journey.

As we have said, our Washo friends were not really boat people. The Truckee River was the largest river in Washo Land and they tended to rate all rivers by comparing them. River of the Feather was rather small, about the same size as the Truckee. Their voyage lasted for many suns. They were continually amazed to find the river ever growing. It got larger and larger, as stream after stream emptied into the water way. Never again would they be able to think of the beautiful Truckee River as big. It would always be beautiful to them, but from now on it would be regarded as hardly more than a stream.

Noah acted as helmsman, steering the craft with his stern paddle. The spring flood waters dashed swiftly along carrying the craft at what seemed like great speed. In the river's higher reaches they encountered places where it narrowed, passing through steep canyons. There were usually great boulders and turbulent white water in these spots. Then, excitement heightened, and Bopo added his strength at the forward paddle to help keep the craft from rotating in spinning whirlpools.

As before, after they became accustomed to the white water and were more adept at handling the clumsy craft, the venture became enjoyable. There was laughter and shouting as the monotony of the smooth flowing river was occasionally broken by a canyon and a stretch of roaring white water.

It wasn't long before our friends were peering anxiously ahead. They looked for the next place downstream, where the ever broadening river would be squeezed into a tortuous narrow canyon. Frequently, after emerging from the white water, Noah would find a convenient sand bar or beach where they could wring out dripping buckskins or stretch cramped legs and eat a hasty meal before resuming the mad flight down river.

In those areas where the river was more placid, moving swiftly without turbulence, our friends were treated to a continuously changing panorama of forests, mountains and meadows. The scene was punctuated here and there by great up thrusting rocky cliffs, over which drifted cottony white cirrus clouds.

The forests were ever changing displays, reflecting every new kind of tree. At each elevation a new variety would emerge. Descending from the high altitude Mountain of Clouds, they were greeted by the twisted, short Fox Tail Pine, the Limber Pine and the White Bark Pine. Next, they started to see Mountain Hemlock, Silver Pine and towering Red Fir.

This was the variety which the mighty ONG was prone to snap like a slender dry stick. As they moved downward Mountain Juniper, White Fir and Lodgepole Pine appeared, interspersed with frequent patches of Quaking Aspen clothed in bright yellow green springtime leaves. The maze of Oak Brush was replaced with Chaparral. Following was Golden Oak, Sugar Pine, Yellow Pine, Incense Cedar and Ceanothus.

Much later as their river journey drew to an end, they began to see the towering Black Oak tree, whose giant acorns were traditionally ground into a wonderful flour. The Washo people traded for the prized Black Oak acorns, which they valued only slightly less than Tah gum.

The River of the Feather grew more and more broad, turning it's course slowly southward. As our friends progressed down stream, the narrow canyons gave way to rolling mountains and the white water rapids became less and less frequent, until at last they were no more. The river had become a giant waterway! Our friends felt as though they were on a tiny leaf, floating on a huge surface without boundaries. It was so wide they were frightened when their cumbersome craft was in mid stream and the bank far away. Noah began to hold near to shore, remaining just out of bow shot. Just in case an enemy should appear. However, Snake seemed more and more remote as they traveled along.

They were alone on a vast river with little or no sign of human life around them. Infrequently, small villages appeared. The occupants looked to be fishermen. They merely stared as the strange boat drifted quietly passed. They offered neither help nor harm as the three Washos drifted by.

On several occasions they encountered small willow covered islands. As they were uninhabited,   the travelers would tarry for a treasured night's sleep on firm ground.

Moving down stream they saw a wide variety of game animals, including deer and antelope, as well as an occasional black bear. Bopo was itching to try out his Atl-Atl on live game. He was all in favor of immediately giving chase, each time they saw one of the lumbering black creatures. However, Noah restrained him with promises he could hunt bear as soon as the water portion of the journey was complete.

They did see large herds of strutting black turkeys. Noah succumbed to a quick bow hunt, which resulted in a much appreciated gobbler feast.

Except for an occasional night spent on a small island in mid stream, it was the usual practice to spend the night adrift. With one person keeping watch, the other two slept as best they could on the crowded deck. It was this night drifting which almost brought disaster to the expedition. As they moved down stream, they encountered more and more floating debris. Uprooted trees were tossed into the river by floods and violent winds. It was just such a fallen tree, with great spreading roots, that almost caused Noah's death by drowning.

The night was pitch black! Noah appointed himself to take the first watch while the other two slept. At length, Noah too began to nod. The strong current shifted the light craft back and forth as a tired Noah's head slumped to his chest. He started to snore softly. His two companions had long since curled up and drifted off into a deep slumber. The swift water twisted and turned as the current slowly rotated the reed craft around and around. It moved imperceptibly closer to a dark shore overgrown with willows.

The river gurgled ominously, as the deep black water nudged the stern of the boat against a soft mud bank. The youths stirred in their sleep but didn't awake, as the boat paused for a moment. The prow caught in an overhanging cluster of willows. Out of the blackness a huge floating tree materialized, its massive roots projected up out of the water. A long slimy tendril of black root entangled the side of the rush boat. It became a part of the floating juggernaut, rotating out into the black hissing water.

At length the swift current forced the boat deck beneath a massive overhanging root. With a violent jerk, the slumped figure of Noah was thrown into the freezing water.

A spluttering Noah finally clawed his way to the surface. Gasping for breath he suddenly became aware of the rapidly disappearing stern of the boat. Noah was an excellent swimmer, but no matter how he tried, he just couldn't seem to close the gap between himself and the distant boat. It was Ai mee who at last awoke. She heard a feeble squawk from a bobbing figure in the water. Arousing Bopo, the two grasped paddles and started to frantically move the boat upstream, against a strong current. After an agonizingly long time, the gap began to close. At last a wheezing Noah was within reach. In what was one of his lesser moments of dignity, Noah was hoisted aboard by a grunting Ai mee, who had taken a firm hold on the seat of his breech clout. It was a short time later when our three friends decided to spend the rest of the night sleeping on shore!

With the dawn the three awoke to find Noah no worse for his unexpected midnight dunking. They discovered themselves in a pleasant clearing, surrounded by dense forest on three sides and broad river on the other. The grass underfoot was a warm golden-brown, not yet ready to assume it's mantle of spring time green. The meadow swept upward in a long steep slope, ending in a rounded hilltop against the forest some distance away. A dense cover of berry brambles crowned the top of the hill. The morning sun was warm. A Meadow Lark shrilled his song nearby.

With a sly look Bopo said. "It's such a beautiful morning, why don't we stay a while. Have a fire and some warm food for breakfast. I'll get some wood. Noah, why don't you light a fire for us?"

"Well" said Noah as Ai mee and Bopo looked on expectantly. "Maybe it would be a better idea if Ai mee made the fire. I'll help you gather wood. You see, my fire pouch doesn't seem to be working so well this morning. In fact, it seems to be just a little damp. Probably because we had a heavy dew this morning. That happens sometimes, you know!"

"Yeah!" said Bopo squinting upward into the sky, "I guess that could happen all right. That morning dew gets pretty bad at times. You never know when it's gonna cause a problem. Of course, if some darn fool were to fall asleep, way out in the middle of a big ole' river. They might end up falling in. That could cause a bit of moisture in the ole, fire pouch too, wouldn't you say?"

"Aw come on Bopo!" said an embarrassed Noah, "So I drifted off to asleep for a minute and fell off that darn boat. That could happen to anybody, you know!"

"Look you two," said Ai mee in exasperation, "You stop it! Go get some firewood. I'll cook us a breakfast that'll make your mouth water. Unless I miss my guess, there should still be some dried berries left in those brambles up on top of that hill. Left over from last year. If you soak dry berries for a while they have a very nice flavor in a venison stew."

"I'm drooling!" grinned Bopo.

"I'll just walk up to the top of the hill, see if I can't find a basket full of nice dry black berries. I'll be back in a little while. You two go find some wood and start a fire. Bopo you quite picking on Noah. He feels badly enough as it is. Of course," she snickered, "He did look kind'a silly when I pulled him out'a the water by the seat of his breach clout."

" Well some people are really cruel !" said a contrite Bopo, "I wasn't even going to mention the part about how silly he looked, coming out of the water."

"Come on Ai mee," said Noah, picking up his bow and quiver of arrows. "I'll go berry hunting with you. I'm quite particular about the company I keep. I can see where a certain person is going to be unbearable all day long."

Bopo began to collect pieces of dry wood all the while snickering to himself. His two companions set off to climb the steep hill in search of dry berries. After assembling a large pile of fuel Bopo started a small fire. He sat cross legged with back to the hill and started work on a new missile for the Atl-Atl.

Each time he test fired the new weapon he learned a little more about it's accuracy. Systematically, he'd gradually shortened the missile body. At the same time he added a small stone weight near the rear of the willow pole. With a grunt of satisfaction he finally held up the latest version of the awesome projectile.

Meanwhile, at the edge of the forest atop the hill, an anxious coyote paced up and down. He studied a pair of berry hunters climbing the hill below him. The coyote was old. It was obvious his feet were hurting something fierce. He limped with a stiff legged gait, walking with his back slightly humped. His coat was mottled with long tatters of winter hair in some places and patches of new spring fur in others. One ear was slightly frayed from an unfortunate encounter with an obstinate badger. His tail was caked with little chunks of river mud, indicating he had recently resorted to the distasteful art of swimming. Every thing considered, he was about the most disreputable looking coyote one could imagine.

At the moment his attention was equally divided between the two Washo youths climbing the hill and something in the middle of the berry patch. Whatever it was in the berry patch, it was causing the brambles to shake violently.

"Lots of times," Ai mee said seriously, "the bears pick all the berries from the top of the bush. They forget about the ones lower down, toward the bottom. Those berries dry out through the winter, but they don't drop off the vine. They're still just as sweet as ever. Even though they've turned brown. If you soak 'em for a while, they taste wonderful!"

As they reached the lower edge of a huge patch of brambles, Ai mee handed her companion one of the little cooking baskets. They got down on hands and knees in search of   dried fruit. Noah proceeded to hunt along the edge of a patch. Ai mee found a corridor leading to the interior of a dense bramble. She moved away on hands and knees. Each time she discovered another heavy cluster of dried fruit she murmured with delight, combing plump brown berries into the waiting basket. Gradually she worked her way out of sight, into the center of the patch.

At the upper edge of the patch, the scruffy looking old coyote paced up and down nervously. He stretched his neck in an effort to see just what it was that shook bushes in the middle of the patch. Mr. Coyote thought he knew what was in there, shaking those bushes so violently. If he was right, he didn't like the idea at all.

Now there was one person who knew even more than Ai mee, about how delicious a feast of dried black berries could be, that was Mr. Bear. If any one was familiar with berries, berries of any kind, berries that were ripe, berries that were dried, berries on the top of the bush or berries on the bottom of the bush, it was Mr. Bear. After all, this particular patch was his very own personal, private place. He'd owned it for many years. He couldn't count on the long shiny black claws of his huge hairy paws, just how many smart aleck young black bears he'd chased out of this particular patch, over the years. But, it was a whole bunch! Of all the fine berry patches in his kingdom, this one was the very best. Had the richest, best flavored berries of all. He wasn't about to share one single berry with anyone.

Now this old black bear was king of the mountain. He was very old and very big. In fact, he was immense. When it came to defending his berry patch, he was very mean. When he was angry he stood up on his huge hind legs and roared. All of the trees shook! All the animals on the mountain shuddered in fear. He was a horrible bear! Right now he was angry, very angry! He could smell something foreign. His eyes weren't so good any more. He couldn't see anything foreign, but he could definitely smell something right here in his personal berry patch. He didn't like it a bit!

Mr. Bear stood on his hind legs, raising to a monstrous height. His huge black head turned slowly from side to side. His shiny black nose twitched. His little pig eyes searched the bushes. Seeking the slightest sign of an intruder. At the first sign of movement he was ready to charge. Ready to tear the intruder to shreds.

Meanwhile, Bopo sat at the bottom of the slope with back turned and head bowed over his work. Completely absorbed, he was oblivious to the world around him. Noah, hidden by bushes, sat with his thumb in his mouth. He was attempting to pull a berry thorn out with his teeth. Ai mee, on hands and knees was deftly placing the last few berries in a full basket, completely unaware she was kneeling in the very shadow of a huge, angry, black bear.

"Well now, isn't this a mess," said the scruffy old coyote, sitting down and shaking his head in disgust. "Just look at them. There's not a shred of common sense in the whole outfit. There isn't one of them who has the slightest idea there's a bear around. Much less a great big mean one, who's about to eat all three of 'em. Well, it's a good thing old Mr. Coyote's on duty. That's all I can say!"

With that he pointed his long nose toward the heavens and gave forth his most mournful and piercing howl.

"Aowwwwoooooooooooooooooooooooo!   Aow ow oooooooooooooooooooooo!"

Pandemonium broke loose! Noah stood up. Immediately assessing the danger, he grabbed his bow and fitted an arrow. He hissed at Ai mee,

"Stay still!"

His brave intention was to drive an arrow deep into the bears chest and then attack with his knife. However, he knew the effort against such a huge monster would have been futile. Hearing Noah's hissed command, Ai mee stood up, only to discover her peril. Immediately she froze where she stood. All she could do was cover her mouth in horror with a small brown hand,

"Ohhh nooooo!"

The mournful howl of a coyote brought Bopo to his feet instantly. Acting instinctively, he grasped Atl-Atl with one hand while fitting the new missile with the other. Reaching far back, so that the mighty missile rested against the ground, Bopo arched his big chest. He emitted a mighty roar that reverberated across the hill side.

"Rrrrooooaaarrrrahh !"

Discovering his enemy for the first time, the immense black bear snarled. He stood erect with great claw tipped fore legs raised high. He answered the challenge with a roar of his own, so fearsome the very trees shook.

"RRRRRRROOARRRRRRRR!"

Bopo's muscular arm flexed like a whip. The missile flashed through the air, across a great distance. The bear dropped from sight. Brush shook and quivered. The air was torn with horrible snarling sounds. The brambles emitted grunts, interspersed with guttural growls and snapping sounds. Then abruptly there was silence, total silence.

The two fellows carefully picked their way through the thorny bushes. With knives drawn, they were ready to run at the first hint of attack. The mighty beast lay flat on his back. His forelegs spread wide, the Atl-Atl missile protruded from the exact center of his great chest.

It was some time before the three youths could calm down and speak normally about what had happened. None of them realized that the mournful howl of a coyote triggered the whole event. They did understand, however, this was a happening of considerable importance.

The Washo, by and large, were sensible people who lived a good life in comfortable harmony with the world around them. They harvested game animals for a portion of their food supply. However, no Washo warrior in his right mind ever looked upon a huge adult male black bear as a source of either food or clothing. They looked upon him with great respect, as something that was very dangerous. Something to be avoided at all costs.

There were a select few who had actually slain a bear, to demonstrate bravery or prowess as a hunter. Bopo would now become a member of that exclusive group. He'd be widely known within his tribe. The bear hide, when suitably tanned, would become a symbol of his prowess.

"Well, it's going to be a big job, Bopo, but this is one trophy you can be really proud of," said Noah, "If your recovered from all the excitement we better get started on skinning this big fella. It's gonna take a lot of time to prepare and tan a beautiful big pelt like this. We're running out of time pretty fast."

Bopo was silently asking the spirits to find a special mountain with a fine berry patch somewhere in the happy hunting ground, for this magnificent animal. Shaking his head, he said "That'll be a monster of a pelt when it's all cured. I'm gonna have all I can do, just to carry it back home. I'm sorry Ai mee, about delaying us while we get the tanning done. Its gonna take several days to do the job. But, it'd be sinful not to do justice to such a beautiful animal. Guess we better get started with the skinning. Sure hope you'll help us with tanning, Ai mee. I've never done anything as big as this before."

"Of course I'll help," said Ai mee, "this is a big event in your life Bopo, maybe the biggest. You need to have a beautifully tanned hide. Just to show everybody how brave you were. Besides that, we're really proud of you, aren't we Noah?"

"Wagh, yes!" said Noah seriously, "My little ole' cousin here, has turned out to be a great big hero of a hunter. I'd be jealous of him if I weren't so busy being proud."

"There wasn't anything brave about it," said Bopo with a frank grin, "I was so far away, and you two were up so close to that angry fella, I figured he was going to eat you two first, if I missed. Then if he started after me, all I'd have to do was jump in the river. Swim down stream. I had that all figured out. While I was settin' up to throw."

They were unable to move the huge beast from the thorns of the berry patch. So, they set to skinning the animal, where it lay. With flint knives, it was a tremendous job. They were one big mass of gore and thorn scratches by the time the pelt was removed from the carcass. The wet pelt was very heavy. It took both of them to drag it down the grassy slope to the river. They peeled off all clothing. Dragging the pelt behind them, they entered the cold water. There, they scrubbed themselves and the hide thoroughly, with hands full of coarse sand.

By the time they emerged, Ai mee had located four long poles of drift wood and was lashing a frame together. Stretching the moist hide out flat over the frame, the three fell to a long and laborious task of scraping away all of the fatty tissue. Every shred had to be removed from inside the hide, with flint scrapers.

The lengthy process of tanning had begun. It would take several days before curing was far enough along to resume their voyage. Later, evenings would be devoted to softening the heavy hide.

Shortly after resuming their journey, they came to a point where the now broad River of the Feather rounded a gradual bend and flowed into that vast body of water known as Great River. The surrounding mountains had flattened to rolling hills and now entered an area of vast level plain. Through it flowed a river much wider than anything seen before. Bopo had glimpsed this great water as a youngster of eight summers. Noah and Ai mee, who had not seen it, were speechless with the spectacle.

"Look at the far bank." said an incredulous Ai mee, pointing into the distance. "It's so far away, no one could ever swim to the other side. I just can't believe there's so much water in one river."

The flat plain they were entering stretched into the west. At a great distance a low laying range of hazy blue hills blended with the sky. Clumps of bright green Cottonwood Trees were sprinkled at random across the broad expanse of rolling grass. Grazing herds of antelope and deer were every where. The sun shown warm on this rich land. Puffy white cirrus clouds drifted lazily across an intense blue sky.

Noahs first thought was, "This land's too open. Too exposed. I wouldn't want'a go out there. Too far from any cover. Nothing except for a few Cottonwoods. There's no place to hide from ONG!"
 Then Noah realized his error.. There is no monster ONG here. This great valley is very far from Washo Land and ONG doesn't venture abroad.

"We're safe here! Well, safe except for Snake. He could be right behind us on the river. That monster will go anywhere to trap us."

Our friends hugged the left bank as they entered Great River. With the added weight of the moist bear hide, the rush boat rode much lower in the water. It was more difficult to handle. Both boys manned paddles now as the current was still quite swift. Stately Cottonwood trees lined the bank. As they moved quickly along, numerous streams emptied into the giant body of water. They watched the bank carefully. Sooner or later Indian River, for which they were searching, would join Great River. At that point the voyage by water would come to an end and they'd embark, abandoning the faithful rush boat.

The three knew only that they were searching for the first "big" river along their route. Ishi's description had failed to specify how great a distance they must cover, before Indian River emptied into Great River. Ai mee and Noah chattered eagerly, anticipating the last overland leg of the journey home. Bopo, however was maintaining a glum silence, as he had for several days.

The morning after the bear was slain, Bopo awoke and rubbed the sleep from his eyes with a grimace. "What an awful dream I had last night," he said, "The dream kept coming back all night long and I woke up over and over again in a cold sweat. I feel terrible now. I'm sure something really bad is going to happen. I just know it! I'm really feeling sick," he said, shaking his head and rubbing his stomach.

"Tell us about your dream," said Ai mee sympathetically.

"Well," groaned the youth,   "it all started when the bear chased me up a big tree. I got out on the end of a skinny little limb, where the bear couldn't follow. So, he started roaring and snarling. He grabbed the limb in his front paws, shook it so hard I fell out of the tree. Then my totem, the Chickaree, was up in the tree screeching away. The bear grabbed him in one great big paw and roared and drooled. He popped the Chickaree in his mouth and ground him up with those big yellow fangs. Swallowed him down! I could still hear my poor ole' totem screaming down inside the bear's stomach. Then I went and jumped in the river to get away. But, the bear came right after me. Just as he grabbed me in his claws, I woke up. What an awful nightmare."

"Your right," said Ai mee, "that was a frightening dream, but it's all over now and you can forget it. Just try to think about something else. Think about   tomorrow. Maybe we'll find Indian River and there'll be the big oak tree. We can climb up to the top. From there we can see the mountains of Washo Land. Think about that!"

"I just can't do it." moaned Bopo. "All I can think of, is how awful that poor Chickaree sounded down inside the bears stomach. Now I don't have any totem. Every one knows! That's the worst medicine a person can have. Now I'm gonna have some sort of awful bad luck. Just you wait and see."

With that Bopo lapsed into a glum silence. Try as they would neither Noah or Ai mee could raise the poor fellow's spirits. For days he maintained an unhappy silence, convinced some terrible calamity was about to befall him.

After entering Great River our friends hadn't long to wait before they arrived at their destination. Drifting around a gentle bend in the broad placid river, an oak covered headland appeared. Beyond, the rapid waters of a " big" river flowed. It created a swirling pattern on the dark surface of the water.

"Hooray!" shouted Noah, "we've found Indian River at last. Let's head for that sand bar on the far side and pull the boat out there."

The spot was just as it had been described many days before, by a wrinkled warrior named Ishi, as they sat clustered around a single ray of sunlight in a gloomy cave, within a dense jungle of Oak Brush. The sand bar led to a beautiful meadow surrounded by Black Oaks. The meadow swept into a steep grass covered hill. At the very top of the hill stood a single spreading oak, with huge twisted branches soaring upward into the sky.

CHAPTER 20   The Mountains of Home

Before a flickering camp fire high in the mountains, a robed figure sat slumped deep in thought. It was Snake, a leaner Snake clad in tattered trail-worn buckskins. His bearskin robe was no longer a symbol of status. Most of the black hair was worn away, leaving only a few isolated tufts down the front. Snake's hair was coarse and unkempt, as was his yellow war paint. It was mostly rubbed away. His face bore the same ugly sneer and the injured ear still hung in shreds. The odor surrounding him was as bad as ever, tainted with the smell of a rattle snake. Two wriggling buckskin bags slung at his waist attested to the presence of his pets. At the moment, he was warming himself before the fire, while awaiting the return of his trusted deputy White Line.

Thoughtfully, Snake chewed on a venison rib bone, which he tossed away into the darkness at the sight of two approaching figures. White Line emerged into the light followed by a shabby near naked figure of an old man. The man was greatly wrinkled, wearing only a breech clout and tattered moccasins. He was painfully thin with long sparse white hair and stooped shoulders.

"This is one of the Taneu. He lives in a small village down by the stream," growled White Line. "While he doesn't speak the Paiute language, he can understand my sign language fairly well, so I'll act as interpreter."

"Tell the old man to sit by the fire and give him some of our food," ordered Snake gruffly. The old man sat, but continued to shiver despite the warmth of the flames.

"He's still afraid of us." said White Line. Someone approached out of the darkness and handed the old man several of the fat venison ribs, which he fell to chewing ravenously. He soon stopped shivering so violently.

Clearing his throat Snake rasped, "Old man, have you seen three young travelers, one girl and two fellows? They're Washo dogs and they're running from me. I don't mean them any harm," he said with a leer. "Just want to talk to 'em for a little while. The girl's my slave. Belongs to me and was stolen by the two dogs. They may be down around the water somewhere. Have you seen them?"

The old man shook his head without looking up and continued to chew on the rib.

"Look at me," thundered Snake. "Have you seen the three Washos?" The old man understood without any translation and was so frightened he almost dropped the venison rib. Spreading his hands palms upward, he shook his head and made the sign for "No see. no see!"

"Have you heard anything, anything at all, about three travelers. Maybe three travelers down around the river. What have you heard old man. Speak!" Again the trembling old man spread his hands and shook his head in denial.

"No see, no hear, no three people." quavered the wrinkled oldster. Then a puzzled look crossed his face. Holding up a finger he said, "I hear a story, it is a tale that just drift by on the wind. Not tell by anyone. Just a rumor. Just drift by, whispered on the wind. A voice say to me, just a voice on the wind, no body, just voice. It say, there is a band. A group, many. They not people. They not Washos. I know Washos. Voice say these are spirits. Spirit people from very far away. Maybe they are from the ancients. The ancient people who come from far away. These spirits are many and they have great powers. They travel far, far across the land. The people are very frightened, they are afraid of the spirits who drift across the land. Spirits with much magic. Great powers. Awful weapons. They can destroy any thing, any one. Most powerful!"

"Tell me old man," hissed Snake. "Are there three of these powerful spirits?" He held up three fingers and his eyes were filled with a murderous light.

Again the trembling old fellow shook his head in negation. "Voice say many, many, spirits. Enough to destroy whole villages. Terrible weapons, great spirit powers, much magic!"

"Tell me about the magic," growled Snake.

Shaking his head, the old man went on. "Many spirits. Much magic. They bring down the evil spirits of the mountains. Very bad. They can call down whole mountains upon their enemies. Make the rocks and the snow and trees and forests, slide down upon their enemies. All they need do is call to the mountain spirit and the great mountain crashes down. Terrible power! They are magic people who come up out of the ground. They live in the Cave of the Ancients and perform evil magic. They have such great powers they command the mighty ONG! Even the ONG fears them and does their bidding. When they wish a person gone, they have but to point and the ONG shakes with fright and leaps to do their bidding. The person is carried off and eaten. They must be spirits of the ancients, their magic is so strong. The whole band of spirits has awful weapons. Many weapons of great power. Power so great they can slay the mighty bear just like that." The old man snapped his fingers for emphasis.

"And, the rumor which drifts by on the wind must be true. The voice says it is easy to recognize each one of these spirits. Because they all wear great black fur robes. The fur of the great Black Bear!"

Now, at the same time Snake was grilling the Taneu high in the mountains, three unsuspecting Washo youths were holding a Council of War down in the flat lands, near the spot where Indian River empties into Great River. They were completely unaware the story of their flight had drifted across the winds and was being whispered around the camp fires throughout the land. They would have been shocked had they known how much the story of their actions had been distorted and magnified.

The faithful rush boat was pulled ashore and left in plain sight along with the paddles, for use by the next traveler. After climbing the great oak and charting their course to the head waters of Indian River, there was some daylight left. The travelers moved a ways up-stream, before selecting a camp site for the night. As always, they chose a site carefully hidden from view and went to considerable trouble to mask the existence of their small fire.

After a spare evening meal, a Council of War was held at Noah's suggestion. "We need to lay plans for the last leg of the trip back to Washo Land."

There had been no sign of Snake and the Evil Five since the encounter in the white water rapids. With each passing sun, hope had risen. Hope that the murderous group had given up the chase, returned to their home village. While our friends still exercised every precaution, the flicker of hope continued to grow.

"Life without fear of Snake! What a relief that would be," chortled an exuberant Ai mee.

Only Bopo remained morose. He still couldn't throw off the effect of a bad dream, which ended with the loss of his totem. After all the loss of one's totem was as serious as the loss of one's soul. Depressed though he was, Bopo hadn't forgotten one of his father's basic rules of survival, when traveling.

"My father always says, wherever you go, you should have a little bit of trading goods tucked away in the bottom of your basket, just in case," said Bopo.

"We're gonna be walking through Taneu country for some time. They're sort of funny people. If you come to trade, you're usually allowed to pass without any trouble. But if your just passing through their lands and they don't benefit in any way, they're just as like as not to stick an arrow or two in you. Their chief, Manu, is a great big fat old guy, with a bad disposition. My father trades with him a lot. He says it's always ticklish. The old guy always acts like he has a stomach ache. You're never really sure he isn't going to turn some of his worst thugs on you."

"Well," said Noah, "I don't want'a go out of my way to have trouble with anybody. On the other hand, I've been pushed just about all I plan to be pushed. Gettin' tired of bein' pushed. What do you suggest we do Bopo? I'm not about to walk all the way around Manu's land. Not worth it, just to avoid his bad disposition."

"I agree. We don't have time anyway. In case Ai mees let you forget, she has a very important date back home, not too many suns from now."

With a rueful grin, Bopo said "No one can ever accuse Ai mee of letting them forget about the first new moon of summer, in fact I see she just happens to have her time sticks with her now."

"You bet I have." smiled Ai mee sweetly. "Got 'em right here!" Turning to Noah she asked, "If we walk straight through Taneu Land, how long do you figure it'll take to get home?"

Holding up the fingers of both hands, Noah said seriously, "At the very least if every thing goes well, it'll take this many suns to walk to Emerald Bay and two more suns fast walk to get to your camp at the head of the Truckee."

"If we can add two more days to that," said Bopo, "I've got a solution. Spend one day in a marsh that's close by. We'll collect some salt. Then spend one more day at Manu's camp, trading. That should get us by Manu. Hopefully everybody'll be friends. How about that? One other thing, we'll get three burden baskets full of Black Oak acorns. That's what Manu'll have to trade. That'll convince my father his sons' a trader!"

And so the council of war reached agreement and our friends prepared to depart for the salt marsh at sunrise the next morning.

Salt was easy to collect at the nearby marsh and our friends filled three heavy bags. The salt was not the same high quality as that obtained in Washo Land, at Antelope alley. That salt was in the form of glistening white crystals with a sharp clean flavor. The salt from the low land marshes was golden in color, in lump form and had a less desirable flavor. Now, the marsh salt was located within a few days walk of Manu's land. His people, the Tan eu, were somewhat lazy and preferred trading for salt to carrying it uphill for themselves.

Dusk found our friends trudging up the trail toward Manu's camp. Their burden baskets were heavily loaded with golden salt.

Manu's camp was located high in the rolling foothills along the shores of the swift Indian River. It was a large village with many grass thatched lodges. Each hut seemed to have a smoking fire and an assortment of frames for curing fish. White fish and trout was the principal food. Beneath the heavy pall of smoke and dust were large groups of shouting children at play, accompanied by many barking dogs. Here and there were small groups of men, engaged in conversation, some standing while others sprawled idly on the ground. Women scurried back and forth, busy with daily tasks.

On a small knoll overlooking the river stood a large oak tree. Beneath it was a lone thatched lodge, somewhat larger than the others. This was the abode of Manu, chief of the village.

Noah, leader of the Washo procession of three, threaded his way through the village toward the lone hut on a hill. All three had donned their clean, freshly washed dress buckskins. They were carefully groomed. Bopo, bringing up the rear, was impressive in his new black bearskin robe. He bore the Atl-Atl in one hand and the long dangerous missile in the other. He was perspiring freely as the day was warm and the robe was heavy. The little procession was followed by a multitude of shouting, screaming, laughing children, which they ignored with studied disdain.

Marching up the slope they arrived before the lone lodge in a thick cloud of dust. Stepping forward, Bopo planted the base of his missile firmly on the ground and shouted at the closed lodge, in a deep booming voice. "Ho the lodge. Ho mighty Manu! Come forth and speak with your friends, traders of the Washo people. We have much salt to trade with you. Much salt of wonderful quality. Come forth!"

The hub bub died, and there was silence throughout the village. Patiently everyone waited, and waited, and waited. At last Bopo cleared his throat loudly and was about to address the lodge again. Abruptly, a deer hide covering the small entrance twitched and was thrust aside. There on hands and knees was a large, very fat fellow. His belly was so monstrous it brushed the ground as he crawled from the doorway. With difficulty he gained his feet. He stood erect and wiped his hands down the front of a greasy vest hanging from his bulging shoulders. Smoothing it carefully, he opened his mouth. He emitting a thundering belch. He rubbed his stomach, grunting in pain.

"We hope the mighty Manu is in good health," said Bopo politely. He went on to introduce Noah as the leader of their expedition. He explained they were on an extended trip, describing their travels at some length. Manu glowered, uttering not a sound. Bopo went on to explain their desire to trade salt for acorns. He stressed the fact they'd return immediately to Washo Land.

"What is the weapon you carry?" grunted Manu with another belch. "I would have that weapon.   That's the only thing for which I will trade."

"That weapon is not for trade," said Bopo in what he hoped was a stern voice. "That's the mighty Atl-Atl , weapon of the ancient Washo people. It has great power and is worth more than all of Manu's acorns. It is not for trade! Watch what I do, Manu. I will show you the mighty power of the Atl-Atl. Manu will see, he would be wise not to offend us. Manu will see, he would be wise to trade with us for salt. Watch!"

With that Bopo turned and pointed to an oak tree on another knoll at least three arrow flights away. He hissed behind his hand to Noah "You and Ai mee unload the bags of salt from all three burden baskets and place them before Manu's door. Then walk slowly over to that tree. Stay out of sight behind the tree. I'll throw the missile. If I'm lucky it'll land right next to where you are. When it lands you grab the missile, so one of Manu's thugs can't get it. Don't move from there, unless it looks like Manu's going to jump me. I case he does, you and Ai mee run like crazy. I'll meet you up the trail somewhere. And Noah, start talking to that totem of yours. Talk to him for both of us. Cause I don't have a totem any more. Good luck!"

When the heavy bags of salt were placed before the entrance of Manu's lodge, Noah and Ai mee slowly walked, with great dignity, to the distant oak and disappeared behind it. Bopo went through quite a ceremony of fitting missile to Atl-Atl and preparing to throw it, all for Manus benefit. He then uttered several mysterious magic incantations, which he had just invented for the occasion. He discharged the missile with a mighty grunt. Unerringly, it flashed through the air and landed within a moccasin length of Noah's foot, which was peeping out from behind the oak tree. There was a gasp from the crowd of onlookers. Bopo, wrapped in the huge black bear skin, with arms folded and back stiff, marched slowly across the meadow and up the slope to where Ai mee and Noah waited.

Noah was grim-faced and he was angry. "You did good Bopo, darned good. But, I'm mad! I don't like being pushed around by that big slob Manu. I don't care if he has got a bunch of thugs. You cover me with that missile of yours. I'm going down there. I'll either get our salt back or I'm gonna get his Black Oak acorns. I don't care which. But I'm gonna get one or the other. He can't push us around anymore."

Without the slightest change of expression, Bopo winked at Ai mee and said, "Ai mee, this fellow just isn't ever going to make a trader. There's just no hope." Turning to Noah he said,

"Cool off Skinny, we won. There's nothing to be mad about. Look!" and he pointed his finger at Manu's lodge. The lodge and the surrounding area was deserted. The entrance to the lodge was closed. The heavy bags of salt had disappeared.

"See, the trades all finished. Manu accepted our offer," grinned Bopo.

"Finished my foot!" exclaimed an angry Noah. "Where's our acorns. How about some acorns?"

"That's simple," said Bopo. "Now we can go out and pick up as many nice fat Black Oak acorns as we can carry. That's Manu's part of the deal. He won't let anyone molest us. Not while we go out and harvest acorns from his land. There's just one thing, we have to harvest 'em at night. That's tradition. Gotta be harvested by moonlight. You see, the way the night business got started was, we don't always trade stuff for acorns. Manu is such a despicable guy, we some times just come down and harvest his acorns without giving him anything in return. It's safer to do it at night cause his people are so lazy.

They don't guard their land at night. Just lay in their lodges and snore. Lazy people!"

" Bopo, maybe your right," said a puzzled Noah. "I'm not sure I'd ever make much of a trader. You guys do things in strange ways."

"Yeah, they do things in strange ways all right. They steal acorns from the Taneu among other things," chortled Ai mee. "Bopo just admitted it! Calls it tradition, Humph!"

Noah chuckled to himself as he moved up the trail at a rapid pace, with burden basket heavily loaded. That basket contained a great many prime Black Oak acorns, which when leached and ground would become a rich flour. Wonderful food! Loaded to the brim, the baskets weight was at least half as much as Noah's body weigh.

In the Washo culture the Black Oak acorn was a tangible form of wealth. Noah and his friends were now wealthy people, much to be admired by their fellow tribesmen. In his minds eye, Noah could picture the scene as they returned home after such a long journey, loaded with wealth. What a happy scene that would be! It all turned out just as Bopo had predicted. Collecting acorns by moonlight turned out to be fun! They hadn't seen a soul as they filled their baskets. Nor was there any evidence of Manu's people as they moved up the trail next morning.

"Bopo did a great job on the whole encounter with Manu," Noah reflected. "Too bad he was feeling so low all the while. Too bad about losing his totem like that. It's a terrible thing to happen to a fellow. Have the bear eat your totem right there in front of you. Hear the poor ole totem screaming down in the bear's belly. That was really bad. No wonder poor ole' Bopo was feeling so low."

Noah and Ai mee just had to find some way to cheer Bopo up. Noah reflected, "Maybe Ai mee would grind some flour and they could have a fine dinner tonight. Sort of an acorn celebration. He'd talk it over with her."

Ai mee smiled and hummed a little tune to herself as she hurried along behind Noah. One needed to move really fast, to keep up with Noah on the trail. In fact, Ai mee almost needed to trot in order to keep up. Despite the hurried pace, she was bursting with happiness. It was a beautiful morning and they were on the trail headed home. At last you could count the number of suns till they'd walk right into camp at the Truckee River. Walk right up to her parents lodge. There'd be her father, Whoop, and her mother Lark.

"Oh my what a fine moment that was gonna be!" Ai mee smiled.

Bopo brought up the rear of the procession. His expression was glum. What future was there for a fellow who didn't have a totem? None!

For the next several days our heavily laden friends moved rapidly up into the high country. Each day drawing nearer to the western border of Washo Land. Noah and Ai mee talked about a celebration to cheer up the disconsolate Bopo. It was decided they'd hold festivities at a spot where the mountain peaks of Washo Land were first sighted. There they'd celebrate Bopo's successful trading venture, as well as their return to the home land. It would be necessary to set up a camp and remain at that spot for a day, in order to gather and prepare suitable food.

After consulting her time sticks, Ai mee agreed there was more than enough time. Toward sunset, a foot sore Noah called the little party to a halt. He pointed ahead saying, "I think this is the spot we've been looking for."

The steep trail turned a bend and emerged into a level area of tall Red Fir. A small stream gurgled around a bed of sharp boulders. Pressing forward through the forest they came to a narrow sand beach that looked out upon a beautiful little mountain lake. Wind riffled the clear waters, which were of the deepest blue.

On the left hand a sheer wall of solid granite rose vertically from the water, attesting to extreme depth. On the right hand a broad shelf swept upward to a point high above the water. There one large and one small juniper tree formed a sheltered wind-break. A pleasant sandy camping spot! It looked out upon the lake and to the mountains beyond. Those mountains were breath taking.

Our three friends stood on the narrow beach. They tilted heads back until their necks were stretched as far as they'd go, surveying the towering peak at the far end of the lake. The lake ended in a narrow grass covered delta, bisected by a winding stream. In the ages to come the tiny stream would gradually fill the lake entirely with silt. The area would become a pleasant high mountain meadow. It was the way of time.

At the head of the meadow a massive head wall of monolithic granite was extruded vertically into the sky. It towered to a height the mind couldn't quite conceive. In the shadows of a precipitous north wall, a glacier hung. It's snows were destined never to melt. And there, to the left and at a great distance behind the towering face, stood a range of jagged mountains glistening in the last rays of a setting sun.

"There," said Noah pointing dramatically. "There, Ai mee are the mountains of Washo Land. If you look very carefully, you can see one peak more sharp pointed than any of the others. It has a long curving tail of glistening white snow. That tail extends down toward your parents camp. Right at the head of the Truckee River. Right where it's born. That's a high mountain peak. Think you can crawl all the way to the top of that mighty peak, Ai mee? That's Rubicon Peak!"

Breathlessly, Ai mee said, "All my life I've dreamed of that climb, and now it's about to come true. I'll take my red elderberry pole to the very highest point. Hide it there in some tiny secret spot. Only I will know the secret."

All three of the young Washo people stood for long moments on the narrow beach. They stood at the foot of a wind swept lake, silently studying the distant mountains they'd traveled so far to see. After a long time Noah heaved a sigh and said to the others,

"It's too windy to camp here, let's move up to that sheltered spot. Beneath those two gnarled old juniper trees. Camp there tonight. Tomorrow we're going to celebrate with a feast."

The next morning a glum Bopo elected to remain in camp and work at building an additional missile for the Atl-Atl. Ai mee and Noah set out to secure delicacies for the evening feast. They'd celebrate Bopo's acorn trade and the sighting of Washo Land.

The two worked their way to the head of the lake. Cautiously, they began to explore the grass covered delta and winding stream. Searching for wild onions, seeds and herbs. At the far end of the delta they entered a marshy pond where Noah was able to bag three fat mallards with his trusty sling. Proceeding onward they came to a cluster of pines and a spot where a second stream emerged from a side canyon.

Turning up the side canyon, in hopes of finding an early bunch of elderberries, they quickly lost sight of the mountain lake and their sheltered camp. For some time they worked their way up the narrow twisting canyon. While they passed numerous elderberry bushes, there was only green berries to be found. They were not edible, the season was just too young for ripe berries.

At length, the sun reached into the western sky. With a start, they realized it was late in the day and time to return to the sheltered camp. Ai mee led the way back. Two junipers screened the sandy ledge hanging above the icy waters of the lake.

Quietly, parting dense olive green juniper foliage, Ai mee peered into the sheltered camp site. She thought to surprise Bopo with a loud, "Booooo!"

Noah, who was following behind, heard her gasp. "Oh, no. What's happened? Where's Bopo?"

Joining Ai mee, Noah beheld a scene of complete devastation. The coals of the camp fire were spread across the sand. One of the new burden baskets lay slashed to ribbons. A hand full of acorns were strewn on the sand, along with slashed remnants of buckskin clothing. Large moccasin foot prints were every where. On the surface of the lake, just below the camp site, the remains of the other two baskets floated lazily in the breeze. They were slashed into shreds. The precious load of acorns gone. Probably at the bottom of the lake.

"Bopo, Bopo, are you here?" called Noah softly. "Bopo, answer, please answer," he pleaded. There was only the soft sigh of breeze in reply.

Slowly, the two looked about the scene of carnage, an icy hand of fear settling upon them. What did it mean? Where had Bopo gone? Again, Noah called out, this time more loudly, this time with desperation in his voice, "Bopo,   Bopo,   if you're here please answer. Please be here," he pleaded.

And then at the same instant, they both saw it. Saw it driven deep into the soft sand.

Standing there quivering in the breeze as if alive! The missile! Bopo's new missile! The point was driven deep into the sand. Dangling from the top of the shaft, swaying slowly in the breeze, Bopo's shiny black pig tail. The black Water Baby Handle! Only that morning, Ai mee had carefully combed and plaited it.

Attached to the very top of the pig tail, was a neat round patch the size of a fist. A neat round patch, that was still dripping blood around the edges. It was Bopo's scalp! The long pig tail was still attached to the scalp.

"Ai mee," gulped Noah, "They've killed him. Killed him and scalped him. Thrown his body in the lake. Bopo's gone! It could only have been Snake. I don't know how he got here, but it had to be Snake. Yes, it had to be Snake! He's taken Bopo's bear skin and his Atl-Atl. He's probably out there watching right now. We can't help Bopo now! All we can do is run! We gotta hide, quick!"

Ripping Bopo's long pig tail from the missile with one hand and grasping Ai mee's hand with the other, Noah ran blindly down the trail.

CHAPTER 21   On Hands And Knees

Noah and Ai mee raced down the trail toward the lake. They felt an agony of terror and grief, all sense of caution thrown to the winds. At last they drew up, gasping for breath. Slowly Noah's senses began to return to normal. His keen ears picked up the sound of soft foot steps and heavy breathing.

"Duck!" he hissed. With not a second to spare they rolled under heavy brush alongside the trail, just as the muscular figure of White Line burst into view, running up the trail. The two Washos held their breath anxiously, as moccasin feet passed within arms reach and receded into the distance.

Shaking his head, Noah puzzled, "I just can't make this out. I just can't believe Bopo's gone. Can't understand how Snake got here. It all happened so fast. Guess I can understand, Snake's here all right. We're in great danger again. But, I just can't believe this," he said, holding up a hand that still clutched Bopo's long black pig tail.

"Maybe, just maybe." Ai mee whispered with a break in her voice, "Maybe he isn't really dead. They must have thrown his body in the lake. But maybe he's hiding in the water somewhere. He'd be along the shore line. If he were trying to hide, he'd wait for us. Let's crawl through the bushes. Go back to the edge of the lake. Watch for some sign of him."

Noah led the way as they cautiously crawled on hands and knees, back to the narrow beach. The wind was rising, roughening the lake surface. Finding a cluster of bushes deep in shadow overlooking the lake, they wriggled into the darkened center. From that spot they had an excellent view of the lake, the delta above and mountains of home beyond. Through the afternoon, they patiently searched every inch of shore line with their eyes. Hoping, always hoping to spot a face or a hand or an unusual ripple in the water. But there was nothing, only silence.

"Quiet, don't move," hissed Noah. Just at dusk, figures suddenly appeared out of the forest. Silently, they slipped into the grass covered delta. No mistaking the big figure of Snake with yellow splashed face, giving orders to his five followers.

"Ugh!" whispered Ai mee. "They're after us now." The Paiutes were obviously searching like a pack of wolves, searching for any sign of the two escaped Washos. Snake motioned with an outstretched arm toward the small side canyon, up which the two had searched for elderberries.

"Search up there." growled a hideous yellow faced Snake. Three of his followers slithered off into the trees to search the canyon. The shadows lengthened and the light was beginning to fail before the three returned. Shaking heads indicated they'd found nothing. Snake pointed to a trampled place along side the trail, near the marshy water. The spot where Noah had bagged three mallards.

The Paiutes proceeded to set up their camp for the night. The camp site was but a short distance from the small side canyon.

"Ai mee, I hate to say this," said Noah sadly. "But, I think we've got to give up. Bopo's lost. If his body is in that lake, it's at the bottom. There's nothing we can do. We're got to try to get out of here and save ourselves. We'll wait till the Paiutes eat and go to sleep. Then we can swim the length of the lake. We'll crawl through the delta grass. Near their camp."

"You mean go right past their camp, to the entrance of that small canyon? Where we hunted berries this morning ? You mean to get that close to 'em?"

"Yup! No other choice. I don't like getting that close, any more than you do. But escape up that canyon's our only way out. Think you can swim that far? In the freezing water? It's an awful long ways?" whispered Noah.

"Sure," said Ai mee, very softly.

There was genuine admiration in his voice as Noah said, "Good Girl!" After a moments serious thought he turned, saying, "You know, Ai mee, some way we're gonna get out of this. I'll admit, right at the moment, I don't know just how we're gonna do it. There's a way and we'll find it. Maybe we're gonna crawl through the bushes. On our hands and knees. All the way to Washo Land if we have to. But, you and I are gonna get there! I promise! We'll do it for Bopo!"

As night settled over the lake, the wind gradually died and the surface of the black water turned smooth. The moon was still below the horizon and the sky was ominously dark. Along the left side of the lake, a sheer granite wall dropped into deep black water. There the shadows were most dense.

Barely perceptible in the gloom, two dark heads moved steadily forward without causing the slightest ripple on the surface. Like otters swimming silently, they moved slowly toward the upper end of the lake. At last they reached an inlet where a delta marked the waters edge. With a faint splash breaking the silence, the dark figures crawled from the water on all fours. Silently, they disappeared into the grass. A line of pines bordered the meadow. Two shadows drifted from pine to pine. They passed a point opposite the dying embers of Snake's two camp fires. They flitted on, to the entrance of the small side canyon.

The glowing coals of one camp fire collapsed upon themselves with a brief flare of sparks and flame, only to die down again. None of the slumbering figures moved in the silent camp.

"This way." hissed Noah, drawing aside a low hanging branch. The two young Washos crept from bush to bush up the canyon, sometimes rising and running quietly from one tree to another. Throughout the night they made their way upward, to where bare granite slopes rose on either side.

The vegetation was more sparse, only a few small bushes here. They crawled across the almost bare stone surface, from bush to bush, slithering like serpents, two silent shadows. At last they attained the head of a canyon. Laying flat on the monolith, it was possible to look out across a vast array of ridges and valleys. They looked out toward Washo Land, to a brilliant point, where the moon was just rising behind Rubicon Peak. The sharp profile of the peak was defined in the moon's blinding white light.

"There it is Ai mee. There's your mountain."

As they lay there, studying the ridges and valleys to be crossed, before they could begin the final assent of Rubicon, realization set in.

"It'll be many, many suns before we reach that distant point." mused Noah. "A time made even longer because we've have to crawl from bush to bush."

"No other way to avoid detection," groaned Ai mee.

"A time made longer because almost all our possessions are lost or destroyed," Noah shook his head in grim agreement.

"Just think," continued Ai mee. " All the food, the spare moccasins and leather. The burden baskets with their loads of acorns. My fire drill and your fire pouch. Everything's gone !"

"On the positive side," said Noah, "I've still got my sling and bow, with a quiver of four arrows and a flint knife. Ai mee you've still got your knife and time sticks, at least"

In a sudden overpowering burst of despair the girl thought to discard her time sticks. It was all so hopeless! Then, with a small bitter smile, she thought, "No, I'll keep those silly old time sticks. If

Noah says we're gonna get there, were gonna get there. I know it!"

The days that followed were long, hard and discouraging. Food was scarce. Noah could not hunt during the daytime for fear of detection. They had to subsist on such roots and herbs as Ai mee could snatch in passing. Moccasins wore thin. They had to be patched with pieces of leather cut from their clothing. Travel was limited to the hours of darkness, when detection was least likely. During the hours of daylight they lay hidden, usually at some vantage point. They maintained a vigil to detect pursuers at a distance. Only one person could sleep at a time. The other stood guard. Sleep was fitful at best.

Hardly a day passed without some sign of Snake. The Paiutes sifted through the country in twos and threes, searching, ever searching, during the daylight hours. They were unrelenting, always sniffing the trail, just behind the frightened pair.

The two youths became dispirited under the constant threat of capture. They grew thin and hollow-eyed from lack of food and sleep. Their cloths hung from them in tatters. Despite the hardship, they became more determined to reach Washo Land with each passing day.

Noah's empty stomach rumbled, reminding him once again he'd not eaten since awaking that morning. He was unable to move for fear of detection. His arms were stretched before him as he lay at full length in the dried grass, chin resting on the firm ground.

Cautiously, he extended two forefingers to part the grass before his eyes. They beheld a small mountain meadow, bathed in early morning sunlight. Golden brown in color, not yet ready to erupt into the bright green of spring. The oval shaped meadow was a jewel set in a great expanse of dark bronze forest.

Beyond the forest to the eastward, were huge expanses of clean gray granite monolith. It rolled smoothly as a liquid flow in places. Abruptly it terminated in a massive up thrust of shattered columns torn into huge blocks. They attested to some awesome inner force from the distant past. Noah's mind roamed back over Crow Woman's tales of the origin of meadows,

(At the head of a meadow a tremendous block of rough granite stood. It had been extruded from the very bowels of the earth. Towering to a great height, it's slopes stripped of all vegetation, it was clean and bright in the morning sun. Long ago a mighty glacier rested against the towering north face. Melting bright blue ice formed a tiny lake as time passed. Through many, many seasons, the weathering effects of driving winter winds and alternate freezing and thawing slowly decomposed tiny amounts of granite surface. A fine silt was formed. Spring floods carried silt down the slope to be deposited in a lake. As many, many more seasons passed, the little lake was finally filled to the brim with the fine silt and a meadow was born.)

Noah studied the far edge of the meadow. Slowly, his eyes examined each element of shadows along the forest edge. There one of the Paiutes might be hidden, waiting to spring at their first movement. Slowly, his eyes studied each blade of grass, each shadowed pine branch, each patch of darkness. Searching, carefully scrutinizing each tiny detail for the faintest hint of something wrong. Something out of place, something that moved ever so slightly, something that indicated the presence of an enemy.

Time seemed to stand still, with only the rumbling of Noah's empty stomach to break the morning silence. Nothing moved along the forest edge across the meadow. A butterfly flickered in the sun light as it drifted from one clump of grass to the next. All was tranquil! Then his searching eyes found just the slightest trace of something that wasn't quite right. A patch in the deepest shadow, a patch that was just a trace lighter than the rest, a patch that was faintly yellowish. And then suddenly, Noah's eyes brought the deep forest shadows into focus. There it was in the gloom. A huge figure, seated silently with murderous eyes of fire staring out of the blackness. Eyes searching the very spot where the two Washos lay concealed in the warm sunlit grass.

In shock, Noah felt Snake's piercing eyes staring straight into his, felt that murderous unwavering gaze penetrating his very soul. His hands clenched in silent agony as he forced himself to realize,

"Snake can see me only if I move." Noah remained rigid in the spot where he lay and hissed at Ai mee behind him,

"Freeze. Don't move so much as a hair. Snake's across the meadow. Staring right at us."

Ai mee was laying flat in the grass, as was Noah. She'd been quietly digging wild turnips and onions from the moist sod. Now, at Noah's whispered command she turned her eyes to the shadowed forest.

"I can't see him. Where is he? How'd you spot him?"

It was a very long time before she heard the whispering voice say, "All's clear. Snake got up and went back into the forest. Let's get out of here quick!"

Silently, the two wriggled back through tall grass toward the sheltering trees. Once in the friendly shadows of the forest they were able to stand. For some time Noah continued to study the far side of the meadow for some additional sign of the enemy, but no one appeared.

"Well Ai mee," said Noah, "I guess we're stuck here till dark. It's just not safe to travel while there's still light. Snake's just too close for comfort. Let's use Ishi's trick and hide in tree tops for the rest of the day. Maybe, if we get up high in the trees, we'll get lucky. Might spot where Snake makes his camp.

"Good idea, then when it gets dark we can circle him and head for the great head wall behind

Daw ow aga." Shaking his head Noah agreed, "If we can get free to travel fast by running, we could possibly make it to the top of the great wall by first light. You know, from there you can look down on Bopo's favorite spot, Eagle Lake. Out beyond, just half a day's walk, is Da ow aga and Emerald Bay."

"At least, Noah, we didn't do too badly today. I was able to dig some turnips and onions out there in the meadow. Enough to keep us from starving for another few days. They aren't the tastiest of foods when eaten dry, but they're better than nothing. You can keep going for a long time on turnips and onions. If you have to."

"Well, I guess right now we have to. Might as well eat turnips and onions and like 'em," shrugged Noah. "But, you know what? After this, I don't ever want to even see those vegetables again. Ever! You know, I'm so darned hungry right now I'd even enjoy a great big steaming hot serving of Bopo's Violet Mushroom Stew."

The first hint of dawn was beginning to pale the eastern sky out over Paiute Land. Noah broke stride and drew to a halt. It was a moment or two before a puffing Ai mee pulled up beside him in the half darkness. The two stood shoulder to shoulder, on the crest of a great bare granite monolith. Directly before them, the smooth stone fell away sharply into shadows of a still remaining night. As far as the eye could see the monster fault formed a crest of the mountain range. This was the western boundary of Washo Land.

A night bird twitted softly, as they stood spell bound watching. Slowly the entire slope of the mountain range began to emerge below them. The first rays of dawn raced across the land. A chain of mountain peaks grew up out of the darkness. One by one they were connected by ridges, forming a vast panorama of hills and valleys. A multitude of glistening silver lakes and streams emerged.

As the light grew, immense forests of velvet textured bronze-green covered the land in an endless expanse of unspoiled wilderness. Before them in the mid distance, the quiet morning waters of Da ow aga took shape and began to sparkle. The first rays of sun light raced across it's blue surface. A soft tracery of wind patterns etched their way across the gleaming expanse. Narrowing, the patterns entered that tiny pocket along the west shore, Emerald Bay! They swept to a stop on the rocky beach of Ominous Island, the home of the monster Water Baby.

"There it is," Ai mee whispered in awe, staring out across the lake with arms outstretched. "Just think of it. After all this time. That big beautiful blue lake, Da ow aga. Right here in the center of Washo Land. Home! If only Bopo could see it too," shrugging her shoulders as if to ward off sad thoughts, she forced a wistful smile.

In silent awe, they watched the story of a fresh new virgin land appear before their eyes. As they looked downward past their feet, down the plunging face of a sheer granite head wall, they discovered a narrow ledge extending across the face.

Clinging to the bare stone of the ledge was a single gnarled Juniper tree. It was very old, weathered by the winds of many a driving winter storm. It stood as a sentinel through eons of time. The tree was so far below them, it appeared tiny, belying it's great age and size.

A single Bald Eagle, with bronze wings stretched motionless, balanced on five finger like feathers at each wing tip. It soared silently, stationary in an updraft, beside the ancient Juniper tree. Far below the hovering eagle, at the foot of a sheer cliff lay a tiny sparkling blue lake. Eagle Lake! A narrow torrent of white water cascaded down the cliff face, to land in spray among tumbled blocks of granite at the lake's edge. Bright green foliage extended to the very shore. In the exact center of the lake was a tiny island, crowned with a single Incense Cedar tree.

"That's Eagle Lake." whispered Noah, pointing with arm extended downward." Bopo's favorite of all places. He used to love to swim over to that little island and crawl up under that cedar tree. Sit and work on his hunting bow. We came here. Camped in a hollow on the ledge. Behind that old Juniper tree. That's where we got the strong wood for our new hunting bows. A dead limb off the old juniper. It'd cured for many seasons. After that, we came here lots of times. Bopo's favorite spot."

"It's a beautiful place," breathed Ai mee, "Sort of seems like Bopo should be siting over there. On the little island. Under that cedar tree. Doing his Ho Ho Ho thing right now."

" Well." said Noah, returning to his practical self, "We'd better stop mooning around here and look out for ourselves. We're really exposed standing out here at the top of this great cliff."

"Yeah, if Snake doesn't come along and spot us, the ONG will. Remember we're back in ONG's country now. I can see several of those little lenticular clouds beginning to form out there over the desert in Paiute country," agreed Ai mee.

"Ole' ONG may be out hunting right now. Let's crawl down the face of this cliff to the ledge. There's a good camping spot behind the old Juniper tree. Out a sight. Trickle of water there. We can sleep till it's dark. Then make our way on down to Da ow aga at night."

The two proceeded to lower themselves down the broken and torn granite cliff face. Weathering had taken it's toll on the face. It was broken into huge blocks of talus. They tumbled in jagged piles like the toys of some giant from another world. In places the blocks were so large they were forced to hang by finger tips and drop in a crumpled heap at the foot. In other places large patches of thick Mountain Oak brush had to be crossed on hands and knees. The terrain reminded them of Ishi and his shadowy passages through the dense stuff.

Much of the morning had slipped away by the time they finally reached the narrow ledge. Their already worn buckskin clothing now hung in shredded tatters. They were a gaunt, a sorry looking pair. They followed the ledge to where it widened out into a sandy spit at the foot of the massive old juniper tree. There against the face of the towering granite cliff, was a sheltering overhang. In the back was a grassy mound, hidden from view. It was the camp spot inhabited by Bopo and his cousin, many moons ago, a perfect place to sleep undetected.

"Noah, I can't go one step farther 'till I have some rest," gasped Ai mee, sinking to the grassy mound.

"That's all right," said Noah, mumbling with fatigue himself. "You go ahead and get some sleep. I'll be back before very long. There's a thing I have to do. Kind a like to just do it all by myself. Private stuff! Just me and Bopo, so to speak. I'm gonna climb on down to that beautiful little lake. Eagle Lake, Bopo's favorite."

"I understand how you must feel," nodded the girl.

"I'll swim out to the island, just like we used to do," continued Noah. " Want a take Bopo's pig tail out there. Build him a small chamber of stone under the cedar tree. Right where he used to sit. I'll put the pig tail in there all safe and dry. Maybe his spirit'll want'a come there. To visit!"

Turning, Noah trudged off down the narrow ledge, a sorrowful figure, shoulders sagging with fatigue. Ai mee, tired though she was, crawled to the edge of the cliff from where she could watch Noah's slow progress downward. Attaining the edge of the lake he quietly slipped into the water and slowly swam to the island, where he disappeared into the bushes. Shortly, he reemerged beneath the cedar tree. Ai mee's eyes were heavy lidded as she watched Noah kneel beneath the tree and begin to carefully build a cavern of stones.

A long ominous shadow fell across Ai mee as she reclined in the warm sunlit sand.

His mission accomplished, a weary Noah plodded down the narrow ledge to the camp spot where the massive old Juniper tree stood.

"Ai mee, Ai mee, where are you? answer me Ai mee, where are you?"

The only answer was silence. And then Noah saw them, there in the sand. Ai mee's time sticks, laying in the sand, dropped in frantic haste. Her cherished time sticks! The notched sticks, carefully guarded and maintained over all that great distance. Ai mee's time sticks! And then Noah's blood ran cold. It froze in his veins. There, beside the tumbled sticks, there was a single large moccasin print in the sand. Clearly defined!

Dropping to the ground, Noah sniffed at the impression in the sand and it was present, that horrible stench, the stench of a rattle snake!

Noah stood at the brink of the cliff, head thrown back and arms rigid against the sky. Shaking clenched fists, he screamed in a voice like flint grating on flint.

"Snake, you fiend! You've taken my friend Bopo! And now you've taken Ai mee from me! I'll kill you! No matter where you go. I'll follow your evil smell. I'm going to kill you!"

CHAPTER 22   Emerald Bay

The sparkling blue waters of Da ow aga slowly turned to a deep angry gray, even though it was mid day. The sun disappeared behind long stringers of wind driven clouds. Very high above a shrieking wind ripped through the heavens, slashing and tearing at the sky. The normal bright midday light faded quickly, leaving a sullen overcast with shadows dark as night. A black line rushed across the surface of the water. It marked a spot at which the slashing wind tore the surface, turning it to driven spray. Huge rolling waves capped with sparkling white foam followed the black line across the water. The crash of waves and the roar of wind obliterated all other sound. Suddenly the Gods were angry and a violent storm descended upon Washo Land.

High in the sky, a fierce ONG soared with wings set against the howling gale. Concealed within the finger like black clouds, he relentlessly stalked some innocent prey. The ONG was famished! When he was driven by hunger, his anger increased to rage. With a scream the furious monster dove toward the heaving surface of the lake. The raging raptor slashed the tip of one extended wing into the water. It created a huge wave which crashed to shore among the rocks.

The ONG extended the hooked talon of one long claw. Lightning flashed from the needle like tip.

It struck a towering pine tree. With an earth shaking crack, the   huge tree trunk split from crown to earth. There, it erupted in fire which quickly engulfed the entire tree. As the monster raptor vented his rage, he spread a howling black storm across the length and breadth of Washo Land, driving fear into the hearts of it's occupants. It was a good time to be hidden in one's lodge or better yet in some sound cave.

Meanwhile, there was a creature who was hidden deep in a pitch black cavern. He felt no fear of the awesome ONG. In fact he felt only disdain for the great bird, as he sat in a deep tomb of glistening black rock. Water dripped down the clammy walls. He crunched the leg bone of an unfortunate warrior in his huge drooling jaws. It was the Water Baby, evil spirit and enemy of any one who dared enter Lake Tahoe. The Water Baby, half Grizzly Bear and half Great White Shark, his favorite of all foods was fat little Washo children. He sought those who disobeyed their parents and strayed too close to the shore of Da ow aga.

The Water Baby lived in Emerald Bay, a beautiful elliptical body of water attached to the shore of the great lake. The bay looked like the mouth of an ancient volcano filled with sparkling blue water. It's steeply sloped sides were richly carpeted in dense forests of green fir and pine. At the center of the bay a jumble of huge stones rose from the deep water to form a tiny island, Ominous Island! The crest of the island was capped with a gnarled old Juniper tree , picturesque with glistening bare white wood, polished and sculptured by many a driving winter storm.

Despite the beauty of the little island, it housed that awful monster the Water Baby. Deep beneath the island, down where the water was black and no ray of sunlight ever penetrated, there was a cave in the stone. A tomb, with walls covered by slippery blackish green moss, made clammy by constantly dripping water. A cold cave with the floor covered by the bleached bones and grinning skulls of his victims. In the center, atop a great black rock sat the monster, growling as he ground a bone in his pointed shark teeth. All the while he cast about, with round black staring shark eyes. He flexed long needle sharp claws, set in the huge hairy black paws of an immense bear. The Water Baby was ravenously hungry and he was about to go out into the deep water. Silently, he began an evening cruise of the shore line. In search of an innocent victim.

Snake and his band moved cautiously down the rocky trail that led through the forest, from Eagle Lake to Emerald Bay.

"Spread out and search along each side of the trail," growled the cautious leader. The Washos could be behind any tree or rock." No longer did the Paiutes move like a pack of hunting wolves, leaning forward from the waist, running from bush to bush, sniffing the wind in search of their prey. Now, they traveled as a band of stealthy warriors in enemy territory, moving cautiously to avoid detection, peering into each shadow. They expected the enemy to appear and attack at any instant.

Snake strode in the center of a pack whose scouts slipping from tree to tree. He was clad in a full length cape of shiny black bear skin, recently stolen from the luckless Washo youth, Bopo. Trudging along behind him, in his shadow, was the small disheveled figure of Ai mee. Her arms tied behind her back and hair hanging down over her eyes. A raw hide rope was knotted about her throat. The other end was tied to a snake pouch at the leaders belt, insuring there would be no escape. The party moved quickly. Their furtive actions made it clear they feared pursuit.

At length the lead Paiute scout raised his hand shoulder high, "Down there," he hissed, indicating there was something to be seen in the trail before him. Cautiously, Snake moved forward and peered over the fellow's shoulder, to behold the panoramic view of Emerald Bay spread out below them.

"That's where we're headed." he grunted with satisfaction. At this point it was still midday and the sun was shining brightly on the beautiful scene of bay and island. The broad waters of Da ow aga were in the background. Even as the group watched, dark fingers of cloud flashed across the waters below them. ONG slashed the surface of the lake with his wing tip releasing the storm's thundering fury. Trembling, the frightened group of Paiutes and their forlorn captive retreated from the trail. They sought the shelter of overhanging forest boughs. Within moments , bright sunlight gave way to the gloomy fury of a stormy sky, almost as dark as night.

"Get back, into the shadows where we can't be seen by that thing." hissed a frightened Snake. Drawing the bearskin robe tightly around himself, he slithered back into the cover of the forest, to avoid detection by the awful ONG. Snake had already gone through the wrenching experience of one close encounter with ONG. He'd barely escaped the murderous claws of the great raptor. He could still remember the pitiful screams of an unfortunate Paiute who was born away by ONG. Shuddering at the memories, Snake ordered,

"Build a fire quick. Maybe it'll drive off that thing." As the fire slowly warmed the band of Paiutes their courage began to return. At length food was passed around, raising their spirits even more. As the ONG didn't reappear, Snake became more confident and decided to address his men. He'd give them a picture of the triumphant ending to the long campaign on which they were embarked.

In the flickering firelight, clad only in breech clout, with stolen bearskin robe thrown open, face freshly decorated with ghastly yellow ochre war paint and shredded ear flapping in the raging wind, the sneering Paiute made a frightening picture. He stood with the cowering figure of Ai mee trembling before him. Shouting at the top of his lungs, so as to be heard above the moaning wind, Snake screamed.

"I'm Snake. Greatest of all Paiute warriors. Through out this entire journey, I've shown every one I am a ruler! Shown I'm the greatest! The most fearless! The mightiest leader of all men. I've sworn to bring back this worthless girl. Sworn to make her a slave for life. A slave of my lodge. I've sworn I'll blind her eyes for ever more. Blind her eyes with fire. This I'll do, before all of the Washo People. They must know I'm the master, to whom they will bow. We'll go to the sacred island. There in the bay below, I'll build a fire at the summit of the island. There are Washo People hiding in the forest all around this sacred bay. They're all afraid of me. They're all watching. They'll all see. I'll take burning coals from the fire and they'll see Snake carry out his promise. They'll see!"

With muscular arm outstretched, he pointed down at Emerald Bay, at the tiny rock island, with the bare Juniper tree gleaming white in the darkness. "There, there at the foot of that dead tree. We'll build a great fire. Come Mighty Paiute Warriors, follow me! Let all the cowardly Washos watch this ceremony of fire. Let them all tremble in fear of the Great Snake. Greatest of all Paiutes!"

Noah was badly shaken when he discovered the print of Snake's moccasin beside Ai mee's discarded time sticks. There could be no question about it. Ai mee was again in the clutches of that evil monster. Noah shuddered at the memory of Snake's threat to blind Ai mee with burning coals.

Now, Noah was normally a taciturn young man who could be counted upon to react calmly to most events, no matter how unexpected. It was his custom to plan his actions carefully, after considering all alternatives. Under normal conditions, he could be counted upon to act in a most conservative fashion. However, at this point in time, there was nothing normal or conservative about Noah's reactions.

The fact of Ai mee's capture slowly registered with chilling effect on Noah's brain. Shaking clenched fists at the sky he screamed in a voice cold as death, "Snake, I'll Kill You!"

Noah was no longer the hunted. From that moment on he became the hunter, a man who's intent was to dispense death. Death to Snake and all of his followers. Searching the trail like a hungry mountain lion, he came upon a patch of damp earth. There in the moist soil the prints of many moccasins clearly told a tale. The war party of Paiutes and their small captive were following the wide main trail downward to Emerald Bay. From the spacing of footprints, it was apparent they were moving fast. Silently, a grim Noah slipped into the shadows of the forest. He avoided the exposure of the trail. Downward he plunged. He'd catch the Paiute war party at Emerald Bay.

The sun was high in the heavens as Noah emerged, a picture of grim determination. Onto an outcropping of granite he drifted, silent as a shadow. He overlooked the beautiful bay, home of the dreaded Water Baby. Shaking his head sadly, he looked down to his left, at the point where the bay's waters entered the big lake. Muttering to himself he said,

"There, where the waters of lake and bay mix, down were those big granite boulders are partially submerged in the shallows. That's where Bopo fell in the water. The time he lost two toes to the Water Baby. That was a long time ago," he thought sadly.

Directly before him was a vantage point overlooking the bay. Far below, Ominous Island thrust up from the deep blue waters. At the very crest of the island stood an old juniper snag, bereft of all foliage, it's sculptured white wood gleamed in the sunlight.

"Strange," mused Noah, "Strange a place so beautiful should house a monster as dreadful as the Water Baby."

Suddenly, the bright sunlight faded, the sparkling blue water turned to an angry dark gray, a thrusting cold blast of air swept across the bare granite outcropping. The gods were angry, a violent storm was racing across dark skies toward him.

Noah's first reaction was to seek shelter. Shelter not only from the storm, but shelter from ONG. One could be sure about ONG, he'd be out hunting on a day such as this. Noah crossed the outcropping to a spot where a giant slab of solid rock projected. It formed a shelter from the roaring wind. Glancing back over his shoulder he was startled to see a husky figure following him. An apparition that staggered with every step, it leaned forward against the driving wind.

"One of Snake's cut-throats trying to sneak up behind me," was Noah's first thought. He quickly fitted an arrow to bow string and flexed the powerful weapon, "In the throat," he told himself. "I don't want him to scream and warn the others. I want'a kill 'em all."

In that last instant before release of the deadly shaft, some inner instinct stayed his hand. There was something curiously familiar about the husky figure staggering toward him out of the gloom of a howling storm. Silently, Noah studied the weaving shape whose long arms were outstretched toward him.

"Bopo? It can't be, Bopo, is that you? I can't believe it, Bopo alive."

The staggering figure collapsed on Noah. The two went down in a heap and rolled on the ground in a groaning, shouting, laughing melee of arms and legs. Sitting up at last, Noah hugged his cousin for a long moment. Holding him at arms length, he examined the broad brown face carefully for what seemed a very long time.

" Bopo, it's really you? You're not dead like we thought? You're alive? You're really alive? You look different, though. You're not the same old Bopo! You're face is different, somehow," gasped Noah.

"Yeah it's me, all right," grunted Bopo with a wry grin. "It's me all right. I'm only about half dead and half alive. Still can't walk very good. Got one leg that sort'a staggers most of the time. Doesn't work very good! You're right, I'm different, a lot different. Look at this!" he grumbled, leaning forward so Noah could see the top of his head. There was a neat round patch of bare white bone. A patch of skull, about the size of a clenched fist, surrounded by shiny black hair, the spot where Bopo's pig tail had once been. He'd been scalped and the wound healed neatly to expose bare skull.

"Scalped by Snake, and now I'm the only bald headed warrior in the whole Washo Tribe," moaned Bopo.

"Tell me about every thing that's happened since Ai mee and I left you at camp. We went hunting for elderberries. Remember, we were gonna have a feast to celebrate the acorn harvest."

"Well," said Bopo, "Seems like ages ago when that all happened. Guess you remember all the trouble I was havin' about my totem. Just couldn't get over those awful dreams, about the bear. He ate my chickaree friend. I couldn't sleep or eat worrying about it. You just can't imagine how bad it is. Lose your only totem. That's bad medicine for the rest of your life."

"I know !" said Noah. "Real bad medicine. A fellow could have awful bad luck for ever more. You sure had some. Bad luck, that is!"

"Anyway, on that last day I really got to feeling sick, sort of feverish. So when you and Ai mee left camp, I went down to the lake. Took a swim in the cold water. You know, see if that'd help the fever. I was sittin' on a rock facing the lake. All of a sudden, this long shadow fell across me. I could feel something was behind me."

"Ughhhh," grunted Noah, shaking his head sadly.

"Sooooo, I started to turn. Take a look. Got just a flash of that dirty yellow face. He was grinning at me! Then the war ax hit me. Hit me in the head. Every thing went black. Next thing I knew, must have been quite a while later, I was floating face down in the lake. The wind was blowin' pretty strong. Couldn't see very good! Hurt! Cold! Drifted into some tall grass."

"Lumpy, ole boy. It's a wonder you're here."

"Guess I was passed out for a long time. Came to, it was dark! I had this horrible head ache and found a gash in my scalp from the ax. It wasn't till a long time later that I found I'd also been scalped. I was so darned weak, I couldn't stand. Just sort'a crawled a ways in the grass. I passed out again."

"Wish I'd been there to help," groaned Noah, shaking his head.

"Even after I came to, I was too weak to stand. Just laid there on my back, in the long grass. At one point Snake and another Paiute came up lookin' for me. They were real close, for a while. Couldn't see me in the tall grass. I was so weak I couldn't make a sound, much less move. Must have been there for two days anyhow."

"Wonder it didn't kill you."

"Anyhow, Snake and his warriors finally went away. Crawled back to camp. Lookin' for you. Nobody! I was afraid you'd been killed! Got my Atl-Atl and the new missile. They were hidden! Snake missed finding 'em, but he sure destroyed the rest of the camp. I thought sure he'd killed you, and taken Ai mee captive. Where is Ai mee, any way? exclaimed Bopo, a note of alarm entering his voice.

"That's what I've been trying to tell you," said Noah dejectedly. Snake's got her! Captured her while I was gone. Went to Eagle Lake. Building a stone shrine for your pig tail. Snake got her! Found the time sticks and Snake's moccasin prints. He's got her! He's headed here to Emerald Bay. Maybe here by now. They were movin' fast! Snake's gonna burn her eyes. Have to find him quick. I'm gonna kill him!"

"I warn you Noah," growled Bopo, "Cousin or not. Soon as I can find Snake, I'm gonna kill him. Don't get in my way. I'll kill him and the rest of 'em too!"

"We'll see about that," said Noah in a flinty voice. "Who ever finds 'em first, gets em. Just make sure they're dead when you leave."

The two Washo youths crouched in the shelter of a big boulder, overlooking the violently turbulent waters of storm tossed Emerald Bay. The island was directly below them, barely visible in the driving storm. Sheets of rain, forced by the screaming wind, wiped out all vision of the scene below. Their eyes searched in vain for just a glimpse of the leering yellow face. Thunder crashed and earth trembled.

The huge dark shape of Water Baby slipped quietly into the black waters. His broad back covered with coarse black hair, the pointed shark fin projecting between his shoulder blades caused an ominous swirl in the dark waters. The smell of human beings was strong in the Water Babies nostrils. The scent of human food came to him on the whistling wind. Human beings were moving about in the night. The slithering black shape moved out into the angry tossing waters. Silently it searched for prey.

High overhead ONG's sharp eyes detected movement in the darkness of a wind driven tempest. He could sense there were humans down there. Warm tasty humans, scurrying about from one shelter to another. Trying to avoid the clutches of howling wind and crashing thunder. Time and again ONG slashed bolts of flaming lightning from his extended talons. He hurled flashing sheets of fire at the tiny figures below, as they scurried from place to place in search of shelter. The mighty wings drove great gusts of air with explosive force against the ground. It tore huge trees from the forest, shattering them against the massive stone walls of the island below. ONG was hunting, hunting for human food!

As the two Washo youths crouched, peering downward at the tiny island, lightning revealed the scene below. There at the crest of the island, where the bare white juniper tree thrust skyward, was a roaring fire. flames lashed by the wind. With his back to them was a large, ominous figure, Snake! Busily he heaped wood on the leaping flames. Standing with back to the tree and arms lashed behind her was a tiny trembling figure, Ai mee!

A short distance down the island slope were three of the Paiute warriors, in full war paint. Obviously, they were assigned to attack anyone who attempted to approach the fire.

With an anguished roar, Noah leaped down the slope toward the island. He disappeared into the darkness, " Snake, I'll kill you!"

Bopo, with the deep throated growl of an angry bear, began to rip the case from his polished black Atl-Atl, " Snake, I'll kill you!"

Snake, the stolen bearskin cape hanging from his powerful naked shoulders, very deliberately selected a large flaming brand from the fire. The sinister figure strode menacingly toward the spot where a cringing Ai mee stood, lashed against the tree. The fire light played across a sneering ugly face with dirty yellow paint and dangling ear. With a growl, Snake leered at the terrified girl.

"I've waited a long time for this. Now, I'll have my vengeance. Look into my eyes. Look at my face. It's the last thing you'll see in this life. Look!" Slowly, Snake began to extend the glowing coals toward the tiny girl's face.

Noah's dripping black hair and tattered buckskin shirt burst up out of the black water in a shower of spray, revealing a face contorted with rage. He moved ashore and up slope toward the fire. His movements were so fast he appeared as a blur to the first Paiute, the one with blue war paint across his broad chest. He turned to intercept the streaking shadow with raised war ax. Noah fainted with his shoulders to the left, as he transferred his flint knife to the right hand. The grinning warrior drove the sharp ax downward in a slash at the exposed junction of his attackers neck and shoulder. Noah deftly slipped aside and drove the thin blade of flint deep into his adversaries heart. Whirling away the Washo youth sped on, before the Paiute realized he was dying.

The second warrior, with gleaming white bands of war paint across his torso, raised his war ax. Noah, without breaking stride whirled on one foot. Back to the enemy, he swung the other foot in a great arc. There was a loud S-n-a-p as the rigid moccasin broke the man's neck. He slipped slowly to the ground.

The third warrior turned to run in terror, as Noah scooped a fallen war ax from the ground and hurled it at the retreating figure. The ax slowly turned end for end in the air and embedded itself in the mans skull. Before the crumpling figure stopped running, Noah flashed by him and reached for Snake's broad back.

The yellow-faced monster's outstretched arm extended a glowing brand toward a cringing Ai mee's eyes.

High up on the hillside across the water, Bopo stood on the outcrop of rock. The island was concealed in the pitch black of a howling storm. Even though he couldn't see his enemy, Bopo knew exactly where he was. Teetering precariously on his injured leg, he fitted the new missile with it's gleaming black war head. Shouting an angry, "Die Snake Die!" he launched the lethal weapon into the howling storm.

High up in the sky, ONG folded his great wings and hurtled earthward. Toward the exact spot where Noah was wrapping bare hands around the neck of his hated enemy, Snake! ONG extended one glistening claw, pointed it at the evil Paiute and released a sizzling white bolt of lightning.

The evil yellow-faced Paiute heard the booming challenge, "Die Snake Die." Opening his ugly mouth in a shout of rage, he turned to face his enemy, only to behold Noah who was upon him. In that very second two things happened. First, Noah heard the hissing scream of Bopo's missile, as it slashed passed his ear and embedded the gleaming black war head at the base of Snake's throat. Second, a searing white bolt of lightning was driven into Snake's open mouth and down through his rigid body to the ground. Curling yellow flames erupted from the soles of Snake's moccasins.

To this day Noah, could not tell you whether it was Bopo's missile or ONG's lightning bolt that killed Snake. He stood there for minutes watching, as Snake slowly shriveled into a smoking pile of black ash. Turning, Noah to untying Ai mee's bonds and the two ran as fast as their legs would carry them, away from the roaring fire. With reluctance they plunged into the crashing waves and swam for the main land, expecting at any moment to feel the sharp pointed teeth of the Water Baby. With a sigh of relief, the two emerged from the water and crawled up the sloping beach to the protection of an overhanging bank.

Looking up Ai mee gasped, "Oh nooooo!" There squatting directly above their heads, with war clubs poised to strike, were the grinning faces of the last two Paiutes. They'd been left to guard the shore, by their deceased leader, Snake. And then, a curious thing happened! The expressions on the two ugly faces changed, from grins of triumph to looks of shocked horror. Two great fur covered paws wrapped glistening black talons around their throats. With a low growl the immense Water Baby emerged from the shadows, it's unblinking shark eyes regarded the two Washo youths for a moment. It rejected them in favor of the struggling Paiutes. Deliberately, it picked up the warriors by their necks and carried them feebly kicking and gasping into the black water.

"Wow!" said a shaken Noah, "I don't care if I never see that thing again. Come on Ai mee, let's get out of here before that thing comes back, looking for us. We'll have to crawl up to that outcropping of rock. Bopo's up there. He's alive! Come back from the dead. He's pretty badly chewed up and can't walk very good. He feels mighty sad about being the only bald headed warrior in the tribe. I'll tell you one thing, he may be banged up some, but, he's still got a throwing arm that works mighty well!"

CHAPTER 23   The Red Dance Stick

The summer camp of the Wel mel ti was located in an area of great beauty! A cluster of snug shelters dotted the shore of Da ow aga, at that spot where the Truckee River was born. It has been the clans traditional summer gathering place for many generations, longer than anyone can remember. The camp site was a grassy meadow, tucked between lake shore and sunny southern bank of the sparkling Truckee River. Behind the meadow, towering forested mountains rose abruptly.

A multitude of summer lodges were scattered at random along the border of the meadow. The dome shaped huts were a slight distance back from the river. The camp was clean and had an orderly look about it. Frames for curing meat , fish and hides were scattered about at random. The lodges would be occupied through the summer months, until it was time to decamp in the fall. Then the Washo people desert Da ow aga and move down slope for the Tagum harvest.

Smoke drifted lazily upward from several of the small shelters. Some made of deer hide, others thatched with grass. At mid day the sun became warm on the soft golden brown meadow grass.

Lark sat alone in the family shelter's dim interior. The leather door cover was closed, to shut away all traces of the outside world. On this day, the Washo mother wished to be alone with memories of her daughter. She sat on the floor with head bowed, a small sad figure. This was the day of the First New Moon of Summer, a time Lark had dreamed of for many years. A time when her first born was to begin the Women Hood Ceremony. But now that the day was here at last, Lark felt only despair. She was alone.

There was a scratching sound and the deer hide door cover shook slightly. Silence! Lark crawled on hands and knees to the cover and pulled it slowly aside. Peering out into the bright sunlight from the east facing doorway, she was unable to see clearly at first and passed a hand across her eyes.

Looking up from her kneeling position, Lark beheld a tall young man, sober of expression, gaunt with hollow cheeks and dark circles under his eyes. Soiled buckskin clothing hung in tatters from his spare frame. He was handsome, despite his haggard condition. Beside him stood a fine looking husky lad, with short hair and equally frayed clothes, he favored an injured leg while leaning on an odd looking, long black weapon of some sort.

With just the trace of a smile, the tall young man said,

"Here's that nice Ai mee girl of yours. Come home to see you!"

Squealing with delight Ai mee, a radiantly beautiful young woman, steped out from behind Noah and fell to her knees, into her mothers waiting arms.

"Mam'ma, Mam'ma."
" My Baby, My little Ai mee!"

Four days later, Ai mee sat before the lodge. The sunlight was warm, as she hummed a happy little tune. Her busy fingers worked at an intricate pattern of turquoise blue quills on a piece of soft gray rabbit fur. Her shiny clean, blue black hair glinted in the sun light as she bowed over the work. A quiet gurgling of the nearby river was interrupted as her empty stomach rumbled. It reminded she'd not eaten in four days. Best to keep one's hands busy and try to forget about food. The ceremony of the Red Dance Stick must be observed.

From a long ways off one could spot the two figures as they amble slowly along the lake shore. Deliberately, they picked their way across the shallow mouth of the Truckee River, a tall slender youth and his slightly limping companion. They move across the meadow and up to the lodge, where a small kneeling figure concentrated on her work. Looking up, Ai mee greeted the two with a smile on her radiantly happy face.

"Brought you a little gift." greeted Noah, holding out a long elderberry pole. "I thought maybe you could use it in the ceremony. Pealed it and dried it very carefully. See, I picked out a pretty long one. Thought it might be easier to find. Just in case anyone looked for it later on, that is."

"Why thank you Noah. That was a thoughtful gift," smiled Ai mee.

"I brought you a gift too," said Bopo seriously, "Actually, it's sort of a gift from my father also. It's a bundle of bright red color for painting the dance stick. My father said to tell you he's been doing some trading with the Paiute people. Since Snake's been gone from the village at Pyramid Lake. The two tribes seem to be getting more friendly. Looks like things'll be back to normal between the Paiutes and the Washos. That's where the red color came from. Paiute Land."

"What a nice gift, thank you Bopo. I've got a little something for you too. Something to thank you for being my good friend through all our travels. I understand there's a certain young lady named Magpie you have been planning to call on and... "

"Guess that's all called off now," interrupted Bopo, "You see, with me being the only bald headed Washo and all, I guess she might not be too glad to see me, after all. So, guess I'll just forget about it."

"Well Bopo, that's where my little gift comes in. I think it'll fix everything just fine," smiled Ai mee, "Now, you just kneel down here before me. See if this doesn't do the trick."

Meekly, Bopo bowed on one knee before Ai mee, as instructed. Placing one small brown hand on each of Bopo's ears, Ai mee leaned over and planted a great big smacker, right in the center of his bald spot. In the very middle of his gleaming bare skull. Then she took out an elegant, round crown of rabbit fur, decorated with turquoise blue porcupine quills. She lovingly placed the soft round patch over her friend's bald spot and gave it a finishing pat.

"Now!" laughed Ai mee, I guarantee Magpie's going to think you're the handsomest warrior in the whole tribe."

"Ho ho ho!" chortled Bopo, "This is great! How come I never thought of this. Thanks a lot, Ai mee. I need to get a look at this. Gotta go find a quiet reflecting pool in the river. So I can get a good look at myself. Thanks again Ai mee, so long, see you later!" With that Bopo dashed off toward the river and it was quite noticeable that his limp was greatly improved as he ran.

Noah and Ai mee stood facing each other, both looking down at the ground before them. A proudly handsome young man, standing tall and erect before a diminutive maiden. Her radiant beauty shone like the pure light of a new moon. Noah was busily drawing circles in the soft dirt with the toe of his new moccasin. For some reason he seemed to be having trouble in finding the right words to say.

"Ai mee, you know, well that is, well what I sort of thought, just maybe that is. Well, what I wanted to say was, when you take that ole' red dance stick up there on Rubicon Peak tomorrow and hide it, maybe you could sort of give me a few clues. About where you left the darn thing. You know, a fellow could spend the rest of his life up there looking for that red dance stick. That's a really big mountain top, you know."

Ai mee looked at Noah out of the corner of her lovely dark eyes. There was just a trace of a smile on her lips, as she said,

"Well, you know, Noah, I thought you just might like to come along with me. When I go up there tomorrow."

On a knoll a short distance behind camp, under a large sage, in the deep shadows, lay a very old, very shaggy coyote. His head rested on his paws, his tongue lolled out the side of his mouth. His eyes were half closed, as he watched Ai mee and Noah. He thought to himself,

"You know, this totem business is a lot of work. Lots of travel! Lots of worry! Never know what's coming up next. I'm getting too old for all this action. Think I'll retire! Just stay home. Find a nice big meadow full of fat field mice. I've earned it!" Shaking his head thoughtfully, he said,

"On the other hand. Come to think of it. That young Noah fella didn't turn out too bad, after all. Maybe I'll just tag along tomorrow. Make sure those two don't get in any trouble."

THE END

Here's an excerpt from Chapter One of the new book by Don La Rue....... THE CLAWS OF ONG

It will be available soon.

CHAPTER 1   Declaration Of War

Runner was the first to see it . Cocking his head to one side, he studied the trail ahead. "Looks like somebody lost a moccasin."

Bopo pulled up behind the big messenger, peering over his shoulder. There was a moccasin some 20 paces ahead, standing upright in the exact center of the trail. Somehow it just didn't look right. If some one just dropped it there, the thing would be on it's side, or pointed at random. Wouldn't be pointed exactly up and down the center of the trail.

"Let's go up closer and take a look. See if there's any sign around it. Maybe there're some tracks to show how it got there. Who left it."

"All right, but be careful not to disturb the soft dirt in the trail around it," grunted Runner.

(Runs Swift is a tribal messenger, know to his friends as Runner.)

The two walked carefully in the grass alongside the trail, so as not to disturb any tell tale sign. Both were expert trackers, among the best in the tribe.

"This thing doesn't look right!" grunted Bopo, after studying the soft dirt in the trail at close range, on hands and knees."

"There isn't any sign around at all. Looks almost as though some body dusted away any footprints. There weren't any marks made when it was dropped," agreed the big messenger. Neither made any attempt to touch the worn sheep hide foot gear. It had obviously covered many a mountain trail on the owner's foot. The stained interior looked as though it had stretched tight over a broad, heavy foot. It gave the impression the owner must have been rather heavy set.

"You know, that looks like a Washo moccasin. Made of sheep hide with the high side and all," pondered Bopo. "What do you think, was it Washo or Taneu?"

"Could be either, you never know. Some of those thugs from Manu's village hunt sheep. The way the hide's cut you just can't tell. Could be either! Besides, what's the difference? What're you so worked up about? Any body could throw away an old worn out moccasin like that."

"Well," Said Bopo, "It just doesn't feel right. A discarded moccasin isn't necessarily an unusual event. I agree with you. At most any other spot around the lake it wouldn't even be noticed. But, consider the facts. First, were on the Maggie's Peaks trail above Emerald Bay. We're headed for the amphitheater where we're supposed to meet the Pine Nut Boss, Stands Tall. Second, the Maggie's Peak area has a long history of invasion. Third, Da ow aga has always teemed with huge, fat lake trout. We've always had an abundant supply of delicious pink trout meat. All of our neighbors envy us such a delicacy. Fourth, on more than one occasion the Taneu have organized raiding parties to Emerald Bay. Want to steal our lake trout. They always come by the Maggies Peak trail."

"I see what you mean," agreed Runner. "There's been quite a number of times when we've had pitched battles with those thug's of Manu. Times when they attempted to steal fish from us and we ambushed 'em. My older brother was killed in one of those battles, years ago."

Glancing over his shoulder to study the deep forest shadows, Bopo whispered, "Suppose there's a big raiding party out there right now, watching us? They could have planted that moccasin in the trail, you know. Maybe left it as some sort of signal"

"Yeah, I see what you mean. They could be all around us right now," whispered his companion, uneasily turning his head from side to side.

"Besides, have you noticed the weather's beginning to change? The water's getting rough down there in Emerald Bay. Sky sure is turning dark all of a sudden. We better get on up the trail to the amphitheater. Stands Tall's probably up there all ready," muttered Bopo.

"I don't like the looks of this at all. Wish there were more of us. Stands Tall's a really nice fellow, every body likes him and all. In fact he's probably one of the most important people in the tribe. But he's older. Kinda fat now. I don't know how much good he'd do in a fight with the Tanue. Wish we had about a dozen heavily armed warriors with us."

"I wish I had my Atl-Atl here right now! It's so powerful it'd make a big difference, in any battle," Bopo whispered. "Only trouble is, I don't have a missile for it any more. Fired the last one at ole' Snake, down there on the island in Emerald Bay.

The night he captured Ai mee. Fired it at the same time as ONG shoved a lightning bolt down his throat. Never really knew which one of us did Snake in. By the time I got down there, he was just a little pile of smoking black ashes. My missile was nowhere to be seen. Maybe ONG's got it! Boy, how I wish I had that missile and the Atl-Atl right now!" muttered Bopo, hastening up the trail toward the amphitheater.

The amphitheater is a small pocket in the face of a steep granite cliff overlooking Emerald Bay, from high above. Big enough to hold several dozen persons, there's a towering wall of Red Fir trees behind it and a massive jumble of boulders forming a rough throne in the center. It's flat sandy floor is frequently the scene of important Washo meetings.

The two worried warriors jogged hurriedly up the steep trail toward the amphitheater. The last vestiges on sunshine disappeared, to be replaced by deep forest shadow. A dark line formed along the length of Da ow aga's east shore. It broadened as it raced across the water toward Emerald Bay, on the west shore. Entering the bay, the rolling dark waves crashed upon glistening black walls of a tiny island. It threw violent white spray high into the air.

The darkening silence was shattered with an ear splitting blast, as the first explosion of thunder shook the ground. Instantly, the world erupted into a searing white light. A huge fir directly behind the throne split open wide, from it's tip downward to the sandy floor of the amphitheater. The base of the huge tree smoked, as flame began to creep up the shattered bark. ONG had struck !

Gasping for breath, Runner and Bopo raced onto the sandy floor of the amphitheater and stopped, frozen in time. A flash of intense white lightning revealed a form seated on the throne-like jumble of gray granite boulders. There, sharply defined, sat the inert figure of Stands Tall. He appeared tiny, with shoulders rested against the towering stone back, arms reclining along the massive rests. One hand dangled, the other grasped his distinctive badge of office, a feathered lance. Below a round belly his lower legs hung limply, with one pale bare foot exposed. The mystery of a moccasin on the trail was solved.

"That's Stands Tall all right. Look at that decorated lance. That's the badge of the Pine Nut Boss. No question, that's Stands Tall. uuuUggggghhh! Very bad medicine!" shuddered Runner.

Bopo stood in the blinding light transfixed, staring upward at the inert figure.

"He doesn't have a head! There's no head! Just a seared black stump of a neck."

Shaking his head slowly as if to brush away the stark scene, Runner said in a whisper,

"The Taneu didn't do this, Bopo. It couldn't have been them!"

"No, not the Taneu. No, it was ONG! No one but ONG could have split that tree from top to bottom. Look here in the sand a my feet. Here's the missile from my Atl-Atl. The one I fired at Snake.

351

The one I never could find afterward. ONG had it all along."

Kneeling, Runner examined the missile. The gleaming black obsidian point was shattered into a pile of glistening shards. The thick missile body of tough juniper was snapped like a twig. The deadly missile looked as though it had been thrown at the figure's feet, as an expression of utter contempt.

"What's it all mean Bopo?" puzzled Runner.

"It's pretty clear. It means ONG has declared war on the whole Washo nation. Singled out one of our most important elders. Just to show he's going to take revenge on the whole tribe. Not a soul will dare to enter the entire Da ow aga basin. Not as long as ONG rules here. This lake, the very center of Washo Land, has been taken from us. ONG won't be satisfied just to eat an occasional Washo any longer. He's out to annihilate the whole tribe, for revenge!"

"Why Bopo? Why... ?"

"Because I fired that Atl -Atl missile. It must have struck and destroyed Snake. Before ONG could wreak vengeance on him! I embarrassed ONG before the whole Washo Nation. Humbled him! So he's declared war, for revenge. It's all my fault!"

"So what 'd you suppose'll happen now?"

"I think the tribal elders are going to be so angry at the loss of the entire Da ow aga basin, they'll banish me. Banish me from the tribe for as long as ONG rules here."

"You mean the elders will throw you out? Just like that?"

"Yup!"